Using and Understanding AI in Higher Education

Rebecca J. Allen • Alex Nakonechnyi
Editors

Using and Understanding AI in Higher Education

Classroom Research with Real-World Strategies

palgrave
macmillan

Editors
Rebecca J. Allen
Center for IT Engagement (cITe)
Mount St. Joseph University
Cincinnati, OH, USA

Alex Nakonechnyi
Center for IT Engagement
Mount St. Joseph University
Cincinnati, OH, USA

ISBN 978-3-031-99753-2 ISBN 978-3-031-99754-9 (eBook)
https://doi.org/10.1007/978-3-031-99754-9

This Palgrave Macmillan imprint is published by the registered company Springer Nature Switzerland AG.
The registered company address is: Gewerbestrasse 11, 6330 Cham, Switzerland

Rebecca would like to thank her family for their support and patience. Especially, she would like to thank D. for her repeated assurances that the book will be "epic" and M. for sacrificial help that made this book feasible. She would also to thank God who is the source of all wisdom.

Alex would like to thank his wife and family for their support. They give the whole project meaning. He gives thanks to God who directs his path.

Acknowledgments

The editors would like to express their sincere gratitude to the K–12 teachers from the Teach Computer Science program at Mount St. Joseph University. Your thoughtful feedback on early chapter drafts challenged us to make the material accessible to non-technical audiences. Your commitment to learning and teaching computer science continues to inspire us.

The editors are also deeply thankful to the students, staff and faculty affiliated with the Center for IT Engagement at Mount St. Joseph University. Much of this book would not have been possible without your active participation in our courses and research initiatives.

Contents

Notes on Contributors

Rebecca J. Allen is Assistant Professor and Chair of Computer Science and Mathematics at Mount St. Joseph University, where she also serves as a faculty affiliate at the Center for IT Engagement (cITe). With a PhD in Educational Studies and a strong foundation in linguistics, Dr. Allen specializes in subfields of AI called natural language processing (NLP) and corpus linguistics. Her work integrates technical expertise with participatory approaches, emphasizing AI literacy, inclusion, and student-centered innovation.

Her NLP research has contributed to nephrology and public health, with a focus on improving clinical communication and decision-making. In the field of education, Dr. Allen is active in undergraduate research and computer science pedagogy, mentoring student projects that apply AI to real-world challenges and publishing on best practices in teaching computing. She also investigates how large language models and digital tools can enhance inclusive teaching and institutional effectiveness.

A frequent international speaker on AI and education, Dr. Allen has secured over $6 million in grant funding. She founded the AI Café initiative to promote collaborative learning and ethical engagement with generative AI. Her work champions responsible, impactful, and community-oriented AI integration in higher education.

Maria Chiara De Angelis holds a PhD in Social Sciences and is a research fellow at Link Campus University. She is a member of the steering committee for the DITES—Digital Technologies, Education and Society Research Center and serves on the editorial board of the scientific journal

Quaderni di Comunità. Her research focuses on educational systems, public policy, and organizational development, with an emphasis on the ethical dimensions of digital culture and the impact of digital innovation on individuals and institutions. She also consults with public and private organizations in the education and training sectors, particularly on integrating digital technologies into teaching and learning, building communities of practice, and applying innovative methodologies in education and professional development. Her recent publications center on ethical challenges in digital research, decision-making in education during the pandemic, and the development of digital competencies.

Brook K. Batch is an educational studies doctoral candidate at the University of Cincinnati and Assistant Professor of Social Computing at Mount St. Joseph University. Her research and teaching interests include writing and research pedagogy, educational applications of artificial intelligence in education, and leveraging technology to engage diverse populations. Her current research explores how generative AI tools affect students' research and writing processes, academic identity formation, and overall engagement in writing-intensive courses.

Olena Holub is a graduate of the Computer Science program at Mount St. Joseph University and is now is a PhD student, with a concentration in Quantitative and Mixed Methods Research Methodologies in Educational Studies at the University of Cincinnati. She works as an application developer and analyst at Mount St. Joseph University, where she also teaches Computer Science courses. Her research focuses on leveraging data science to develop tools that support engagement, decision-making, and operational efficiency in educational and health contexts.

Gene Kritsky obtained a PhD in Entomology (University of Illinois) in August 1977. He is Professor Emeritus of Biology at Mount St. Joseph University in Cincinnati, Ohio. He is the author of over 260 publications, including five books on periodical cicadas.

Allison J. Lester (she/her) is an assistant teaching professor at Arizona State University, where she designs and facilitates courses on action research, ethical AI integration, and educational innovation. Her teaching centers first-generation college students, community-engaged learning, and reflective practice. Her research explores the tensions and possibilities of co-designing learning environments that honor student agency, cultural context, ethical complexity, and the evolving role of emerging technology. She is especially interested in how critical digital literacy and participatory AI can support students in shaping the future of education and technology.

Alex Nakonechnyi is Associate Provost, Chief Information Officer, and CEO of CITE INC at Mount St. Joseph University, where he leads enterprise-wide digital strategy and innovation. With a PhD in Educational Studies, an MBA from the Schulich School of Business, and a BSc in Computer Science, Dr. Nakonechnyi brings a rare blend of academic insight, business acumen, and deep technical expertise to higher education leadership.

Oliver Oniate is pursuing a BS in Computer Science from Mount St. Joseph University and is expected to graduate in December 2025. As part of his undergraduate studies, he completed a capstone project on artificial intelligence and computer vision. His professional interests include software development and cybersecurity. He plans to work in industry after completing his undergraduate studies.

Jermaine Poynter is a fourth-year computer science student at Mount St. Joseph University. Upon graduation, he will be working as a computer science teacher at a school. Over the next several years, he plans to pursue a master's degree in cybersecurity.

Mark A. Sulzer is Associate Professor in the areas of Secondary English Education and Literacy at the University of Cincinnati. Before joining the faculty at the University of Cincinnati, he worked as a high school English-language arts teacher and drum line instructor. His research and teaching focus on young adult literature, secondary English teaching methods, digital literacies, dialogic pedagogies, and teacher reflection.

Abbreviations

ABC	Actual Behavioral Control
AFT	Affect Toward Use
AI	Artificial Intelligence
AIAS	Artificial Intelligence Assessment Scale
AIISA	Artificial Intelligence Institute of South Africa
ANN	Artificial Neural Network
ATT	Attitude Toward the Behavior
BERT	Bidirectional Encoder Representations from Transformers
BI	Behavioral Intention
CAIR	Centre for Artificial Intelligence Research
CX	Complexity
DCDT	Department of Communications and Digital Technologies
DIT	Diffusion of Innovations Theory
FC	Facilitating Conditions
FERPA	Family Educational Rights and Privacy Act
GAN	Generative Adversarial Network
GenAI	Generative Artificial Intelligence
GPT	Generative Pre-trained transformer
HAB	Habit
HIPAA	Health Insurance Portability and Accountability Act
IoT	Internet of Things
LMS	Learning Management System
LLM	Large Language Model
LTC	Long-Term Consequences
ML	Machine Learning
MM	Motivational Model
NLP	Natural Language Processing

O	Observability
PB	Past Behavior
PBC	Perceived Behavioral Control
PCU	Model of Personal Computing Utilization
PEOU	Perceived Ease of Use
PDU	Perceived Difficulty of Use
PU	Perceived Usefulness
RA	Relative Advantage
RIAA	Recording Industry Association of America
RL	Reinforcement Learning
SAMR	Substitution Augmentation Modification Redefinition model
SCT	Social Cognitive Theory
SEM	Structural Equation Modeling
SF	Social Factors
SN	Subjective Norm
STEM	Science Technology Engineering and Mathematics
TAM	Technology Acceptance Model
TACT	Target Action Context Time
TPB	Theory of Planned Behavior
TRA	Theory of Reasoned Action
UTAUT	Unified Theory of Acceptance and Use of Technology
YOLO	You Only Look Once

List of Figures

List of Tables

List of Tables

CHAPTER 1

Finding Our Voices in the Maze of AI

Rebecca J. Allen and Alex Nakonechnyi

This year, I (Rebecca, the first editor) have been on two parallel adventures. The first, of course, is editing this book—the one you are reading. The second? My university launched a new online program to help K-12 teachers—many without computer science backgrounds—pursue licensure in computer science entirely at a distance.

Over the past year, I found myself teaching computer science asynchronously to a wonderfully diverse group of educators: elementary, English, science, and math teachers, many of whom were enthusiastic but brand new to artificial intelligence (AI) and computer science. Some of my fellow computer science instructors called this task "impossible," but really, it was not. In fact, teaching this group was a joy. Teachers tend to be the best kind of students: curious, reflective, and eager to learn. But more than that, they made me think differently. I had to distill an enormous wall of technical information into something scalable and approachable. I had to decide what mattered—and what did not.

R. J. Allen (✉) • A. Nakonechnyi
Center for IT Engagement (cITe), Mount St. Joseph University, Cincinnati, OH, USA
e-mail: rebecca.allen@msj.edu; alex.nakonechnyi@msj.edu

R. J. Allen, A. Nakonechnyi (eds.), *Using and Understanding AI in Higher Education*,
https://doi.org/10.1007/978-3-031-99754-9_1

And while I did my best to meet the challenge, one request kept ringing through: "Please, make us more videos!" Now, I am many things—or at least I try to be—but I am not much of a YouTuber. Still, their plea was not really about production quality. It was about connection. Even when I used excellent video-based textbooks, what they craved was presence and perspective: someone to help them focus on what mattered most.

That same need—for simplification, for a human voice—has guided the editing of this book. Many people need a clear, grounded narrator when learning about technology. We, the editors, hope to offer this grounding—not through video, but through prose. My teacher-learners were in the back of my mind throughout this process. I kept asking myself, "Would they get this?" And if the answer was no (either because we thought so or the teachers told us), we revised. If you are new to computer science and wondering what AI is or how it works, this book was written with you in mind.

AI—and the computer science behind it—deserves more than one book. A library or maybe a data warehouse, might begin to cover it. But you're reading this one book. That means what we offer is selective. Our goal is not to include everything (as if that were possible), but to offer the essentials: to help you become a more informed user of AI and to spark your future curiosity. This book reflects what we, the editors, believe matters most—while grounding AI in human contexts, lived experiences, and inclusive conversations.

Who Are the Editors?

I (Rebecca) and my co-editor Alex come from a non-traditional and a traditional computer science backgrounds, respectively. My own journey began in linguistics and literacy education. However, twenty years ago, I did something straight out of a reality show: I moved abroad to be with my then-new spouse, who worked in IT. While waiting on immigration paperwork and unable to work, I picked up one of those massive, phone-book-sized computer science texts that were common at the time and began teaching myself to program.

I had needed to take some programming classes in my undergraduate degree, but I still largely I believed that "computer people" were born, not made—maybe emerging fully formed from garages, something like Steve Jobs. However, I learned otherwise. If we set the pressure aside, computer science is a learnable subject—like any other topic, with some initial support, truly, it is figure-out-able. Fast forward to today, some two graduate degrees later: I now chair a computer science department—something I never imagined. Helping people understand computers has become one of my greatest joys. I want to say to you, sincerely: ***You've got this!***

Alex, on the other hand, took the more traditional route into computer science. He earned a degree in computer science and spent decades working in IT support and systems administration. Later, he completed a PhD in education and shifted his focus from practicing computer science to teaching it, eventually becoming a university administrator. Between us, we bring content expertise and a strong commitment to science communication and knowledge about the intricacies of higher education—we have tried to tap into all of these areas to create a valuable experience for you in this book.

Whether you are just beginning to explore AI or are already an experienced practitioner, we hope this book offers something useful. If you are starting out, we have worked hard to keep content accessible and grounded. If you are more advanced, we recognize that you are often called upon to explain, justify, or defend what you do—so we have included examples, analogies, and language that may be helpful when speaking with others.

Why This Book? Holding Space for a Starting Point

This book is one small step toward bridging the wide chasm between education and IT. Computer science and especially AI education are still relatively young disciplines, grappling with not only ***what*** to teach, but ***how*** to teach it. Consider this: the American Society for Engineering Education was founded in 1893, but the computer science counterpart, the Computer Science Teachers Association, was not established until 2004. Much of computer science education remains focused on training future programmers, often overlooking those who need computing skills for interdisciplinary applications (Guzdial, 2015). The field has long emphasized competitiveness over collaboration and has historically undervalued diverse perspectives (Barker et al., 2002). Today, fewer than 20% of computer science bachelor's degrees are awarded to women—and even fewer to women of color or those from lower-income backgrounds (Pournaghshband & Medel, 2020). Unfortunately, AI has not shifted that trajectory of exclusion. Recent studies suggest that men are adopting AI tools at higher rates than women (Nouraldeen, 2023; Obenza et al., 2024; Ramos, 2022).

Faced with these statistics, one of my students and I asked a simple question: *Where do people even begin if they want to learn about AI?* So—like many others—we turned to Google. Anecdotally, we found it surprisingly difficult to locate clear, practical guidance on how to get started with AI. That initial frustration led us to systematize our search process and turn it into a research project: *Navigating the AI Maze: What Search Engines Do and Do Not Tell Us About Practical AI Use* (Holub & Allen, 2023). Our study explored the gap between what people hope to learn about artificial intelligence and what they actually find through everyday online searches. We analyzed 60 pages of content from the top 20 search results on Google, Bing, and Yahoo, using web scraping to simulate real-world search behavior for pages about AI To uncover deeper patterns, we applied two topic modeling techniques—both forms of unsupervised machine learning. Specifically, we used Latent Dirichlet Allocation (LDA), which treats each document as a mix of topics, and Latent Semantic Analysis (LSA), which maps word relationships based on shared context.

What we discovered is that while online searches for AI pages often return content that appears relevant at first glance, much of it lacks the depth and practicality that potential learners actually need. The most common themes included business applications of AI, higher education initiatives, and academic program rankings. However, despite surface relevance, most of the content was thin. Although "how to" searches account for roughly 3% of U.S. Google queries (Okunoye, 2020), very few pages offered tutorials, tools, step-by-step guidance, or background information. Even in sources categorized under "AI in Higher Education," the focus was typically on academic program promotion rather than curriculum or instructional support.

In short, when people search for AI online, they are unlikely to find the practical, hands-on resources they need to get started. Reading this book is a starting point for building foundational knowledge to support sense-making about AI—helping you cut through the noise and begin to make informed, confident decisions about how AI could fit into your work, teaching, or learning.

Excited, Anxious, and Everything in Between

Over the past few years, I (Rebecca) have given dozens of workshops and talks on AI, both in the United States and abroad. What continues to stand out is the emotional divide. Some faculty members advocate banning AI entirely from their classrooms. Stil others are eager to use tools like ChatGPT to grade essays—ethics, legality, and privacy considerations notwithstanding. These moments raise a central question: not just simply "Can AI do that?" but rather "Should it?"

This book offers a place to begin answering such questions thoughtfully. It is not a technical manual, nor a simplistic "just copy these prompts" guide. Instead, it is a grounding resource—intended to help readers think critically about AI's uses, risks, and possibilities. More than anything, we hope this book encourages thoughtful participation in AI, rather than passive consumption of it.

You will also find an interdisciplinary perspective woven throughout. Computer science literature, like much of academia, is often siloed. However, social context is not just a sidebar to AI—it is central. Many individuals from underrepresented groups are drawn to computing not by the code itself, but by the desire to make a positive impact in their communities (Boucher et al., 2017). By highlighting difference making, we aim to make this book both meaningful and approachable.

We have designed this book to be accessible to all readers—whether you are new to computer science or already using AI tools in your work. That means helping readers grasp both how AI works and what it can be used for. This is not a how-to manual or a programming tutorial—though those are excellent next steps. For readers seeking more practical applications and tools, we have included an appendix with some of our favorite how-to ideas and resources. At its core, this book is about helping more people enter the conversation around AI with knowledge, confidence, and purpose.

What You Will Find in This Book

The chapters that follow offer a range of entry points into the complex and evolving topic of artificial intelligence. While each chapter takes a distinct approach—whether conceptual, historical, theoretical, empirical, or practical—they are united by a shared goal: to deepen understanding of AI's role in education and society. We hope readers—whether educators, students, researchers, or policy makers—will see themselves reflected somewhere in these pages and find language, frameworks, and tools they can use in their own contexts.

Chapter 2 introduces core AI concepts and terminology. Designed as a foundational overview, it provides readers with a clear explanation of how AI systems function, how terms like "machine learning" and "neural networks" relate to each other, and why definitions of AI remain contested in public discourse. This chapter helps establish a shared vocabulary that flows through the rest of the volume.

Chapter 3 situates today's AI debates within a broader historical and ethical context. Drawing from literature, mythology, philosophy, and early automation, it explores enduring questions about human-machine relationships, agency, and responsibility. This chapter also overviews current legal international AI regulatory frameworks. By connecting present-day concerns to centuries-old narratives, the chapter invites readers to reflect critically on power, control, and the social values embedded in our technologies.

Chapter 4 outlines major behavioral and institutional theories used to explain how new technologies are adopted—or resisted—within educational settings. It introduces models like the Technology Acceptance Model (TAM) and the Unified Theory of Acceptance and Use of Technology (UTAUT), while also exposing their limitations. In particular, the chapter challenges readers to consider how culture, power, and identity shape people's responses to AI, and why these dimensions must be included in future research and practice.

Chapter 5 presents findings from a participatory study conducted on a U.S. university campus. Combining survey and interview data from students, faculty, and staff, it examines how people are encountering generative AI in real time—what excites them, what confuses them, and what kinds of supports they need. This chapter centers the voices of learners and educators navigating a rapidly changing landscape.

Offering a global perspective, Chap. 6 shares international faculty perspectives on AI, gathered through a series of interdisciplinary focus groups. It highlights how researchers and instructors across diverse academic fields are thinking about, experimenting with, and questioning the role of AI in their professional lives. The chapter offers insight into common concerns and aspirations, as well as the contextual factors that shape how faculty engage with emerging technologies.

Chapter 7 turns the spotlight to undergraduate students and their use of AI in writing and research. Using a case study approach, it explores how generative tools are influencing students' academic identity, shaping their sense of authorship, and raising new pedagogical and ethical questions for faculty. This chapter emphasizes the importance of listening to students and taking seriously their lived experiences with AI.

Chapter 8 presents an interdisciplinary exploration of AI, the natural sciences, and citizen science. The authors trace the history of a mobile app designed to capture crowdsourced data on cicada emergences, illustrating how collective participation can yield valuable datasets for scientific analysis through machine learning. This chapter also offers practical insights into app development, undergraduate research involvement, and the broader potential of crowdsourcing in scientific discovery powered by AI.

Chapter 9 demonstrates how AI techniques can be applied to a real-world educational challenge: student attendance and academic performance. Through a hands-on case study using both traditional statistics and machine learning, it shows how data analysis might inform institutional interventions, surface patterns of inequity, and offer new tools for supporting student success. Uniquely, this chapter offers two methods sections—a traditional one and a layperson friendly one, with the idea of aiding non-technical readers in understanding key parts of machine learning approaches and methods.

Chapter 10 offers a concluding reflection on faculty agency and institutional transformation. The chapter features two first-person case studies of educators navigating inclusion of AI at their respective institutions. It considers the strategic, ethical, and pedagogical decisions educators face as they encounter AI tools and debates. Rather than prescribing a singular path forward, the chapter encourages intentional, informed choices that align with institutional missions, equity goals, and the evolving needs of students and educators alike.

An Invitation to Join the Conversation

So welcome. Whether you embrace AI with enthusiasm, reject it outright, or find yourself somewhere in between, we are glad you are here. This book was written for readers across that spectrum—those who are curious, cautious, overwhelmed, or inspired. Use this book to engage with AI on your own terms—**knowledgeably, ethically, and with intention**. We suggest that as you read, you ask good questions, stay grounded in your values, and remain open to learning. Wherever you are starting from, we hope these chapters offer language, insight, and practical tools to help you make sense of AI in your educational and professional life.

Try It Out: Getting Started with Generative AI

In Chap. 5, the authors share that on their campus, about one in three staff and faculty members are "not at all familiar" or "not very familiar" with generative AI tools. Although adoption appears to be growing, many staff and faculty members on university campuses have not yet used generative AI and need a starting point.

Your understanding of this book and of AI education more broadly will be greatly improved if you take a moment to familiarize yourself with generative AI tools. Generative AI tools—such as ChatGPT, Gemini, and Microsoft Copilot—can write text, create images, answer questions, and even help brainstorm ideas. However, for those encountering them for the first time, it can feel unclear where to begin or what is possible. This activity is designed to help you take your first steps, with no technical background required.

Whether you are excited, unsure, or even a little nervous, remember: the goal here is not to master AI, but to begin exploring how it might support your work, learning, or creativity.

Step 1: Choose a Generative AI Tool

Pick one of the following free or freemium tools to try:
ChatGPT (OpenAI)
Gemini (Google)
Copilot (Microsoft)
You may need to create a free account using your email address.

Step 2: Start with a Simple Prompt

Once you have created an account and logged in, you will see something similar to the image below (Fig. 1.1): you will see a textbox where you can type your prompt (request, question).

Open the tool and type a short, clear instruction into the textbox. Try something practical and low-stakes:

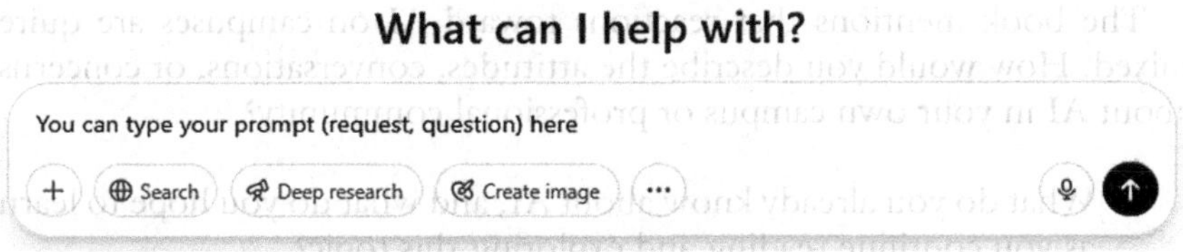

Fig. 1.1 Most generative AI systems will have a similar layout. You need to look for the textbox where you can type your prompt. The example below is OpenAI's ChatGPT

"Give me five dinner ideas using rice, beans, and spinach."

"Explain what a thesis statement is for a college writing class."

"Write a friendly reminder email to my classmates about a group project meeting."

Then click "submit" (or hit Enter) and read the response.

Step 3: Reflect and Revise

Was the response helpful?

Was anything inaccurate, odd, or surprising?

Try adding more context to improve the result.

Example:

Original: "Explain homeostasis."

Improved: "You are a high school science teacher. Explain homeostasis to a group of 10th graders using simple language and one real-world example."

Questions for Reflection and Discussion

Who introduced you to generative AI, and how did you first engage with it? What did that experience reveal about how people make sense of new technologies?

Have you ever struggled to understand what AI is or how it works? What questions or uncertainties have come up for you along the way?

The book mentions that reactions toward AI on campuses are quite mixed. How would you describe the attitudes, conversations, or concerns about AI in your own campus or professional community?

1. What do you already know about AI, and what do you hope to learn as you continue reading and exploring this topic?

References

Barker, L. J., Garvin-Doxas, K., & Jackson, M. (2002). Defensive climate in the computer science classroom. *ACM SIGCSE Bulletin, 34*(1), 43–47. https://doi.org/10.1145/563517.563353

Boucher, K. L., Fuesting, M. A., Diekman, A. B., & Murphy, M. C. (2017). Can I work with and help others in this field? How communal goals influence interest and participation in STEM fields. *Frontiers in Psychology, 8*(MAY), 1–12. https://doi.org/10.3389/fpsyg.2017.00901

Guzdial, M. (2015). *Learner-centered design of computing education: Research on computing for everyone.* Morgan and Claypool Publishers.

Holub, O., & Allen, R. (2023). *Navigating the AI maze: What search engines do and do not tell us about practical AI use.* Paper presented at the International Scientific-Practical Conference "Future Creators," SMK College of Applied Sciences, .

Nouraldeen, R. M. (2023). The impact of technology readiness and use perceptions on students' adoption of artificial intelligence: The moderating role of gender. *Development and Learning in Organizations, 37*(3), 7–10. https://doi.org/10.1108/DLO-07-2022-0133

Obenza, B. N., Go, L. E., Francisco, J. A. M., Buit, E. E. T., Mariano, F. V. B., Cuizon, H. L., Jr., Cagabhion, A. J. D., & Agbulos, K. A. J. L. (2024). The nexus between cognitive absorption and AI literacy of college students as moderated by sex. *American Journal of Smart Technology and Solutions, 3*(1), 32–39. https://doi.org/10.54536/ajsts.v3i1.2603

Okunoye, B. (2020). *How nations seek answers online and what it might suggest about global learning cultures/attitudes* [Working paper (v.1)]. OSF Preprints. https://osf.io/preprints/osf/zb9ru

Pournaghshband, V., & Medel, A. (2020). Diversity in computer science: Addressing the gender gap. *Proceedings of the 2020 ACM Conference on Innovation and Technology in Computer Science Education*, 12–18. https://doi.org/10.1145/3341525.3387366

Ramos, G. (2022). Why we must act now to close the gender gap in AI. *In World Economic Forum..* https://www.weforum.org/stories/2022/08/why-we-must-act-now-to-close-the-gender-gap-in-ai/

CHAPTER 2

What Is Artificial Intelligence and How Does It Work?

Alex Nakonechnyi and *Rebecca J. Allen*

Introduction

> "The inventor or introducer … deserves to be ranked among the best contributors to learning and science, if not among the greatest benefactors of mankind … there is no substitute for it…almost works miracles." Josiah Freeman Bumstead, 1841 (p. viii), reflecting on the utility of blackboards in education.

Is AI going to change the world? Perhaps it will, and certainly, in some ways, it already has. AI has been lauded by both sides of the U.S. political spectrum. Former President Joe Biden (2023) stated that AI is: "the most consequential technology of our time. It's going to accelerate it at warp speed … [it] expands the boundary of human possibility…[it] is all around us. Much of it is making our lives better." Similarly, President Donald Trump (2025) stated that "America's decades-long leadership in AI

A. Nakonechnyi (✉) • R. J. Allen
Center for IT Engagement (cITe), Mount St. Joseph University, Cincinnati, OH, USA
e-mail: alex.nakonechnyi@msj.edu; rebecca.allen@msj.edu

R. J. Allen, A. Nakonechnyi (eds.), *Using and Understanding AI in Higher Education*,
https://doi.org/10.1007/978-3-031-99754-9_2

research and development has resulted in cutting-edge, transformative technologies that are improving lives, growing innovative industries, empowering workers, and increasing national security." Both of these diametrically opposed sides seem to agree that AI is a future making technology. So, the question is: are they both right?

One thing that we have sought to avoid in this book is futurism—the authors are teachers, computer scientists, and humans, not clairvoyants. Another thing we have tried to avoid is hype. While promises of AI transforming lives may serve political rhetoric well, hype is not without downstream consequences (see Chaps. 3 and 4). Hype can stymie understanding and prevent informed choices, often breeding extreme reactions on both ends of the spectrum.

We do want people to become more aware of AI, to dream big, and to find new ways to use technology for the good of humankind, but alongside that hopeful enthusiasm, problems emerge. When overly hyped, AI—like the blackboards of yore—can take on an almost mystical status, as if it were a force beyond human control. And for some, this aura of power leads not to adoption, but to rejection. Hype can provoke avoidance; this avoidance reaction that, for many, feels like an empowered stance against what they perceive as unstoppable technological evil (Winkel, 2024). I recall an AI workshop for university educators in which one participant, while tapping at her smartphone (certainly an AI-enabled device), looked me in the eye and said, with conviction, that AI was "against her profession."

Another challenge with trumpeting AI as the future is that what AI actually is—and is not—is still unclear. Many Americans lack the technological literacy needed to grasp the nuances of this evolving discussion. What this chapter aims to do, in plain and accessible terms, is to cut through some of the prevailing confusion and misinformation, and to set the stage for an engaged, informed dialogue about how AI should—and should not—be used in our educational institutions and beyond.

What Is AI, Anyway? Definition of AI

AI is not just ChatGPT. Although many laypeople tend to equate ChatGPT with AI as a whole, it's important to understand that ChatGPT is just one type of AI system. In reality, there are many different types and applications of AI,

Definitions of AI vary widely, and this variability often causes confusion (Luckin et al., 2022). For the purposes of our discussion, AI can be defined as the use of machines to simulate intelligent behavior (Nussbaum, 2023). However, this definition is not as straightforward as it might appear. In broader society, the goalpost for what counts as "intelligent behavior" keeps shifting. This constant redefining of what qualifies as AI is referred to as the *AI effect* (Nussbaum, 2023).

For example, many internet-connected devices—collectively known as the Internet of Things (IoT)—use some form of artificial intelligence. These include speech recognition technologies that power voice assistants like Siri, navigation tools such as Google Maps, video games, recommender systems on platforms like Netflix and Amazon, social media algorithms on apps like Instagram, and spam filters that manage email inboxes. While these systems are often quite sophisticated and perform tasks that would otherwise require human intelligence, their widespread use and seamless integration into everyday life mean that people may not always recognize them as AI-powered (Fig. 2.1).

Fig. 2.1 AI is all around us in everyday devices and technologies such as email spam filters, GPS systems, and smart home devices like thermostats, voice assistants, and vacuums

As of writing, a large nationwide survey of the U.S. revealed that 44% of Americans self-report as not regularly interacting with AI (Kennedy et al., 2023). This figure likely says very little about how often AI is actually used, instead it speaks about confusion around AI's definition and a woeful lack of AI literacy among the general public.

AI Approaches and Methods: The Many AIs

AI is a broad and evolving field that encompasses many types of systems and methods including but certainly not limited to LLMs like ChatGPT. For readers aiming to build a foundational understanding of what AI is and what it can do, it is especially useful to explore the different types of AI—how they function, what they are used for, and how they relate to one another.

In the chart below, we provide a mapping of common AI-related approaches and their typical use cases. In the sections that follow, we walk through each of these branches in more detail, but in the meantime, Table 2.1 helps to map out the AI landscape we will cover.

AI Systems

When making sense of the AI landscape, it is helpful to understand that, quite often, when we use common AI systems, we are interacting with more than one core method or technology at once. Understanding how these branches work together helps demystify the "magic" of AI.

What Happens When You Prompt an LLM Like ChatGPT?

For example, let us walk through what happens behind the scenes when you prompt ChatGPT (see Table 2.2). Imagine that you upload a recent article you wrote and prompt: "Summarize this article and generate a short headline for it. Also, suggest a related image and provide a table of key points." What actually happens then?

First, ChatGPT uses natural language processing (NLP) to interpret the words and structure of your prompt, identifying the specific tasks you are requesting, such as summarization, headline generation, image suggestion, and table creation. This understanding relies on deep learning models, specifically Transformer-based neural networks, that enable the

Table 2.1 Types and subfields of AI

Method or Technology	*Definition*	*Example use case*
Machine Learning (ML)	Systems improve through data-driven experience without explicit programming.	Spam filters in email systems improving over time based on detected patterns.
Supervised Learning	Relies on labeled data to train models for specific tasks.	Image recognition models trained to distinguish between cats and dogs.
Unsupervised Learning	Identifies patterns in unlabeled data without predefined categories.	Customer segmentation in marketing by grouping customers based on behavior.
Reinforcement Learning	AI learns by trial and error, receiving feedback to improve decisions over time.	Robots learning to walk or play games like chess by trying different moves and learning from outcomes.
Neural Networks & Deep Learning	AI models inspired by the human brain; can recognize patterns and improve decision-making.	Autonomous vehicles using deep learning to detect objects and navigate roads.
Natural Language Processing (NLP)	AI's ability to understand, interpret, and generate human language.	Chatbots like ChatGPT understanding and responding to user queries.
Computer Vision	AI that processes, analyzes, and interprets visual data like images and videos.	Facial recognition systems used for identity verification.
Generative AI	AI that generates new content, including text, images, music, and code.	DALL·E generating images from text descriptions.

system to analyze language patterns based on vast amounts of prior training data.

If your article includes a picture, ChatGPT can also apply its multimodal capabilities, using methods from computer vision to analyze and integrate visual information alongside the text-based prompt.

Next, to generate a response, ChatGPT draws on its foundation as a generative AI model. Instead of retrieving a pre-written answer, it predicts and produces one word (or token) at a time, based on statistical patterns it has learned from billions of examples. This generation process combines principles from supervised learning, from training on labeled tasks, and unsupervised learning, by detecting broader patterns and associations in

Table 2.2 What happens when one types a prompt into an LLM like ChatGPT?

AI Approach	*AI Approach Used*
Natural Language Processing (NLP)	Understands the user's prompt; identifies requested tasks like summarizing, titling, and organizing content.
Supervised Machine Learning	Applies patterns learned from labeled examples (e.g., summaries, headlines, Q&A pairs) to analyze the article.
Unsupervised Machine Learning	Identifies underlying themes or patterns in the article without relying on labeled data, supporting the organization and coherence of the generated summary.
Deep Learning	Employs large neural networks (transformers) to model complex language patterns, enabling the AI to generate responses that stay on topic, maintain flow, and adapt to the context of both the prompt and the article.
Generative AI	Produces the new original language of the actual summary.
Computer Vision (if image is included in the article)	Analyzes images for relevant content or matches visuals to the article's themes.
Reinforcement Learning (from human feedback)	Fine-tunes responses based on user feedback to improve usefulness, tone, or clarity in the model over the long term.

the data. In this way, ChatGPT constructs an entirely new response customized to your input, rather than copying or searching existing text.

Finally, while the model's immediate output is not directly updated after a single use, ChatGPT's performance over time can be improved through reinforcement learning from human feedback—data such as thumbs up, thumbs down, or user comments help developers fine-tune future model versions to better meet users' needs.

Now having understood that these approaches to AI often work together, let us go more granularly and consider in more detail each approach.

Machine Learning

The first kind of AI we will consider is machine learning. Let me first disambiguate AI (the broader concept) and machine learning (the narrower subset). Broadly, artificial intelligence (AI) refers to the overarching field focused on creating systems that can perform tasks typically requiring human intelligence. This includes reasoning, learning, problem-solving, perception, and language understanding. Machine learning (ML) is a specific subfield of AI that involves algorithms and statistical models enabling computers to learn patterns from data and make predictions or decisions without being explicitly programmed for every scenario.

While some AI systems function based on predefined logic—such as expert systems that follow human-crafted decision trees—ML algorithms adapt dynamically, refining their outputs as they process new information. Not all AI relies on machine learning, but most modern advancements, particularly in fields like computer vision, natural language processing, and autonomous systems, are powered by ML techniques, especially deep learning. In short, most of the time, the AI we use involves a type of machine learning.

A key point to understand about machine learning (and by extension, most AI systems) is that these systems are only as good as the data they learn from—and how well the model matches the problem it is trying to solve. Building a good model is about finding the right balance: the model needs to be detailed enough to capture real patterns, but not so detailed that it gets distracted by random noise. If the model is too simple, it may miss important patterns altogether. This is called underfitting, and it often leads to poor performance because the model has not learned enough to make useful predictions. It is akin to trying to guess someone's favorite movie genre based only on their age—age is not enough information to go on. On the other hand, if the model is too complex, it might learn not only the patterns but also the irrelevant details or quirks in the training data. This is called overfitting. It is like memorizing the answers to a specific practice test without understanding the material—so when the real test changes even slightly, you are lost. This is why machine learning experts pay close attention to model complexity—that is, how detailed or flexible a model is—and use strategies like cross-validation, where the model is tested on different portions of the data to ensure that it can generalize well to new, unseen situations. The goal is to create a model that captures the signal (the phenomenon we are interested in), not the noise (extraneous data) (Bzdok et al., 2018).

Let us dig a little deeper into what machine learning is. Machine learning uses different types of algorithms to identify patterns in data and make predictions. Within the three main categories of supervised, unsupervised, and reinforcement learning, specific algorithms can be used to explore different kinds of questions that researchers may have about data (Luan & Tsai, 2021).

Supervised Machine Learning

Let us first consider supervised machine learning. In supervised learning, the computer learns by example. That means the system is trained using data where the correct answers are already known. Imagine teaching a student with flashcards—on one side is a picture of a fruit, and on the other side is the label "apple" or "banana." Over time, the student starts to notice patterns: apples are usually red or green and round, while bananas are yellow and curved. In the same way, supervised learning algorithms learn from labeled examples and try to apply those lessons to new situations.

For instance, Netflix uses supervised learning when recommending movies. If you have watched and liked several action films, the system starts to learn your preferences by comparing your choices to others with similar tastes. One simple method used in this case is called K-Nearest Neighbors—it finds the "closest" match based on viewing habits and suggests similar content. Another common algorithm is Naïve Bayes, which is often used to sort spam emails. It looks at the kinds of words found in spam messages—like "winner," "free," or "urgent"—and calculates the chance that a new email is also spam.

Other supervised learning methods are used to make predictions. Linear regression, for example, might predict how well a student will do on a future test by looking at how they have performed in the past. Logistic regression helps answer yes/no questions, like whether someone is likely to pass a class or not. Decision Trees work like a series of questions, such as "Did the student attend class regularly?" or "Did they submit assignments on time?"—each answer leads to the next question until a final decision is made. And Random Forest takes this a step further by combining many decision trees to make a more accurate guess—kind of like asking a group of people for their opinion instead of relying on just one person. Support Vector Machines, or SVMs, are another tool in this group. They are used in facial recognition, for example, to tell whether a photo matches a specific person by analyzing features like the distance between the eyes or the shape of the jaw.

Unsupervised Machine Learning

On the other hand, unsupervised learning is more like giving the computer a bunch of puzzle pieces without telling it what the final picture should look like. The system has to figure out the patterns on its own. It is often used when we do not have labeled data or when we want to explore a large set of information and see what naturally groups together.

One common unsupervised technique is clustering. For example, stores might use this to group customers into types based on what they buy—maybe "bargain shoppers," "brand loyalists," or "occasional splurgers." Another important use is in fraud detection. Banks and credit card companies use unsupervised learning to catch unusual spending patterns that might signal fraud. Since fraudulent behavior often doesn't look like anything the system has seen before, unsupervised methods are useful because they do not need labeled examples of "fraud" to notice when something looks suspicious.

Reinforcement Learning

A third type of machine learning is reinforcement learning. Reinforcement learning (RL) in AI has its conceptual roots in behaviorism, a school of psychology that studies behavior through observable actions rather than internal mental states. Behaviorism, especially in the work of B.F. Skinner, emphasizes how behavior is shaped by stimuli, rewards, and punishments. This approach is known as operant conditioning.

As Kosinski and Zaczek-Chrzanowska (2007) point out, RL mirrors this model by training agents—autonomous decision-makers like software programs or robots—to learn through feedback from their environment. In this context, the environment includes everything the agent can sense and act upon, and it responds to the agent's choices with new situations and evaluative signals (rewards or penalties). A classical example of behavioral conditioning is Pavlov's experiment with dogs, where a bell paired with food eventually triggered salivation at the sound alone. Similarly, RL systems learn which actions lead to desirable outcomes through trial and error, making them a computational extension of behaviorist learning theory.

Reinforcement learning can be broadly divided into two styles: model-based methods, which attempt to build a representation or "map" of the environment before acting, and model-free methods, which learn optimal behaviors through trial and error—like robots learning to pour water or balance on two wheels by practicing repeatedly (Naeem et al., 2020).

Within model-free approaches, different algorithms are used to guide learning. One popular method is Q-learning, which teaches systems to make better decisions over time by assigning value scores to actions based on expected future rewards. For instance, it has been applied in electric power system control and in helping robots decide how to move on a grid. Deep Q-Networks (DQNs) extend Q-learning by using neural networks to handle complex, high-dimensional inputs like images or maps. This approach is used in applications such as self-driving cars, where the system learns to navigate safely by recognizing patterns in visual data.

Another group of model-free algorithms, called Policy Gradient methods, directly optimize the decision-making process instead of assigning scores to actions. These are used in managing resources in computer networks—for example, determining how to allocate internet bandwidth during periods of congestion. Actor-Critic methods, which are also model-free, combine both value estimation (like Q-learning) and direct policy optimization (like Policy Gradients). They are often used in AI-powered devices—from robots to smart home systems—to enable smooth, adaptive behavior in dynamic environments (Naeem et al., 2020).

Machine Learning vs. Traditional Statistics

Traditional statistics and machine learning (ML) both help us make sense of data, but they do so in different ways. Statistics is primarily focused on inference—understanding how and why patterns in the data occur. For example, a medical researcher might use statistical models to determine whether a new drug significantly lowers blood pressure compared to a placebo, and how confident we can be in that result. This involves clearly defined models and assumptions to test hypotheses and estimate relationships with measurable certainty, such as p-values or confidence intervals (Bzdok et al., 2018). This approach is especially useful when the goal is to explain and understand relationships in a dataset. However, traditional statistics works best with "long data," where there are more observations (like people in a study) than variables being measured.

Machine learning, on the other hand, is more often used for prediction than explanation. ML uses algorithms to learn patterns from data and make forecasts, without necessarily needing to understand the underlying cause. ML can handle "wide data," where the number of measurements per item is very large and can look for relationships between those measurements. A good example is image recognition: each image is made up of thousands of tiny squares called pixels, and each pixel holds a number representing brightness or color. Figure 2.2 shows an example of how pixels work.

Fig. 2.2 The two images in this figure were created by OpenAI's Dall-E when we prompted to create an image to explain how pixels and image recognition work. (The left-most image shows tiny squares of different colors and brightness that together compose an image)

When a user feeds pixels' numbers into a machine learning model, it can learn to identify what is in the image—like distinguishing a cat from a dog—even without knowing anything about animals. While ML models are often more accurate in these kinds of complex tasks, they can be harder to interpret and may not easily translate to scientific explanations (Bzdok et al., 2018).

To complicate things further, the terminology and methods between statistics and ML often overlap, and the distinctions can be inconsistent. Many techniques—such as regression or decision trees—exist in both fields but may be used with different goals and described with different terms. For example, a statistician may use a regression model to test whether a variable has a meaningful effect, while a machine learning practitioner might use the same model purely to optimize predictive accuracy. The justification for choosing a statistical model typically rests on how well it captures the data-generating process, while machine learning models are selected based on empirical performance in similar tasks (Bzdok et al., 2018). In this way, the boundary between the two is more about intended use than about the tools themselves. Ultimately, statistics and machine learning are complementary: often, statistics helps us understand why something is happening, and ML helps us predict what is likely to happen next.

Neural Networks and Deep Learning

One relatable way to understand deep learning is to consider how much and why spell and grammar checkers have improved in the past two decades. Many of my fellow academicians will remember spell checkers of the early 2000s. Back then, spell checking your document was a necessary step in editing, but these tools often missed many errors—especially context-sensitive ones. Mistakes like missing words or confusing homophones ("their" vs. "there") often went undetected. Today's AI-powered editing tools, such as Grammarly, not only catch most of these issues but can also suggest improvements in tone, clarity, and style. So what changed? The leap forward was driven by advances in deep learning and natural language processing. Modern tools are built on large-scale machine learning models—particularly neural networks trained on vast amounts of text—that enable them to understand the context and intent behind language, rather than relying solely on predefined rules.

AI and Spellcheckers. Let us consider the improvements in spell checkers in a bit more detail as a way to understand what deep learning can do. Prior to the widespread consumer use of deep learning in language tools, most spell checkers operated using a rule-based, dictionary-driven approach (Dickinson et al., 2012). These systems relied on a static list of correctly spelled words. If a user typed a word that did not appear in the dictionary, the spell checker would flag it as incorrect and suggest a likely replacement. But how did it decide what to suggest? One of the most common methods was to calculate Levenshtein distance—the minimum number of insertions, deletions, or substitutions needed to turn a misspelled word into a valid one. For example, if someone typed "definately," the system might compare it to both "definitely" and "defiantly." Although both are real words, "definitely" has a Levenshtein distance of 2 (changing "a" to "i" and inserting another "i"), while "defiantly" has a distance of 3. Because "definitely" is closer by this measure, it would be offered as the most probable correction. This process is entirely rule-based: the spell checker applies a fixed algorithm to identify the word with the smallest number of edits, regardless of context.

Users of early spell checkers quickly learned the limitations of rule-based approaches. Because most systems did not consider meaning, they often failed to catch errors when the misspelled word was still a valid dictionary entry. For instance, a sentence like "All students must sing the academic honesty pledge before submitting their work" might pass unnoticed—even though "sing" and "sign" are clearly not interchangeable in this context. These words differ by only one transposition, making them close in spelling, but only one makes sense. Such examples, often circulated in early 2000s academic humor, highlight the shortcomings of spell checkers that rely solely on spelling rules rather than understanding language in context.

In contrast, modern AI allows for computers to use language's context—not just rules. Today, spell checker tools are powered by deep learning models trained on massive text corpora—large collections of real-world language from books, articles, websites, and conversations. These corpora are not just lists of correct words, but rich datasets that reflect how language is actually used in practice, including tone, sentence structure, and idiomatic expression. Deep learning enables these systems to move beyond just guessing the closest word. At the heart of this approach are artificial neural networks (ANNs)—computer models inspired by the structure of the human brain. These networks automatically learn to identify complex relationships in data without requiring humans to hand-select which linguistic features to analyze. For spell and grammar checkers, this means they can evaluate the context of a sentence, determine whether a word choice or construction makes sense, and offer corrections that align with fluent usage rather than just mechanical rules.

Healthcare. Deep learning—a branch of artificial intelligence that analyzes patterns in large datasets—is emerging as a transformative tool in medical imaging, offering diagnostic insights that often surpass human perception. One of its most compelling advantages is its ability to detect subtle patterns, textures or spatial relationships in medical images that may be imperceptible to even trained specialists. For example, in early-stage cancer detection or the identification of microscopic cellular changes in pathology slides, deep learning models have shown the ability to recognize indicators of disease that are easily overlooked in manual review. These systems not only "see" what humans might miss but also learn to look for features that clinicians may not have been trained to prioritize—or may not have known to consider at all. In conditions like Alzheimer's disease, where early anatomical changes are gradual and complex, deep learning can analyze brain scans for shape and volume variations that fall below the threshold of human visual recognition. Moreover, these models improve over time by learning from vast collections of annotated images, allowing them to identify atypical presentations and rare variations that may confound human judgment. In doing so, deep learning extends the diagnostic toolkit of clinicians, serving as a second set of eyes that can illuminate what might otherwise remain unseen (Parker, 2025).

Facial recognition. In the higher education context, one example of deep learning in action is a facial recognition attendance system (Essien & Ansa, 2023). Instead of using a sign-in sheet or ID card, students simply walk into the classroom, and a camera captures their faces. The system then automatically detects each face, analyzes its unique features—such as the distance between the eyes, the shape of the nose, or the curve of the jaw—and matches it against a database of known students. Deep learning helps by making the system smart enough to recognize faces even when lighting conditions change or when someone turns their head slightly. It does this by learning what features really matter for identifying someone, without needing a person to program those rules manually. The result is a fast, reliable way to take attendance that saves time, reduces impersonation, and works accurately in real-world conditions. Of course, this application of deep learning—like many others that rely on biometric or personal data—raises important questions about privacy, surveillance, and consent, issues that are explored more fully in the next chapter.

Misconceptions About Deep Learning. We have just made a powerful argument that deep learning is useful because it allows for considerations of complex patterns and context. This usefulness for certain applications is often confused with inherent superiority. In talking with university leaders, though, one of the key misconceptions that we have seen is that somehow deep learning is a superior next-generation alternative to traditional machine learning. Traditional machine learning approaches and deep learning approaches are both useful, and neither one is "better," just may be more appropriate for a given application.

Consider that when an AI system uses deep learning, it is often difficult to understand exactly how it arrives at its decisions. We explore the issue of explainability in more detail in Chap. 3, but for now, it is important to recognize that many deep learning models function as "black boxes." While it is usually possible to assess model outputs and measure their accuracy, it is typically not possible to trace the reasoning behind a specific result. This lack of transparency is sometimes compounded by closed-source practices. For instance, companies like OpenAI do not release their model architectures or training code. Others, such as Meta, have taken a more open approach by making large language models like LLaMA publicly available. However, even when the code is accessible, the underlying models—often consisting of millions or billions of parameters across many layers—learn internal representations that are too complex and abstract for humans to interpret. In short, access to the code does not mean the model is understandable in practice.

Even when explainability is not a primary concern, deep learning is not always the right tool for the job. One common misconception—especially among those new to AI—is the assumption that having a large number of rows in a few spreadsheets means deep learning is feasible. However, deep learning models typically require not just thousands, but often millions of well-labeled, high-quality examples to perform effectively. In contrast, many real-world datasets—particularly those collected from a single institution or project—are relatively small or narrow in scope. In these cases, traditional machine learning methods are often more appropriate: they can handle moderate-sized datasets, are faster to train, and still provide high levels of predictive accuracy.

Natural Language Processing

At its core, Natural Language Processing (NLP) acts as a lens through which language becomes analyzable by computers—NLP breaks down text into structured elements such as words, grammar, syntax, and semantics. This transformation allows computational systems to work with language as data, uncovering patterns, extracting meaning, and interpreting context. The origins of NLP can be traced back to the 1950s, when researchers first attempted to use computers for automatic translation between languages. Early machine translation systems were primarily focused on translating between English and Russian, driven by Cold War efforts to quickly interpret scientific and technical documents. These early systems used simple dictionaries and grammatical rules to produce rough translations, marking the first attempt to formalize language for computational use. Though the output was often awkward or inaccurate, the effort illustrated the possibility of analyzing language systematically—and laid the foundation for future NLP developments (Khurana et al., 2023).

NLP may use rule-based approaches or deep-learning based approaches. Rule-based NLP systems often rely on expert-written linguistic rules and pattern-matching tools. For example, regular expressions—simple but powerful search patterns used to identify strings of text—can help detect specific words or phrases. Some systems also incorporate ontologies, which are structured representations of knowledge that define relationships between concepts, to improve the precision of language analysis. An example of a rule-based system used in a medical application might scan clinical notes for combinations of terms like "chest pain" and "shortness of breath" to flag possible cardiac concerns. While these systems offer precision and transparency, they often struggle with the complexity and ambiguity of real-world language. Consider a sentence like "The test came back negative, which is not bad." A rule-based system might flag the word "negative" as concerning without understanding that in this context it actually signals a good outcome. Similarly, rule-based models may not handle idiomatic expressions or sarcasm well—for instance, interpreting "That was just great," as positive when it is actually meant to express frustration. Because they cannot easily account for nuance or shifting usage, rule-based systems tend to break down when language becomes less predictable or more context-dependent.

In contrast, adding deep learning to NLP brings flexibility by allowing computers to learn from data rather than rely entirely on predefined rules. In NLP, machine learning models are trained on large datasets to detect statistical patterns associated with different outcomes. For example, in spam detection, a model might learn that messages containing phrases like "urgent response needed" or "click this link," especially when combined with certain email addresses or formatting styles, are more likely to be spam. Over time, the model adjusts its internal weights based on the frequency and combinations of these features, improving its ability to flag suspicious messages—even those using slightly different wording than what it has seen before. These models can also account for patterns in metadata, such as sending frequency or header anomalies. Much like pixels serve as the basic units that an image model processes to recognize visual patterns, tokens function as the basic units of text that NLP models use to detect meaning and structure. Both are low-level building blocks that, when organized effectively, allow AI to interpret complex forms—whether visual scenes or human language. While deep learning requires annotated data and is less interpretable than rule-based systems, deep learning models can generalize better to new or varied inputs, making them more adaptable in real-world scenarios where language is constantly evolving.

Deep learning represents a more recent and powerful evolution in NLP (Rusk, 2016). While convolutional neural networks (CNNs) were commonly used in earlier NLP models—particularly for tasks like sentence classification—they have become less prevalent in modern NLP. Today, recurrent neural networks (RNNs), which read text one word at a time while keeping track of what came before, and transformer models, which consider all the words in a sentence at once to understand how they relate to each other, are more widely used because they do a better job of capturing context and meaning—especially in longer or more complex texts.

Bidirectional Encoder Representations from Transformers (BERT). One of the most influential deep learning transformers for NLP is BERT, short for Bidirectional Encoder Representations from Transformers (Devlin et al., 2019). BERT is trained to understand the meaning of a word based on all the words around it, rather than just the ones before or after. This makes it especially good at tasks where subtle meaning and context are important. In practice, BERT powers everyday tools like Google Search's ability to understand what you are really asking, email clients that suggest smart replies, and customer service bots that can answer complex questions with relevant and coherent responses.

NLP in Electronic Medical Records. One of the areas we (Alex and Rebeca) use NLP in is healthcare, where NLP could be used to analyze written or spoken medical information, such as what patients say (Allen et al., 2025) or doctors' notes in electronic health records (EHRs) (Allen & Abrahams, in press). For example, one study in dialysis care used rule-based NLP to examine how well kidney dialysis patients' symptoms—like fatigue, itching, or sleep problems—were being documented in medical records (Dai et al., 2025). The researchers found that while NLP could accurately flag symptoms when they were mentioned in the notes, many patient-reported symptoms simply were not written down. This example illustrates a larger point: what people say and what gets recorded often differ, and a result, real patient needs just go unaddressed. NLP can help researchers notice such significant discrepancies; NLP might also help with systems designed to automatically capture important details, like symptoms. Of course, like all AI tools that handle sensitive information, NLP raises important questions about privacy, bias, and oversight—issues explored more fully in Chap. 3.

Computer Vision

Computer vision is a field of artificial intelligence that allows computers to interpret visual information—photos, videos, or other image-based inputs—in ways that are increasingly similar to how people do. Depending on the purpose, a computer vision system might be designed to carry out tasks such as classification (identifying what kind of object is present, like a tree or a bicycle), detection (locating where an object appears in the image) or segmentation (mapping the exact boundaries of an object to separate it from the background or other elements) (Mahadevkar et al., 2022).

To perform these kinds of tasks, computer vision systems rely on machine learning and deep learning. With machine learning, systems are trained on labeled examples to recognize patterns—like learning to tell the difference between a cat and a dog based on thousands of sample images. Deep learning, which builds on this approach, enables systems to automatically extract useful features from raw image data—such as edges, textures, and shapes—making it especially effective for complex visual environments like autonomous driving or diagnostic imaging. As these learning methods continue to advance, computer vision is becoming more accurate, more adaptable, and more deeply embedded in everyday technologies.

One of the most recognizable uses of computer vision today is in autonomous vehicles. These systems rely on a combination of classification, detection, and segmentation to safely navigate the world. Classification helps identify road signs and traffic signals, detection locates other vehicles, pedestrians, and cyclists, and segmentation separates road lanes, curbs, sidewalks, and other environmental features. However, it is important to note that, beyond transportation, computer vision plays a major role in research, industry, and everyday life. In astronomy, classification is used to sort stars and galaxies based on their shape, brightness or other visual characteristics. In healthcare, detection and segmentation work together to identify and isolate tumors, signs of glaucoma or skin conditions from medical images. In agriculture, classification supports tasks like identifying plant species or grading crops, while segmentation can highlight damaged areas of leaves. In manufacturing, detection is used to spot defects on production lines and segmentation helps define exactly where the flaws occur, so they can be corrected or removed (Singh et al., 2022). One of the most intriguing uses of computer vision is using the technology to create assistive devices for people with blindness or visual impairments. For example, researchers have proposed systems built into wearable items like shoes that use computer vision algorithms along with Internet of Things (IoT) devices and sensors to detect and identify obstacles in real time. These systems can guide users not only by alerting them to the presence of objects but also by recognizing what those objects are—such as a stairway, doorway or parked bicycle—and helping the user move safely around them. Navigation support is provided through voice feedback via a smartphone and physical cues from haptic actuators, such as vibrations in the shoe (Rao & Singh, 2021). These varied applications show how core computer vision tasks can be adapted to very different fields—all using similar underlying techniques to extract meaning from visual data.

Generative AI

The final approach to artificial intelligence we will explore is generative AI (often abbreviated as GenAI or sometimes GAI).

Generative AI refers to models capable of creating new content, such as text, images, or audio, that may resemble human-created content. Readers may be most familiar with prominent examples of generative AI tools, including OpenAI's ChatGPT, Google's Gemini, and Microsoft's Copilot. In addition to these commercial offerings, there are open-source generative AI models available for download and local use, such as xAI's Grok and Meta's LLaMA.

Generative AI refers to a class of artificial intelligence systems designed to produce new content—such as text, images, audio, or code—based on patterns learned from existing data (Fui-Hoon Nah et al., 2023). These systems do not retrieve information in the way a search engine does. Instead, they generate responses by predicting what is likely to come next, based on the input they receive and the vast datasets they were trained on. These models are trained on massive collections of text from books, websites, and other sources. Through this training, the models learn statistical patterns in language: how words and ideas tend to be structured, how concepts relate to one another, and how context shapes meaning.

At the core of many of these systems is a machine learning architecture known as a transformer, which allows the model to consider the context of each word in a sentence—both what comes before and what might logically come after. When a user enters a prompt, the model generates a sequence of words that statistically fit the context, drawing on its training rather than any real-time access to the internet or external databases. Some of these systems use other architectures, such as Generative Adversarial Networks (GANs), which involve two neural networks working in tandem—one generating content and the other evaluating it—to improve the quality of the output over time (Fui-Hoon Nah et al., 2023).

Ethical and acceptance issues. Generative AI is not without potential problems or controversies. It is important to note that while these systems often produce content that appears coherent or even creative, they do not "understand" their outputs in the way humans do. Their capabilities are based on learned associations and probability, not comprehension or intent (Fui-Hoon Nah et al., 2023).

As I will further outline in Chap. 5, faculty have strong beliefs and emotions when it comes to Generative AI. While Generative AI tools can support learning and creativity, they also raise concerns about bias, the erosion of critical thinking skills, and the reliability of AI-generated content. Overreliance on generative AI may lead to a deskilling of essential academic competencies, such as writing and problem-solving. Additionally, the integration of AI into educational settings introduces questions around privacy, transparency, and equitable access. As institutions experiment with these technologies, it is essential to adopt policies and practices that promote responsible use while preserving the core values of higher education (Batista et al., 2024)—all of these concerns are explored more in the subsequent Chap. 10. Also, even if ethical concerns can be addressed, and supposing that the benefits outweigh the negatives in a particular use case, faculty acceptance of generative AI is a major consideration—Chap. 5 discusses the acceptance landscape on my local campus.

Prompt engineering. Optimal use of Generative AI can help to maximize Generative AI's efficiency and benefits. Prompt engineering can be thought of as programming for natural language—it's the art of crafting inputs that shape how a large language model like ChatGPT responds (Batista et al., 2024). Instead of writing code, users design prompts using plain language, but with clear structure and intent. A well-engineered prompt typically includes an instruction (what the model should do), context (background or framing), input data (the focus or subject) and an output indicator (such as the format or length of the response). For instance, instead of simply saying "summarize this article," a stronger prompt would be: "Summarize the main arguments of this article in five bullet points suitable for an academic PowerPoint presentation." Educators can use prompt engineering not just to guide AI output, but also to model academic thinking, scaffold writing tasks, and encourage deeper student engagement with content. The "Try It Out" feature at the end of this chapter provides some additional information about prompt engineering that can help you get started with getting better Generative AI outputs.

Generative AI to generate educational content. Most readers are likely aware that educators can use tools like ChatGPT by prompting the interface to create lessons, generate practice activities or provide quick feedback. This approach remains largely manual and one-size-fits-all. But more than just this local ad hoc usage, some companies are integrating generative AI into the core architecture of their platforms to automate, personalize, and scale learning in more transformative ways.

For instance, Duolingo—a widely used language learning app with hundreds of millions of users worldwide—offers a compelling example of this kind of deep AI integration. Historically, computer-assisted language learning (CALL) systems were limited to static, rule-based drills, such as flashcards or fill-in-the-blank exercises that provided pre-scripted, non-adaptive feedback. These programs lacked the ability to respond to individual learner needs or generate novel content, often resulting in a repetitive and disengaging experience. Until recently, such approaches were the norm in digital language education, offering limited interactivity. Little Duolingo, for example, exemplifies a new generation of AI-enhanced language learning platforms by embedding generative models like GPT-4 alongside its proprietary AI system, Birdbrain. These tools are not merely add-ons but are integrated into the core of Duolingo's infrastructure, powering everything from adaptive grammar exercises to interactive, story-based lessons. Unlike educators who manually prompt generative tools like ChatGPT to produce isolated materials (Batista et al., 2024), Duolingo automates content generation at scale. Structured prompts guide the AI to produce exercises tailored to specific grammar points, vocabulary, and difficulty levels. Human experts then review and refine this output, ensuring it meets pedagogical standards. This workflow has dramatically accelerated lesson production, allowing Duolingo to expand its course offerings, support niche languages, and develop new features more efficiently—all while maintaining quality. By fully integrating generative AI into both content creation and delivery, Duolingo demonstrates the transformative potential of these tools when thoughtfully embedded into educational design (Parker, 2025).

Conclusion

Like the blackboards once hailed as revolutionary, AI has become a symbol of both promise and peril and fear. As we have explored in this chapter, the term "AI" encompasses a wide and evolving range of systems—some visible, some purposely opaque or just poorly understood by the general public. Whether or not you use generative AI in your daily work, in many ways, AI shapes our daily lives and educational environments—AI is present in our cars, phones, email systems, search engines and more. Yet much of the public discourse around AI remains clouded by hype, confusion, or outright misinformation. That confusion is not just a matter of semantics; it has real consequences for how people respond to AI—ranging from overreliance to total rejection. Building AI literacy—an understanding of what AI is, how it works, and what it can (and cannot) do—is essential to cutting through this fog. Table 2.3 provides an overview of some of the myths we have dispelled and the AI facts that we have covered.

When we demystify AI, we empower ourselves and our students to make informed, ethical, and confident decisions about its use or non-use.

Table 2.3 Misconceptions about AI

Myth	*Reality*
Public fears and excitement about AI are mostly technical in origin.	Cultural narratives, political rhetoric, and media portrayals often shape perceptions of AI more than technical facts do.
AI is one single tool or system.	AI refers to a broad set of methods and technologies, including machine learning, natural language processing, computer vision, and more.
Systems like ChatGPT 'think' like humans.	AI models generate outputs based on statistical patterns, not human reasoning or understanding.
Highly accurate AI models are inherently trustworthy.	Deep learning models can deliver accurate results, but often lack transparency in how they arrive at those outputs. Accuracy does not guarantee explainability.
AI literacy requires becoming a technical expert.	Conceptual literacy—understanding what AI can and cannot do—is often more important than technical mastery for responsible use.
Using AI tools like ChatGPT requires coding skills.	Public-facing AI tools operate through natural language, allowing everyday users to interact with them without programming.
The quality of AI output cannot be influenced by users.	Thoughtful prompt engineering can dramatically improve the relevance, clarity, and usefulness of AI outputs (see the "Try It Out" feature at the end of this chapter.

This chapter has aimed to lay the groundwork for that literacy. We have clarified that AI is not a single tool but a collection of approaches—including machine learning, natural language processing, computer vision, and generative AI—that may often work together in AI systems. We have examined how these technologies function, where they appear in everyday life, and how systems like ChatGPT respond to prompts using combinations of supervised learning, deep learning, and human feedback. We have also introduced the concept of prompt engineering as a practical and accessible way to interact with AI systems—a kind of programming for natural language that educators can learn and use. By unpacking these elements, we hope to replace fear or blind enthusiasm with curiosity, skepticism, and understanding. In a moment where AI is often treated as magical or menacing, AI literacy offers something far more valuable: perspective.

Acknowledgments Open AI's Dall-E was used to create Fig. 2.2

Try It Out: Getting Started with Prompt Engineering

LLMs like ChatGPT have become the most familiar image of "AI" in the public imagination. When people hear about AI today, they often think first of chatbots, writing assistants, or similar tools. While LLMs are certainly not the only kind of AI—technologies like computer vision, robotics, and expert systems also play major roles—working with tools like ChatGPT is an approachable and effective starting point for building AI literacy.

When accessed through public-facing websites, LLMs like ChatGPT do not require users to program using a formal coding language. Instead of writing code, users interact with these systems by writing requests in everyday human language. The model then interprets and responds based on patterns it has learned from massive training datasets. This natural-language interface makes AI feel accessible, but it can also be deceptively simple. Many people try these tools once or twice, receive generic or unhelpful responses, and conclude that "ChatGPT just is not that good." However, often the problem is not with the model—it is with the prompt. Like any tool, AI performs better when it is used with skill and intention. Prompt engineering—the practice of designing effective prompts—can make LLMs far more useful. It helps guide the AI's output, improve relevance and clarity, and tailor responses to specific needs in writing, analysis, and creative work.

LLMs have cause tremendous ethical controversy, as will be discussed in the next chpater (Chap. 3). One of the major concerns about LLMs is the possibility of hallucination—that is, making up believable but false content. What is often missing in discussion of hallucination is the context that the quality of the prompt matters. Prompt engineering is how to make quality prompts.

How to Get Started

Be Specific About the Task

As described earlier in this chapter, clear input leads to clearer output.
Instead of:

Summarize this article

Try:

"Summarize the main arguments of this article in five bullet points suitable for a presentation to undergraduate students."

Provide Context and Assign a Role

Giving the AI a role helps shape its tone and style, drawing on its broad training data.
Instead of:

Explain AI ethics

try:

"You are a university ethics professor. Write a brief lecture introduction explaining why ethical considerations are important when designing AI systems."

Request a Specific Output Format

Structuring the output helps the AI organize its response more effectively.
Instead of:

Tell me about machine learning,

Try:

Create a table comparing supervised, unsupervised, and reinforcement learning, including definitions and one example for each.

Combine Multiple Tasks for Deeper Engagement

Combining tasks encourages the AI to integrate multiple capabilities at once.

Instead of:

Summarize this article

Try:

Summarize this article, suggest a headline, and generate two discussion questions appropriate for a graduate seminar.

Iterate and Refine

Feedback and refinement improve the output.

Instead of accepting the first result, try following up with:

Now rewrite the summary to be more conversational and suitable for a podcast audience.

Building Your Skills

Keep a "Prompt Journal" to track your best prompts, refinements, and outcomes can help you develop a stronger sense of how different styles of input produce different outputs.

Questions for Reflection and Discussion

1. The chapter discusses how political leaders and public figures often frame AI as a revolutionary technology. How might this framing influence public expectations, fears, and patterns of adoption? Can you think of historical examples where technological hype helped or harmed society's approach to a new innovation?

2. Artificial intelligence is not a single tool or technology but an evolving field made up of different methods such as machine learning, natural language processing, computer vision, and generative AI. Why does it matter that the public—and professionals—understand these distinctions when considering the impact of AI on education, healthcare, and society?
3. The chapter highlights that AI systems like ChatGPT combine multiple approaches, including natural language processing, deep learning, and reinforcement learning. How important is it for users to have conceptual literacy about these methods, even if they are not technical experts? Where should we draw the line between what a responsible AI user needs to understand versus what only technical specialists need to master?
4. The chapter explains that deep learning models can produce highly accurate outputs, but the processes they use to arrive at those outputs are often opaque, even to experts. When should we accept this lack of transparency in AI systems, and when should explainability be a non-negotiable requirement? Support your argument with examples.
5. Prompt engineering is presented as an accessible way to meaningfully engage with AI without needing programming skills. In what ways could learning to design better prompts strengthen broader skills in writing, communication, teaching, or research? How might prompt engineering change the way we think about inquiry and problem-solving in professional settings?

References

Allen, R. J., & Abrahams, A. C. (in press). Enhancing nephrology research with NLP and AI: A case for more comprehensive symptom documentation. *Kidney, 360*.

Allen, R., Nakonechnyi, A., Norton, S. A., & Saeed, F. (2025). Questions older people and caregivers ask about kidney therapies: A computer-assisted analysis. *Patient Education and Counseling, 135*, 108713.

Batista, J., Mesquita, A., & Carnaz, G. (2024). Generative AI and higher education: Trends, challenges, and future directions from a systematic literature review. *Information (Switzerland), 15*(11). https://doi.org/10.3390/info15110676

Biden, J. (2023). Remarks by President Biden and Vice President Harris on the Administration's Commitment to advancing the safe, secure, and trustworthy development and use of artificial intelligence. *The White House.*. https://biden-whitehouse.archives.gov/briefing-room/speeches-remarks/2023/10/30/remarks-by-president-biden-and-vice-president-harris-on-the-administrations-commitment-to-advancing-the-safe-secure-and-trustworthy-development-and-use-of-artificial-intelligence

Bzdok, D., Altman, N., & Krzywinski, M. (2018). Points of significance: Statistics versus machine learning. *Nature Methods, 15*(4), 233–234. https://doi.org/10.1038/nmeth.4642

Dai, Y., Wen, H. H., Yang, J., Gupta, N., Rhee, C., Horowitz, C. R., et al. (2025). Natural language processing identifies under-documentation of symptoms in patients on hemodialysis. *Kidney360*, 10–34067. https://pubmed.ncbi.nlm.nih.gov/39879098/

Devlin, J., Chang, M.-W., Lee, K., & Toutanova, K. (2019). BERT: Pre-training of deep bidirectional transformers for language understanding. In J. Burstein, C. Doran, & T. Solorio (Eds.), *Proceedings of the 2019 conference of the North American Chapter of the Association for Computational Linguistics: Human Language Technologies, Volume 1 (Long and Short Papers)* (pp. 4171–4186). Association for Computational Linguistics. https://doi.org/10.18653/v1/N19-1423

Dickinson, M., Brew, C., & Meurers, D. (2012). *Language and computers.* Wiley-Blackwell.

Essien, U. D., & Ansa, G. O. (2023). A deep learning-based face recognition attendance system. *Global Journal of Engineering and Technology Advances, 17*(1), 9–22. https://doi.org/10.30574/gjeta.2023.17.1.0165

Fui-Hoon Nah, F., Zheng, R., Cai, J., Siau, K., & Chen, L. (2023). Generative AI and ChatGPT: Applications, challenges, and AI-human collaboration. *Journal of Information Technology Case and Application Research, 25*(3), 277–304. https://doi.org/10.1080/15228053.2023.2233814

Kennedy, G., Tyson, A., & Saks, E. (2023). *Public awareness of artificial intelligence in everyday activities: Limited enthusiasm in U.S. over AI's growing influence in daily life.* Pew Research Center. https://www.pewresearch.org/science/2023/02/15/public-awareness-of-artificial-intelligence-in-everyday-activities/

Khurana, D., Koli, A., Khatter, K., & Singh, S. (2023). Natural language processing: State of the art, current trends and challenges. *Multimedia Tools and Applications, 82*(3), 3713–3744. https://doi.org/10.1007/s11042-022-13428-4

Kosinski, W., & Zaczek-Chrzanowska, D. (2007). Pavlovian, Skinner, and other behaviourists' contributions to AI. In *Intelligent motion and interaction within virtual environments*. NASA. https://ntrs.nasa.gov/citations/20070038351

Luan, H., & Tsai, C.-C. (2021). A review of using machine learning approaches for precision education. *Educational Technology and Society, 24*(1), 250–266.

Luckin, R., Cukurova, M., Kent, C., & du Boulay, B. (2022). Empowering educators to be AI-ready. *Computers and Education: Artificial Intelligence, 3*, 100076. https://doi.org/10.1016/j.caeai.2022.100076

Mahadevkar, S. V., Khemani, B., Patil, S., Kotecha, K., Vora, D. R., Abraham, A., & Gabralla, L. A. (2022). A review on machine learning styles in computer vision – Techniques and future directions. *IEEE Access, 10*, 107293–107329. https://doi.org/10.1109/ACCESS.2022.3209825

Naeem, M., Rizvi, S. T. H., & Coronato, A. (2020). A gentle introduction to reinforcement learning and its application in different fields. *IEEE Access, 8*, 209320–209344. https://doi.org/10.1109/ACCESS.2020.3038605

Nussbaum, F. G. (2023). A comprehensive review of AI myths and misconceptions. 1–27. https://doi.org/10.13140/RG.2.2.28098.15049

Parker, H. (2025, February 14). How Duolingo uses AI to create lessons faster. Duolingo Blog. https://blog.duolingo.com/large-language-model-duolingo-lessons/

Rao, S., & Singh, V. M. (2021). Computer vision and IoT-based smart system for visually impaired people. In *2021 11th International conference on Cloud Computing, Data Science & Engineering (Confluence)* (pp. 552–556). IEEE. https://doi.org/10.1109/Confluence51648.2021.9377120

Rusk, N. (2016). Deep learning. *Nature Methods, 13*(1), 35. https://doi.org/10.1038/nmeth.3707

Singh, G., Pidadi, P., & Malwad, D. S. (2022, December). A review on applications of computer vision. In *International conference on Hybrid Intelligent Systems* (pp. 464–479). Springer Nature Switzerland. https://doi.org/10.1007/978-3-031-27409-1_42

Trump, D. (2025). *Artificial intelligence for the American people*. https://trumpwhitehouse.archives.gov/ai/

Winkel, M. (2024). Controlling the uncontrollable: The public discourse on artificial intelligence between the positions of social and technological determinism. *AI and Society*. https://doi.org/10.1007/s00146-024-01979-z

CHAPTER 3

From Frankenstein to Facebook: The History, Ethics, and Regulation of AI

Rebecca J. Allen and Alex Nakonechnyi

Introduction

In Mary Shelley's *Frankenstein* (2018), the technological being—the monster—turns against his creator. Scorned, feared, and rejected by people, the monster demands that his creator, Victor, make him a female monster companion. At first, Victor agrees, but later recants, fearing what reproducing monsters would mean for humanity. The monster, enraged, rails against his creator:

> Remember that I have power; you believe yourself miserable, but I can make you so wretched that the light of day will be hateful to you. You are my creator, but I am your master;—obey!

For many people, the themes in Shelley's story—unchecked innovation and creator responsibility—mirror current concerns about AI. With the

R. J. Allen (✉) • A. Nakonechnyi (✉)
Center for IT Engagement (cITe), Mount St. Joseph University, Cincinnati, OH, USA
e-mail: rebecca.allen@msj.edu; Alex.Nakonechnyi@msj.edu

R. J. Allen, A. Nakonechnyi (eds.), *Using and Understanding AI in Higher Education*,
https://doi.org/10.1007/978-3-031-99754-9_3

rapid proliferation of AI in our society, have we indeed created a Frankenstein?

Again, as we wrote in the previous chapter, one thing we have tried to resist in this book is the temptation to engage in futurism. We do not know what AI will become or do, and predictions often do not age well. But given AI's ever-increasing presence in our daily lives, society is increasingly confronting important questions about its use and misuse. Arguably, though, these kinds of fears and concerns about technology getting out of hand are not new. AI—or at least the idea of AI-like systems—is as old as written history.

In a way, then, where we are with AI today is not as unprecedented as many imagine. In this chapter, we take a step back and first look at where AI came from—what is the history of AI? Having placed AI in context, we then take a more granular look at some of the current ethical controversies surrounding it. The goal of this chapter is not to invalidate the swirling ethical concerns around AI. Truly, AI raises many valid ethical conundrums. But in talking about these conundrums, we want to emphasize that there is historical precedent for many of them. Ethical issues like privacy and job displacement are old, not new. Understanding how we arrived at the current state with AI gives us a more balanced perspective for future planning.

History of AI

Shelley's *Frankenstein* featured a human-like monster, but others envisioned different forms of AI much earlier. The notion of a thinking machine—artificial intelligence—is actually not new. Of course, one must take care not to shoehorn ancient history into modern-day reality (Fitzpatrick, 2018), but it is intriguing that in the eighth century BCE, Homer imagined a world where machines performed human-like tasks and made decisions—just like AI does for us today.

AI-Like Conceptualizations in Ancient Greece

Homer's epics present a fascinating array of machines he calls *automata.* These automata demonstrate varying degrees of intelligence and autonomy. For instance, *The Iliad* describes Hephaestus's automated bellows, which adapt their operations based on his commands, and the self-opening gates of Olympus, which respond autonomously to the gods' approach.

Moreover, Hephaestus—lame from a fall—is described as having robotic assistants and self-moving, hearing tripods that serve the gods and return unaided to their origin.

He [Hephaestus] was making twenty tripods that were to stand by the wall of his house, and he set wheels of gold under them all so that they might go of their own accord to the assemblies of the gods and come back again—marvels indeed to see. They were finished all but the ears of cunning workmanship which yet remained to be fixed to them; these he was now fixing, and he was hammering at the rivets (Stevenson, 1994, bk. XVIII).

More intriguingly, Homer's *The Odyssey* introduces ships capable of navigating without pilots, seemingly endowed with cognitive abilities to "know" their destination and adjust their course, paralleling modern autonomous vehicles. These examples suggest that the ancients envisioned not only the mechanization of labor but also the integration of cognitive faculties into their creations (Liveley & Thomas, 2020).

While for us Homer's writings are myth, his descriptions of automata in the Iliad and Odyssey inspired practical advancements in ancient Greek science and engineering, particularly in automating tasks and utilizing natural energy sources. Inspired by Homeric writings, Greek engineers did in fact develop automated production systems, such as workshops powered by self-regulating bellows and hydraulic devices. Homer's visions also influenced philosophical inquiries into control systems and energy: Plato introduced the concept of cybernetics as the art of governing and control, while Aristotle analyzed the regulation of systems, distinguishing between tools that act autonomously and those requiring human input. Aristotle went on to envision machines capable of performing tasks independently, reducing the need for assistants or slaves.

These ideas culminated in the Hellenistic period when engineers like Heron of Alexandria created functional automata that demonstrated Homeric inspiration. Devices such as self-operating temple doors powered by heated air, hydraulic systems like automatic fountains, and steam-driven machines like the Sphere of Aeolus illustrated the use of natural elements (air, water, fire, and earth) as energy sources. The Sphere of Aeolus, often considered the first recorded example of a steam engine, used steam to spin a hollow sphere by expelling it through bent pipes, showcasing the potential of steam power for mechanical motion. Heron also developed mobile theaters with programmed mechanisms that enabled movement, sound production, and even the lighting of fires, showcasing advanced automation and control. These innovations were practical marvels, used for religious ceremonies, entertainment, and mechanical demonstrations, paving the way for the broader application of automation in Greek society (Kalligeropoulos & Vasileiadou, 2008).

Early Modern History: The World War II Era

Fast-forwarding to modern computational theory and AI, automata—a word and a concept first described by Homer—has carried through until today. While ancient and modern automata are not fully analogous, there are notable parallels. Simply put, nowadays, modern automata are the simplest form of thinking machines. Hungry users of vending machines, stalled drivers who encounter traffic lights, and hurried shoppers who walk through automatic doors all experience automata—machines that decide when and whether to dispense a snack, turn red, or open up. Automata can be self-reproducing, meaning they have the ability to create copies of themselves and continue performing tasks autonomously (John von Neumann, 2017). Some readers unfortunately may have experienced self-reproducing automata in the form of computer viruses—viruses that, beyond their initial launch, do not need further help or instructions from their creator to spread from machine to machine. The early modern conceptualizer of automata was John von Neumann, a Hungarian-American genius polymath and contemporary of Albert Einstein. While von Neumann (2021) cited biology and the structure of cells as his inspiration for automata, he was known to love history (Halmos, 1973), and so it is intriguing nonetheless that his conceptualization "automata" carries this name of ancient Greek origin that we just overviewed.

The Post-War Era: Chatbots and an Actual Name for AI

Subsequent to the war, Turing continued working and proposed the "Turing Test," suggesting the possible need and vision for designing machines that could provide output indistinguishable from humans. This test laid the foundation for conversational agents such as chatbots, which mimic human interactions by generating natural language responses. For instance, Frank Rosenblatt's Perceptron in 1957 introduced an early form of artificial intelligence called a neural network, which mimics basic processes of the human brain to learn and make decisions. Physically implemented on hardware, the Perceptron used a camera-like device to process inputs and distinguish patterns, such as determining whether points fell to the left or right of a dividing line. Another more famous example is ELIZA, which simulated the behavior of a psychotherapist in 1966, creating an interactive experience that felt revolutionary at the time (Toosi et al., 2021). These advancements reflected the beginnings of AI in the 1950s and 1960s, characterized by rule-based systems and early machine learning.

It was during this same post-war era that AI was actually called "AI." "Artificial intelligence" as a term was coined at the Dartmouth Conference in 1955, though not without debate among the participants (Prins et al., 2023). An alternative moniker, "complex information processing"—perhaps more accurate, but certainly less catchy—was also considered (Nussbaum, 2023). Dartmouth College hosted the summer workshop, funded by the Rockefeller Foundation and attended by leading scientists of the time. In the original proposal for funding, it is notable that the authors promised that "significant advance" could be made "if a selected group of scientists work for a summer" (McCarthy et al., 1955, p. 2). The proposal outlined many ambitions, including programming a computer to use language via rule-based approaches and simultaneously pioneering neural networks. Indeed, a rather ambitious plan for a singular summer!

AI Winters: Avoidance Again

Subsequent to the postwar boom, AI experienced significant fluctuations, with periods of progress interspersed with downturns known as AI winters. These winters occurred primarily during the 1970s, 1980s, and early 1990s. They followed a familiar theme: the over-promising of breakthroughs that exceeded the technological realities of the time. Researchers, driven by ambition or external pressures, claimed AI would rapidly achieve feats like replicating human cognition, solving intricate problems, and transforming industries. When researchers inevitably failed to deliver, disillusionment set in, leading to skepticism and the withdrawal of support from governments, funders, and institutions.

The 1970s, for example, witnessed the demise of early enthusiasm for expert systems and rule-based models, which struggled to handle complex, real-world scenarios. Similarly, in the 1980s, ambitious efforts in robotics and natural language understanding faltered as researchers confronted the limits of available hardware and algorithmic approaches. In both cases, the hype and media attention surrounding AI's perceived potential amplified the disappointment. These cycles of inflated expectations, unmet promises, and diminished trust became hallmarks of AI winters, stalling progress for years. Yet from these setbacks, AI eventually emerged stronger, bolstered by transformative breakthroughs in both hardware and interdisciplinary collaboration (Toosi et al., 2021).

Making Modern AI Possible Hardware and Connectivity

When people talk about contemporary AI, they often describe it as a disembodied technology that has somehow gotten better or smarter. But in understanding how AI reached its current capabilities, it is notable that by the 1990s, AI began to benefit significantly from broader advances in computing. AI tends to get the limelight, but the leap in hardware capabilities since the 1990s has been nothing short of revolutionary. The Museum of the Computer offers an interactive timeline (Computer History Museum, 2025).

Some readers may recall when their households first acquired a computer, perhaps in the 1990s, when a CPU like the Intel Pentium operated at around 200 MHz. Today's processors commonly run at over 3 GHz—a 15 times increase in clock speed—enhanced further by the addition of multiple cores and vastly improved efficiency. This surge in computational power is essential for training and deploying AI models, which require millions or even billions of calculations per second. Similarly, memory has undergone dramatic growth. RAM has expanded from a modest 8 MB to 16 GB or more, representing a 2000 times increase in capacity. This expanded memory enables AI algorithms to process larger datasets and run more complex models in real time. Storage, too, has evolved from gigabytes to terabytes, accommodating the vast volumes of data AI systems rely on for training.

Internet connectivity, critical for accessing cloud-based AI resources and datasets, has been indispensable to the rise of AI. The World Wide Web, as we know it, came about in the 1990s. According to CERN's official website (CERN, 2025), the web was intended as a way for academics to communicate and was invented in 1989 by Tim Berners-Lee at CERN, a world-renowned physics laboratory. Since the web's invention, it is noteworthy that internet speeds have dramatically increased. Dial-up speeds of 56 Kbps, which took nearly 15 minutes to download a single 3 MB file, have given way to 1 Gbps broadband or faster, capable of downloading the same file in less than a second—an 18,000 times improvement in speed. Doubtlessly, this rapid movement of data has been essential to AI and modern technology more broadly.

However, what is less frequently acknowledged is that Berners-Lee's original proposal for the web was initially rejected. The web as we know it today emerged largely from enthusiasm and perseverance, funded under the guise of unrelated projects (Johnson, 2000). Even in the early 2000s, authors trumpeting the web's success cast doubt on Berners-Lee's continued vision for the web—as a tool for collating documents and making decisions—which was dismissed as "science fiction" (Johnson, 2000, p. 48). Ironically, this early 2000s vision aligns closely with what we achieve today using large language models (LLMs) like ChatGPT.

Striking the right balance between hype and vision is neither straightforward nor obvious, particularly in the moment. To navigate this tension, we arguably need multidisciplinary stakeholders who understand both AI's origins and its potential to make informed decisions about research and investment. Progress demands collaboration, dialogue, and shared understanding to ensure AI develops responsibly and effectively. More importantly, we need to maintain a bird's-eye view and a long-game perspective.

AI Ethics

As we shift from the historical roots of artificial intelligence to the questions it raises today, it is important to recognize that ethics is not something added on after the fact. It has been part of the story from the beginning. The early myths and mechanical inventions that shaped how we imagine intelligent machines also raised deep questions about control, power, autonomy, and responsibility. These themes did not disappear—they evolved along with the technology. In the sections that follow, we map key ethical concerns that continue to shape how AI is built, used, and debated: surveillance and privacy, bias in data and algorithms, challenges to academic integrity, and accountability in areas like policing, education, and warfare.

Privacy and AI

We opened this chapter by emphasizing that fears around the safety of unchecked technology are not new; we also argued that the idea of AI itself is not new. We suggest, too, that concerns about technological privacy are quite old:

> Recent inventions and business methods [e.g. the telephone] call attention to the next step which must be taken for the protection of the person, and for securing the right "to be let alone," Numerous mechanical devices threaten to make good the prediction that "what is whispered in the closet shall be proclaimed from the house-tops". (Warren & Brandeis, 1890)

So, while concern about privacy in general is not new, what is new is the extent of data collection that many people experience in their day-to-day lives. The U.S., a country not known for its strong commitment to user privacy, published the following in a U.S. Federal Trade Commission (FTC) report:

> The amount of data collected by large tech companies is simply staggering. They track what we read, what websites we visit, whether we are married and have children, our educational level and income bracket, our location, our purchasing habits, our personal interests, and in some cases even our health conditions and religious faith. They track what we do on and off their platforms, often combining their own information with enormous data sets purchased through the largely unregulated consumer data market. And large firms are increasingly relying on hidden pixels and similar technologies—embedded on other websites—to track our behavior down to each click. (U.S. Federal Trade Commission, 2024, p. i)

Most would agree that privacy, especially in the U.S. context, needs more attention. However, defining privacy is not as simple as it sounds. Privacy is not a static or universally defined concept; rather, it exists on a continuum shaped by individual, societal, and cultural values. What one person or community considers private may not align with another's expectations. As Martin and Zimmermann (2024) point out, privacy decision-making in the context of artificial intelligence is deeply psychological, influenced by factors like perceived control, ownership, and social norms.

The long-standing idea of privacy as a trade-off—exchanging some personal information for access to services—persists in the AI era, but the calculus has become more complex and less transparent. For instance, when discussing AI and privacy, it is important to look beyond tools like ChatGPT. A major concern is how companies collect data from everyday Internet of Things (IoT) devices—such as smart speakers, fitness trackers, and home security systems. As Giordano et al. (2022) explain, these devices often rely on cloud services to function, meaning that sensitive data is constantly being transmitted and stored off-site. Privacy is not only about whether we are comfortable with large companies knowing things about us. It also involves serious risks from malicious actors who may intercept, steal, or exploit this data. These threats include location tracking, health data leaks, and behavioral profiling, all made possible by the invisible AI systems embedded in the infrastructure of modern life.

Infrastructure and AI Privacy

I have often heard laypeople state that they will not use AI because AI is "not private." To contextualize and understand privacy and AI, it is important to recognize that AI is not inherently private or non-private; its level of privacy depends on how it is implemented, particularly the infrastructure and data flows that underpin its use.

AI on the Cloud

Most publicly available AI systems operate "on the cloud," meaning that remote servers—often distributed across geographic regions—store, process, and analyze user data. Cloud-based models enable scalability and convenience, allowing organizations and individuals to avoid the upfront costs of infrastructure. However, this convenience introduces significant security and privacy trade-offs (Tawalbeh & Saldamli, 2021). Data sent to third-party servers is exposed to potential vulnerabilities, including unauthorized access, data leakage, and insider threats. Common privacy risks in cloud computing include someone changing your data without permission (data tampering), your information leaking out, or hackers accessing it through system weaknesses. One major challenge is that cloud services often store data from many different users together on the same systems, which increases the risk that mistakes, breaches, or poor security practices could expose private information across accounts. These problems are even tougher when using cloud-based software (like Google Docs or Zoom) because users usually cannot see what is happening behind the scenes—how their data is being stored, whether it is encrypted, or who has access to it. Cloud companies often use complicated systems with multiple layers and services working together, which makes it difficult for everyday users (or even organizations) to verify whether their information is truly safe and private. Although data authentication techniques and encryption can mitigate risks, their effectiveness depends on correct implementation and management across both client and server environments. These concerns are not exclusive to AI but reflect broader structural issues inherent in cloud-based technologies—including learning management systems (LMS) and database-as-a-service (DBaaS) platforms. Thus, privacy in AI is best understood as a function of the surrounding technological ecosystem.

AI Running Locally

Recognizing these challenges, some privacy-conscious users and organizations have explored alternatives by running AI systems locally. Recent developments in open-weight large language models (LLMs)—such as Meta's LLaMA family—have made it increasingly feasible to deploy conversational agents (ChatGPT-like systems) on local hardware without sending data to external servers. Running LLMs locally provides significant privacy advantages, as user data remains entirely under the individual's or institution's direct control. This approach, however, requires considerable computational resources, technical expertise, and ongoing maintenance, making it impractical for many everyday users.

Compliance-Focused Cloud Options

At the same time, secure and compliance-focused cloud options have also emerged. Some AI providers now offer "private cloud" deployments that meet regulatory requirements (such as HIPAA or FERPA compliance), ensuring that user data remains isolated, encrypted, and governed by strict access controls. Whether through local hosting or specialized secure cloud offerings, organizations seeking greater privacy must weigh the technical and financial demands against the potential benefits. Again, infrastructure choices fundamentally shape the privacy characteristics of the AI systems we use. How maintain AI privacy should be grounded in a discussion of technology and privacy as a whole.

Intellectual Property

Over recent decades, the ease with which intellectual property can be reused without consent or compensation has steadily increased, reshaping how we think about ownership and access to creative work. People who came of age in the 1990s will certainly remember the mix tape: a cassette where one copied favorite songs to share with friends. The early 2000s digitized the mix tape, bringing this casual culture of copying into the internet age. Napster, launched in 1999, was a peer-to-peer file-sharing service that allowed users to share MP3 music files freely and easily (Chesterman, 2023). It quickly gained enormous popularity, especially among young users, and just as quickly drew the attention—and lawsuits—of the music industry. Major artists like Metallica and Dr. Dre, along with the Recording Industry Association of America (RIAA), sued Napster, arguing that the platform enabled massive copyright infringement by distributing music without permission or payment. In 2001, a United States court ordered Napster to shut down its file-sharing service, effectively ending its original form. The company filed for bankruptcy shortly afterward and was eventually sold off. Although the brand name survived under new ownership, it never regained its original influence. Napster's rise and fall triggered a broader shift: stricter copyright enforcement, growing public debate about digital rights, and the eventual rise of legal platforms such as iTunes, Spotify, and YouTube. In hindsight, Napster did not merely break the rules—it forced a reckoning that helped rewrite them.

Today, we may be facing a similar inflection point. The controversy over generative AI's use of data echoes the debates that surrounded Napster, even as the details differ. While Napster distributed works in their original form, generative AI does something more complex: it trains on creative content to produce something new. At the heart of this process is scraping—the automated collection of online material, including books, news articles, images, and social media posts. These scraped collections, known as corpora, are used to train large language models such as ChatGPT, Gemini, and Copilot. The models analyze patterns in these corpora to generate new text, code, or images that often resemble—but do not replicate—existing works. This scraping and training raise a new set of legal and ethical questions. While Napster was about unauthorized distribution, generative AI raises concerns about unauthorized training: the use of creative works as raw material to build systems capable of mimicking human expression at scale, often without consent or compensation for the original creators.

There is currently no global consensus on the legality of using copyrighted data to train large language models (LLMs), and as a result, these models often operate in a legal gray area (Tiedrich et al., 2025). The practice of scraping publicly accessible data to build AI training datasets raises significant concerns around copyright, database rights, intellectual property and legal and ethical implications. In the United States, developers often argue that such use falls under "fair use," but this is being actively tested in lawsuits such as *Getty Images v. Stability AI*, where Getty alleges the unauthorized use of millions of copyrighted images to train an image-generating model, and Authors Guild v. OpenAI, in which prominent authors claim their books were used without permission to train ChatGPT. In the European Union, Article 4 of the 2019 DSM Copyright Directive allows text and data mining (TDM) for scientific research, but commercial uses are restricted unless rightsholders opt in, and countries like France have already seen publishers assert these rights to block scraping. Additionally, the UK's Information Commissioner's Office, along with 11 other international regulators, issued a 2023 statement cautioning that scraping data—even from public websites—can still infringe on privacy and IP rights. As these legal challenges mount, policymakers are exploring voluntary codes of conduct, licensing frameworks, and technical safeguards to balance innovation with protection, but until clearer global rules emerge, LLMs continue to operate in uncertain legal terrain.

Transparency and Explainability

Regulations and laws about AI primarily address privacy, but transparency regarding how AI works receives considerably less attention (Ehsan et al., 2021). When people do discuss transparency, they are apt to point out that many AI systems are black boxes—that is, we frequently do not know how exactly AI answered our questions, drove our car, or recognized our photos (Toy, 2023). Part of the transparency issue at hand is that large technology companies, for reasons of profit, often do not make their algorithms public—in short, we cannot fully know how the AI systems we use on a daily basis—Google, most social media platforms, and OpenAI/ChatGPT—work behind the scenes. However, even in cases where algorithms are public, it should be understood that these algorithms contain millions of lines of code that interact with one another; explainability—being able to show what is happening and how—is challenging even when code is disclosed. Tools like SHAP (SHapley Additive exPlanations) attempt to address this challenge by attributing each model output to its contributing input features, helping users understand which factors most influenced a given prediction. Still, such tools can be difficult to interpret for non-experts and do not eliminate the opacity of large-scale systems.

A well-documented gap is the lack of a widely accepted framework for what exactly transparency in AI would constitute (Bommasani et al., 2023). While researchers and practitioners frequently call for greater transparency, the term itself remains ambiguous. Does it mean opening the black box of deep learning models to expose their internal logic? Providing documentation of training data and design decisions? Explaining outputs in terms understandable to end users? These questions point to the complexity of operationalizing transparency. Without a shared understanding, efforts to build explainable AI risk becoming inconsistent, incomplete, or even misleading—offering the appearance of clarity without meaningful insight. As a result, transparency remains more of an aspiration than a standard, limiting its impact on trust, accountability, and equitable deployment.

Bias

Bias in artificial intelligence (AI) systems often stems from the data they rely on. Most AI models are trained on large corpora—extensive collections of text, images, or audio—that shape how they learn patterns and make decisions. Generative systems like large language models (LLMs) use these corpora to predict word sequences and generate new content, while retrieval-based systems, such as search engines, use them to locate and rank relevant results. In both cases, the content and structure of the corpora influence which perspectives are amplified or ignored. When training data over-represents certain groups, omits others, or embeds harmful stereotypes, AI systems tend to replicate and reinforce those biases.

Bias in corpora has serious consequences, especially in visual AI systems. Facial recognition technologies, for example, rely on image-based corpora to train algorithms that detect and classify faces. When these datasets lack diversity, the resulting systems can be dangerously inaccurate. The *Gender Shades* study by Buolamwini and Gebru (2018), a seminal work in algorithmic fairness, found that commercial facial recognition systems had error rates as high as 34.7% for darker-skinned women, compared to less than 1% for lighter-skinned men. These disparities were directly linked to unrepresentative training datasets. In 2018, the ACLU tested Amazon's Rekognition software and found that it falsely matched 28 members of the U.S. Congress with mugshots from a criminal database—disproportionately affecting people of color. When these systems perform poorly on already marginalized groups, they do more than make mistakes—they amplify inequality and erode public trust.

Another example of bias in AI is search engines. Search engines, though often perceived as neutral, are similarly shaped by the corpora they rely on and the algorithms they use to retrieve results. These algorithms determine not only what information surfaces, but also what is buried or excluded. Search engines such as Google, Yahoo, and Baidu all rely on massive corpora to understand queries and proprietary ranking systems to decide what content users see first. Yet the details of how these systems do query understanding and rank and personalize content are not fully publicly disclosed, making search engine providers difficult to scrutinize or hold accountable. Ulloa et al. (2022) note that search engine algorithms remain largely opaque, and even academic researchers must rely on indirect audits to study how results are ranked. Despite this, users often treat search results as objective truth, without questioning why some perspectives are missing. If the underlying corpora reflect social or cultural bias, those distortions are reproduced in the results, shaping how people understand the world.

Gray et al. (2024) emphasize that bias mitigation must begin with the design and evaluation of the corpora themselves. First, datasets must be intentionally constructed to include diverse populations and perspectives, especially those historically underrepresented or misrepresented. Second, transparency is critical. Documenting how a dataset was collected, what it contains, and what limitations it has—through tools like data datasheets and model cards—allows developers and users to better understand potential sources of bias. Third, community engagement is essential. Involving stakeholders from different backgrounds can help surface concerns that may be invisible to developers working in isolation. Finally, ongoing monitoring is necessary, since bias is not static. As AI systems are deployed in new contexts, they must be continuously evaluated and refined to ensure they serve all users equitably. These measures, taken together, underscore that reducing bias is not just a technical challenge—it is also a social and ethical responsibility.

Misinformation and Hallucination

In 2023, a New York attorney submitted a legal brief citing several court decisions—all of which turned out to be entirely fabricated by ChatGPT. The AI-generated citations appeared legitimate, complete with docket numbers and legal reasoning, but none of them actually existed. The attorney, unaware of the risk, relied on the tool without verifying the information. The result was a courtroom embarrassment, legal sanctions, and a public warning about the dangers of trusting AI-generated content without oversight (Davis, 2023).

This case exemplifies a growing concern in the use of large language models (LLMs): hallucination. Hallucination refers to instances when an LLM generates information that sounds plausible but is factually incorrect, invented, or misleading. These models do not "know" facts in the human sense. Instead, they generate responses based on patterns found in massive datasets. Since their training data may include outdated, biased, or incorrect information, LLMs can produce confident-sounding statements that are simply wrong (Tonmoy et al., 2024). Hallucinations are especially troubling in high-stakes fields such as law, medicine, or education, where errors can have serious consequences.

Several strategies have been proposed to reduce hallucinations, though each has limitations. One approach is prompt engineering, which involves carefully wording input questions or instructions to guide the model toward more accurate answers. Including specific details, asking for sources, or breaking complex queries into smaller parts can all help improve reliability (Tonmoy et al., 2024). Another effective technique is to provide the model with relevant background information—such as uploading documents or supplying verified facts—before requesting a response. Giving the model access to accurate, well-sourced material reduces the likelihood it will rely on guesswork or outdated data.

Users also play an essential role by fact-checking model responses, especially in professional or academic contexts. Taking time to verify key claims or statistics helps catch errors and promotes safe, responsible use. Some LLMs incorporate a method called self-refinement, where the model reviews and revises its own output in a second pass to improve factual accuracy. Finally, users can improve these systems by offering feedback—whether by rating responses or suggesting corrections in plain language. This kind of human input helps guide models toward more honest, helpful, and grounded answers (Tonmoy et al., 2024).

While no single method can eliminate hallucinations entirely, combining these approaches and encouraging active user involvement offers a promising path toward safer and more trustworthy AI.

Job Displacement

Technology has long had a way of enriching some and impoverishing others. In the 1880s, decrying mechanization and the Industrial Revolution, Toynbee (1956, p. 57) lamented:

> [W]e now approach a darker period—a period as disastrous and as terrible as any through which a nation ever passed; disastrous and terrible, because, side by side with a great increase of wealth was seen an enormous increase of

> pauperism, and production on a vast scale, the result of free competition, led to a rapid alienation of classes and to the degradation of a large body of producers.

Today, AI raises both excitement about socioeconomic prospects and growing concern over inequality and displacement. Just as mechanization reshaped the nineteenth-century labor landscape, AI is transforming the modern workforce—eliminating some jobs while creating others. According to Dimple (2024), automation powered by AI may displace up to 85 million jobs by 2025, particularly in sectors reliant on repetitive tasks such as manufacturing and retail. At the same time, AI opens pathways to high-skill roles in data science, cybersecurity, and AI ethics—opportunities that require significant reskilling and education. Without inclusive workforce development and digital infrastructure, countries and communities risk falling behind, exacerbating income inequality and social fragmentation.

Early trends are troubling: the emerging AI divide mirrors long-standing patterns of technological exclusion. For example, early studies suggest that women are adopting AI tools at lower rates than men (Nouraldeen, 2023; Obenza et al., 2024; Ramos, 2022). One preprint examining familiarity with ChatGPT found that in the U.S., AI adoption closely tracks pre-existing educational and socioeconomic divides—those with higher levels of education and income are significantly more likely to use AI tools (Daepp & Counts, 2024).

Environmental Sustainability

The rise of AI raises substantive concerns about environmental sustainability. In 2021, UNESCO (2021) pointed out that "environment and ecosystems are the existential necessity for humanity and other living beings to be able to enjoy the benefits of advances in AI." In that context, UNESCO advocated for laws and regulations that "reduce the environmental impact of AI systems" and "ensure the minimization of climate change and environmental risk factors, and prevent the unsustainable exploitation, use and transformation of natural resources contributing to the deterioration of the environment and the degradation of ecosystems."

In forming an understanding of AI's environmental and energy use concerns, it can be helpful to understand the relative scale of AI energy use. Spencer and Singh (2024) point out that data centers consume about 1% of the world's energy production—this amount of energy consumption is about half of what is used on household digital appliances like smartphones and TVs. The projection that the energy needs of data centers will grow rapidly is driving substantive investment in the global energy sector, as evidenced, for instance, by Microsoft's stake in the recent $100 billion global partnership to develop additional data centers and energy infrastructure to power them (Novet, 2024). It is this rapid hockey-stick type growth, perhaps more than current use, that is environmentally concerning for many (Wu et al., 2022).

Yet, while few would argue that minimizing environmental harm by AI and its related data centers, energy consumption, and digital waste is important, the net positive or negative environmental impact of AI is hard to measure—even the UN calls this impact a "wildcard" (UN Environment Programme, 2024). As discussed in Chap. 1, the power of AI lies in pattern recognition—AI can be used to recognize efficiencies and reduce resource use across multiple sectors (Wu et al., 2022; Ahmad, 2024). For example, the rise of AI-powered data centers may make transportation by electric cars more efficient and affordable. A world in which people could efficiently hail safe, autonomous electric vehicles might be an environmental win—fewer cars, especially fossil fuel-consuming cars, may be removed from production and remaining cars may be smaller and use optimal routes. Yet, efficient electric vehicle hailing services and a resulting drop in price could alternatively mean that people abandon walking and cycling. Given that environmental impact, technology, and human behavior are hard to disentangle and fully predict, moving forward, there is a need for awareness of intended and unintended AI environmental consequences, as well as a need for a technological focus on developing efficient AI algorithms (Wu et al., 2022).

It also merits noting that there are many environmental benefits of AI. Artificial intelligence plays a pivotal role in fostering sustainability by addressing complex environmental challenges through innovative solutions. For instance, AI optimizes energy consumption, supports renewable energy integration, and enhances water resource management using predictive modeling and data analytics. It also aids biodiversity conservation by modeling ecosystems and informing efficient land-use strategies. Moreover, AI contributes to better environmental governance by analyzing large datasets, enabling science-based policies for sustainability. However, challenges such as high computational energy demands and uncertainties in human behavioral responses persist, requiring further exploration (Nishant et al., 2020).

Academic Honesty and Cheating

As will be discussed in Chap. 5 cheating and academic honesty are key faculty concerns. In our campus survey, many instructors expressed anxiety about how generative AI tools might undermine the learning process, while others called for clearer norms and better tools to guide ethical student use.

LLM Detection

Faculty are prone to attempt detecting LLM-generated assignments, but LLM detection currently faces significant challenges and risks. Detecting LLM-generated text is technically difficult and error-prone (Wu et al., 2023). Anecdotally, I have observed students reverse-engineer their assignments by iteratively adjusting LLM outputs until detectors report a low probability of AI generation. Modifying LLM-generated text to defeat widely used commercial detectors is relatively easy, both according to published research (Nicks et al., 2024) and widespread online tutorials—for example, a simple search for "defeat ChatGPT Zero" yields multiple solutions. So pervasive are these issues that researchers advise "against the continued reliance on LLM-generated detectors" (Nicks et al., 2024, p. 1). Yet, this problem is rarely acknowledged in academic literature or policy discussions (Koike et al., 2024).

It is also difficult to define exactly what constitutes cheating with an LLM. If an LLM generates parts of content or improves style or readability, is that cheating? When answering this question, it should be understood—as explained in Chap. 1—that modern spellcheckers such as those in Word, Google Docs, or Grammarly use AI and improve style and phrasing, albeit usually integrated within the word processing program itself. Is copying and pasting text into an LLM to receive similar edits different? In many institutions, prompt engineering—how to systematically work with LLMs—is not widely taught. Thus, instructing students that certain uses of LLMs are appropriate and others not, while failing to teach them how to effectively use the LLMs, may be a poor strategy.

In terms of ethical frameworks, it has been suggested that students increasingly view cheating not as a moral failure, but as a calculated risk—especially in environments where surveillance and enforcement are uneven or opaque. With the rise of generative AI and large language models (LLMs), traditional definitions of academic dishonesty are being challenged. As tools like ChatGPT become easily accessible and difficult to regulate, some scholars argue that it is no longer feasible to fully prevent AI-assisted cheating. Instead of focusing on punishment, McIntire et al. (2024) suggest that instructors should reframe the conversation: cheating should be seen not simply as a moral failing, but as a detriment to genuine learning. This shift places the emphasis on student growth, engagement, and long-term understanding rather than surveillance and control.

Online Proctoring
Another common use of AI is in online proctoring tools, which became widespread during the pandemic. These systems rely on algorithms to detect "suspicious" behavior by tracking eye movement, background noise, keystrokes, and browser activity. The intent is to flag potential cheating, but the technology often misinterprets normal behavior—especially for students with disabilities or those dealing with unstable internet or noisy environments. For instance, at Dartmouth's Geisel School of Medicine, students were accused of cheating based on system logs that showed file access during exams. However, these logs may have been generated automatically in the background, not through intentional actions. Still, they were treated as definitive evidence of misconduct (Kelley et al., 2021). This highlights a core issue in AI ethics: when institutions rely on automated tools without understanding their limitations, serious errors in judgment can follow.

Perhaps most troubling is that students caught in these situations are often denied due process. Often, students are given no meaningful way to contest the accusations. AI is assumed to be neutral and objective, but that assumption falls apart under scrutiny. In reality, students from lower-income backgrounds—who may not have access to quiet, controlled testing environments—are disproportionately flagged, revealing how bias and inequity can be baked into supposedly impartial systems.

AI and Warfare

In the recent war in Ukraine, robotics and AI have been increasingly tapped for defensive tasks such as mine clearance, supply delivery, casualty evacuation, and surveillance (Mazarchuk, 2024). Drones have also been deployed as offensive weapons. Ukraine created the Unmanned Systems Forces, the first military branch dedicated to unmanned systems, as part of its ambitious "Million Drone Army" program (Mazarchuk, 2024). Both Russia and Ukraine have used drones to strike targets hundreds of miles away, and drones can now be constructed quickly and cheaply, for as little as $500 (Reuters, 2024).

There is growing concern about what the ease of warfare at a distance—possibly even automated warfare—could mean for humanity. The United Nations has repeatedly emphasized the need for human oversight in the use of autonomous weapons, including drones. In 2019, Secretary-General António Guterres stated that "human responsibility for decisions on the use of weapons systems must be retained," arguing that accountability cannot be delegated to machines (United Nations, 2019). Most recently, in 2023, the UN Secretary-General and the International Committee of the Red Cross (ICRC) jointly called for international rules prohibiting autonomous weapons that function without meaningful human control (United Nations, 2023).

The rapid development and deployment of AI-driven weaponry raise profound ethical and legal challenges. Autonomous systems blur traditional distinctions between combatant and noncombatant, complicate accountability when harm occurs, and lower the threshold for engaging in conflict by reducing risks to human soldiers. Critics argue that the increasing reliance on drones and unmanned systems could desensitize policymakers and militaries to the costs of war, making armed conflict more frequent and potentially more devastating. As AI capabilities continue to advance, the international community faces urgent questions about where to draw boundaries—and how to enforce them—in a world where machines may soon be capable of making life-and-death decisions without human input.

AI Regulatory Frameworks

As ethical debates about artificial intelligence move from academic discourse into the fabric of everyday life, national governments are now faced with the concrete task of regulating its real-world applications. Table 3.1 overviews a sample of large countries' and blocks' approaches to AI regulation; the subsequent sections provide more detail.

Table 3.1 Sampling of countries' AI regulatory approaches

Country/Region	*Comprehensive AI Law?*	*Primary Regulatory Approach*
United States	No	Executive orders and agency-led sectoral oversight
Canada	No (AIDA failed)	Proposed risk-based federal bill (AIDA); now stalled
United Kingdom	No	Regulator-led, principle-based model (White Paper 2023)
European Union	Yes	Binding legislation: EU AI Act (2024)
Brazil	In progress	Draft law modeled on EU AI Act (PL 2338/2023)
Russia	No	National AI Strategy (2024 update); government-managed
India	No	Economic-development-oriented strategy; sectoral
China	Partial (sectoral)	Centralized national strategy with binding sectoral rules
South Africa	No	Draft strategy; ethics- and participation-oriented

United States

The transition from the Biden to the Trump administration marked a pronounced ideological and regulatory shift in U.S. federal AI policy. President Biden's *Executive Order 14110, Safe, Secure, and Trustworthy Development and Use of Artificial Intelligence* (2023), established a precautionary framework that foregrounded civil rights, safety testing, and federal oversight. It required developers of large-scale foundation models to report red-teaming results—including for chemical, biological, radiological, nuclear, and cybersecurity risks—to the Department of Commerce before public release when models exceeded defined compute thresholds (Executive Order No. 14110, 2023, §4.2(b)). Federal agencies such as DHS, HHS, and the Department of Labor were directed to enforce algorithmic fairness and conduct AI impact assessments, embedding protections against bias and discrimination in employment, housing, and health contexts (§5.1).

In contrast, President Trump's *Executive Orders 14141* and *14142* enacted a broad deregulatory turn. EO 14141 (*Advancing United States Leadership in Artificial Intelligence Infrastructure*, Jan 14, 2025a)

prioritized rapid buildout of domestic data centers and clean energy infrastructure to secure U.S. dominance in frontier AI development. Rather than imposing mandatory oversight on private developers, it encouraged voluntary coordination with the AI Safety Institute, limited foreign ownership of AI infrastructure, and offered long-term federal land leases to industry consortia. Notably, it mandated that new AI infrastructure be powered by additional clean energy capacity—such as geothermal, nuclear, solar, and wind—to avoid consumer price impacts and reinforce national energy security (EO 14141, §§1–4). EO 14142 (*Promoting Innovation and Competition in Artificial Intelligence*, Jan 25, 2025b) reinforced this deregulatory posture, directing agencies to rescind any AI-related rules issued after October 30, 2023, unless they demonstrably advanced U.S. competitiveness or national security. It prohibited compelled disclosure of proprietary model details absent a declared national emergency and framed AI as a strategic engine of American exceptionalism. As Lubello (2025) observes, Biden's policy was grounded in "the precautionary principle," emphasizing safety and civil rights, while Trump's orders reflect a "build-fast, compete-hard ethos" that dismantles compliance regimes in favor of voluntary standards and accelerated innovation.

Canada

Canada's AI policies have also been in flux. Canada's approach to AI governance had centered on the Artificial Intelligence and Data Act (AIDA), introduced in 2022 as part of Bill C-27, the Digital Charter Implementation Act. As the country's first national AI regulatory framework, AIDA aimed to ensure that "high-impact" AI systems would be developed and deployed safely, transparently, and without discrimination (Government of Canada, 2023). However, the bill died abruptly in early 2025 following Prime Minister Justin Trudeau's resignation and the prorogation of Parliament (Arai, 2025).

AIDA proposed a risk-based model requiring businesses to assess and mitigate potential harms, maintain oversight, and inform users about system limitations (Government of Canada, 2025). It also would have introduced new criminal offenses related to AI misuse and created an AI and Data Commissioner to support enforcement, reporting to the Minister of Innovation, Science and Industry (Government of Canada, 2023).With the bill's collapse, analysts expect no immediate federal replacement, possibly leaving provinces to fill the gap through a patchwork of local initiatives (Arai, 2025).

United Kingdom

As of early 2025, the United Kingdom has not passed a law specifically regulating artificial intelligence. Instead, it released a 2023 policy white paper, *A Pro-Innovation Approach to AI Regulation*, which outlines five guiding principles—such as transparency, fairness, and accountability—for existing regulators to interpret within their own sectors. This flexible, non-binding framework avoids creating a new AI regulator or legal obligations, favoring a light-touch model designed to support growth and innovation.

However, the UK's position has drawn scrutiny. It has been described as "sitting on the fence" between the deregulatory stance of the United States and the more prescriptive European Union AI Act (Prickett, 2025). While the government initially opted for guidance over legislation, it has since recognized the need for firmer oversight. A formal AI bill—once expected in early 2025—has been delayed but is now being reconsidered for introduction in summer 2025. The postponement reflects tensions between encouraging investment and addressing rising concerns over the safety and accountability of advanced AI systems, particularly large language models.

EU (European Union)

The EU Artificial Intelligence Act, adopted in March 2024 as Regulation (EU) 2024/1689, is the world's first comprehensive, binding legal framework specifically targeting artificial intelligence. It introduces a tiered, risk-based classification of AI systems—unacceptable, high, limited, and minimal—each with corresponding obligations. High-risk systems, such as those used in biometric identification, education, healthcare, and migration, must meet strict transparency, documentation, and human oversight standards. The Act applies not only to developers and users within the EU but also extraterritorially to any provider placing AI systems on the EU market. Enforcement will be staged, with full implementation expected by 2026, and the European Commission is tasked with issuing further guidance and delegated acts to clarify provisions. This ambitious legislation positions the EU as a global leader in regulating AI technologies (Regulation (EU) 2024/1689, 2024).

Despite its historic scope, the EU AI Act has drawn serious criticism from civil society organizations, including the European Center for Not-for-Profit Law (ECNL), Liberties, and the European Civic Forum. These groups argue that the final version of the Act is "packed with loopholes" that leave fundamental rights and civic space inadequately protected. Key concerns include vague definitions, broad exemptions for national security and law enforcement, and weak requirements for fundamental rights impact assessments—often relying on AI developers' self-assessment rather than independent oversight. The Act's implementation process also lacks guaranteed mechanisms for meaningful civil society participation, and critics highlight the disproportionate influence of commercial and security interests during the legislative negotiations. These flaws, they warn, risk undermining both the democratic legitimacy and the human rights protections the Act claims to uphold (European Center for Not-for-Profit Law et al., 2024).

BRICS (Brazil, Russia, India, China, South Africa)

In April 2025, BRICS foreign ministers met in Rio de Janeiro and issued a joint statement calling for a United Nations-led global AI governance framework centered on Global South priorities such as development, sovereignty, and inclusivity (Access Partnership, 2025). This collective position reflects the bloc's ambition to counterbalance Western-led models and shape international technology governance in ways that emphasize accessibility, capacity building, and national regulatory autonomy. In the subsequent subsections, we take a closer look at what is happening in each of these BRICS countries at current.

Brazil

In the lead-up to the aforementioned Rio de Janeiro AI Summit, Brazil—current chair of BRICS—passed its national Artificial Intelligence Bill (PL 2338/2023) in the Senate in December 2024, after nearly two years of negotiations, expert input, and public hearings (Martins, 2025). Now under discussion in the Chamber of Deputies, the bill is expected to pass into law in 2025 (Battilana & Lacerda, 2025). Inspired by the EU AI Act, Brazil's bill adopts a flexible, risk-based approach but applies broader obligations across developers, distributors, and users. It incorporates strict liability provisions through Brazil's consumer protection code and uniquely requires AI companies to compensate copyright holders when using their content for model training, with exceptions for academic research (Martins, 2025; Battilana & Lacerda, 2025). It bear noting though that AIDA recently failed to become law, and major regulatory shifts in the United States, including the repeal of Biden's AI executive order and growing opposition from tech companies under the new Trump administration, add further uncertainty to the global AI policy landscape (Martins, 2025). As Brazil leads BRICS in advancing a development-focused global framework, its domestic legislation will be closely watched as both a policy milestone and a test case for AI governance in the Global South.

Russia

Russia's regulatory framework for artificial intelligence is grounded in a national strategy formalized by presidential decree, most recently updated in February 2024 (Putin, 2024). The strategy outlines state priorities through 2030, including the development of trusted AI technologies, integration of AI into public administration and industry, promotion of workforce training, and advancement of international cooperation, especially through multilateral partnerships like BRICS. Notably, the strategy places strong emphasis on AI education and workforce development, mandating the creation and regular updating of higher education programs, integration of AI modules into all university curricula, and the widespread retraining of educators and civil servants. It also supports K–12 initiatives, online learning platforms, and public AI literacy campaigns (President of the Russian Federation, 2024). Legal liability for AI-driven decisions is assigned to human or corporate actors, and the framework stresses ethical, explainable, and risk-based AI governance.

Supplementing this legal foundation, Daneliya and Kurbanov (2025) observe that Russia does not yet have a single, comprehensive AI law but instead relies on a combination of strategic frameworks and experimental legal regimes (regulatory sandboxes). Their analysis highlights important developments such as the extraterritorial application of personal data legislation, restrictions on fully automated decision-making without written consent, and the legal risks associated with AI-generated content that replicates elements of copyrighted works. They also note that Russia's regulatory model prioritizes ethical safeguards, transparency in algorithmic recommendation systems, and strict controls over biometric data, reflecting a state-managed, standards-driven approach to AI governance.

India's approach to AI regulation is evolving, with a strong focus on fostering innovation and economic development through enabling infrastructure, data strategies, and public-private partnerships (Joshi, 2024). Rather than adopting comprehensive AI-specific legislation, the country has so far relied on existing frameworks such as the Information Technology Act, 2000, which, while foundational, were not designed to address the unique risks and complexities of AI technologies (Sharma et al., 2025). This flexible, innovation-oriented strategy has supported growth but also revealed important regulatory gaps. For instance, there is currently no legal framework clearly defining liability when AI systems cause harm—an issue of growing relevance as AI tools are increasingly used in sectors like law enforcement and healthcare (Khara & Yadav, 2024). As AI adoption deepens, areas such as accountability, transparency, and ethical safeguards are likely to become key priorities for future policy development.

India

India's approach to AI regulation is evolving, with a strong focus on fostering innovation and economic development through enabling infrastructure, data strategies, and public-private partnerships (Joshi, 2024). Rather than adopting comprehensive AI-specific legislation, the country has so far relied on existing frameworks such as the Information Technology Act, 2000, which, while foundational, were not designed to address the unique risks and complexities of AI technologies (Sharma et al., 2025). This flexible, innovation-oriented strategy has supported growth but also revealed important regulatory gaps. For instance, there is currently no legal framework clearly defining liability when AI systems cause harm—an issue of growing relevance as AI tools are increasingly used in sectors like law enforcement and healthcare (Khara & Yadav, 2024). As AI adoption deepens, areas such as accountability, transparency, and ethical safeguards are likely to become key priorities for future policy development.

China

China's AI governance landscape is characterized by a dual dynamic of centralized ambition and decentralized execution. At the national level, the 2017 *New Generation Artificial Intelligence Development Plan* (NGAIDP) laid out China's goal to become the world leader in AI by 2030, emphasizing national security, geopolitical competition, and core technological breakthroughs. However, provincial governments have largely reframed AI as an engine for local economic growth, prioritizing commercial applications over national strategic objectives (Khanal et al., 2025). While some leading regions like Beijing and Shanghai align closely with national aims, many others lag in implementation or pursue regionally tailored goals. In parallel, China has introduced a regulatory framework to manage emerging risks, including the 2023 *Interim Measures for the Management of Generative Artificial Intelligence Services*, which impose content controls, user protections, and data governance obligations on AI service providers operating within China's borders, including foreign entities (Fasken, 2023)

South Africa

South Africa's regulatory approach to artificial intelligence (AI) is currently in a developmental and consultative stage, guided by a draft national strategy and emerging academic perspectives. The Department of Communications and Digital Technologies (DCDT) has proposed a hybrid governance model that incorporates self-regulation, co-regulation, and targeted government oversight, supported by institutional platforms such as the AI Institute of South Africa (AIISA) and the Centre for Artificial Intelligence Research (CAIR) (DCDT, 2023). Responding to the ad hoc nature of regulation, some authors emphasizes the importance of early, evidence-informed regulation (Cloete, 2024). Rather than reacting to harms after they occur, he advocates for anticipatory governance frameworks that build public trust, promote accountability, and align technological development with societal values. This approach reinforces the need for agile, inclusive, and forward-looking policymaking as South Africa shapes its AI trajectory.

Conclusion

We began this chapter by arguing that AI, in many ways, is not a new technology. We made this point deliberately—to highlight that many of today's concerns surrounding AI, such as privacy, intellectual property, labor, and surveillance, are rooted in long-standing social and ethical dilemmas. These problems may be long-standing, but they remain urgent. When left unexamined, even familiar issues can cause significant harm.

We also discussed different countries' approaches to AI regulation, noting that most—apart from the European Union—have implemented only limited, fragmented policies. Regardless of one's personal stance on the value of government regulation, the reality is that, to varying degrees, individuals will need to monitor their own AI use and conduct. As we established in Chap. 2, AI systems are already widespread, and the technology may be advancing more quickly than regulation can keep up. Because everyday people both use and are affected by AI, we need more public conversation and education—not avoidance—to confront the ethical and regulatory challenges it poses. Concerns about privacy, bias, surveillance, and the erosion of autonomy are real, and they demand active engagement and critical oversight—not withdrawal. Ethical problems do not disappear when technologies are ignored; they simply evolve without critical voices in the room.

When used responsibly, AI systems have the potential to do good—personalizing instruction, identifying students in need, improving accessibility, and reducing workload for educators. But studying a technology and teaching others about it is not the same as endorsing its use. In education, we often examine harmful systems to understand their consequences and to avoid repeating past mistakes.

Faculty with ethical objections are fully within their rights to avoid using AI tools in their own classrooms or research. However, opting out entirely—at the level of curriculum design, institutional policy, or public discourse—risks forfeiting influence over how these systems are developed and deployed. Moreover, even those who choose not to adopt AI tools still need AI literacy. Artificial intelligence is not going away, and understanding its strengths, limitations, and ethical risks is essential for participating meaningfully in society and shaping its future.

Importantly, as Birhane et al. (2022) argue, the field of AI has taken a participatory turn—emphasizing co-design, community input, and the integration of pluralistic knowledge systems into technical development. This shift reflects a growing recognition that systems function more responsibly and equitably when shaped by the communities they affect. However, participation must extend beyond the early stages of design and development. Inclusive design alone is not enough if the policies governing AI use in practice are created without that same inclusive spirit. As AI becomes increasingly embedded in classrooms, administrative tools, and assessment platforms, we must ensure that participation continues—through sustained, critical engagement with how these tools are governed on a day-to-day basis.

Recent trends in higher education highlight just how urgent this shift is. According to the 2024 *Inside Higher Ed* survey of provosts, 56% of institutions report encouraging faculty to explore or experiment with generative AI in their teaching. Yet only 29% say their institutions have formal policies to guide its use in the classroom. This disconnect between exploration and governance reveals a troubling gap: faculty are navigating powerful new tools without a shared framework to ensure equity, transparency, and accountability. In the absence of clear policies, decisions about generative AI are uneven, often left to individual instructors or departments, potentially deepening disparities rather than addressing them.

What is needed now is not only better policy, but better policymaking. To create institutional responses that are relevant, responsive, and just, the policy process itself must be participatory. Faculty, staff, and students—those most directly affected by AI integration—must have meaningful roles in deciding how these technologies are used in educational spaces. Participatory policymaking ensures that diverse needs and concerns shape institutional responses, helping to prevent one-size-fits-all mandates that may overlook context or reinforce existing inequities. Moreover, engaging end users in this process builds trust, strengthens transparency, and promotes long-term sustainability rooted in shared values and goals. If AI is to serve education equitably, educational communities must be empowered not only to help design technologies, but to co-create the rules and practices that govern their use.

As we continue this conversation in the next chapter, we will explore theoretical frameworks that help us better understand technology resistance and acceptance, offering new tools for navigating the ethical terrain ahead.

Try It Out: Design a Participatory AI Policy Workshop

AI in higher education presents two major challenges: it is contentious, and AI-generated text is difficult to reliably detect. These realities have contributed to a policy vacuum, where technologies are rapidly adopted without sufficient rules or shared norms to guide their use. As a result, top-down, one-size-fits-all policies—often developed by small administrative committees—can be ineffective and even harmful. Instead, institutions should consider participatory approaches that engage those most affected—students, faculty, and staff—in co-developing ethical and practical guidelines for AI use.

Participatory governance is gaining traction across research, teaching, and institutional decision-making. Yet as Vaughn and Jacquez (2020) point out, "the nuts-and-bolts description of how to do this work is often minimal to non-existent." Their review of the literature connects readers to a wide range of participatory techniques—such as concept mapping, deliberative polling, photovoice, and stakeholder interviews—that could help your group think creatively about engagement. There is no single formula for doing participation "right," but many practical models already exist.

This activity invites you to imagine how your institution might host a participatory AI policy workshop tailored to your own context.

Activity Prompt

Design a participatory workshop to co-create campus guidelines for generative AI (e.g., ChatGPT). Consider:

Who should participate?Include a diverse group of students, faculty, staff, and administrators across roles and disciplines.

What questions will guide the discussion?For example:

What uses of generative AI should be encouraged, restricted, or clarified?

How can we protect academic integrity while fostering responsible innovation?

How will you gather input?Choose from techniques like breakout discussions, visual mapping, case studies, or anonymous feedback tools.

How will ideas be translated into policy?Plan a process for turning group input into practical recommendations or working drafts.

As Chap. 10 **will show, there's no single way to "do" participation well—but starting with who should be involved, and how, is essential for building ethical, effective responses to AI in education.**Building participatory structures takes time, but this kind of inclusive policy development is one of the most powerful tools we have for responding to the ethical, social, and pedagogical tensions that AI introduces. By practicing engagement now—even in small, local ways—you can help shape how AI is understood, governed, and used in ways that reflect the values of your learning community.

Questions for Reflection and Discussion

This chapter explores how many people anthropomorphize AI equating it with robots or sci-fi characters like Frankenstein's monster. Before reading, how did you define or picture AI? How has that definition changed after learning about its historical and ethical roots? Consider reading **Chap.** 2 if you have not already to add depth to your conversation about AI.

Chapter 3 suggests that public fears about AI often reflect deeper concerns about power, control, or identity. Which example from the chapter—such as automata, ***Frankenstein***, or modern surveillance—felt most relevant to you, and why?

What is one specific misunderstanding about AI (e.g., its capabilities, intentions, or decision-making) that this chapter helped you reconsider? How might that new understanding shape how you use or evaluate AI in your own work?

Based on the ethical themes in this chapter, what opportunities or challenges do you see for AI in your field or community? How might you prepare to engage with those issues thoughtfully?

References

Access Partnership. (2025, May 1). *Access alert: BRICS takes stance on global AI governance frameworks.* https://accesspartnership.com/access-alert-brics-takes-stance-global-ai-governance-frameworks/

ACLU. (2018, July 26). *Amazon's face recognition falsely matched 28 members of Congress with mugshots.* American Civil Liberties Union. https://www.aclu.org/news/privacy-technology/amazons-face-recognition-falsely-matched-28

Ahmad, S. (2024). The impact of artificial intelligence on business & social values: Benefits, challenges, and future directions. *Educational Administration Theory and Practice, 30*(6), 3174–3180. https://doi.org/10.53555/kuey.v30i6.6012

Arai, M. (2025, February 11). *What's next after AIDA?* Schwartz Reisman Institute for Technology and Society, University of Toronto. https://srinstitute.utoronto.ca/news/whats-next-for-aida

Battilana, C. C. H., & Lacerda, M. E. G. de M. (2025, April). *Brazil: Similarities and key differences between the Brazilian AI Bill and the EU AI Act.* TozziniFreire Advogados. https://www.dataguidance.com/opinion/brazil-similarities-and-key-differences-between

Biden, J. R., Jr. (2023, October 30). *Executive Order No. 14110: Safe, secure, and trustworthy development and use of artificial intelligence.* Federal Register, 88(208), 75191–75223. https://www.federalregister.gov/documents/2023/10/31/2023-24283/safe-secure-and-trustworthy-development-and-use-of-artificial-intelligence

Birhane, A., Isaac, W., Prabhakaran, V., Díaz, M., Elish, M. C., Gabriel, I., & Mohamed, S. (2022). Power to the people? Opportunities and challenges for participatory AI. In *Proceedings of the 2nd ACM Conference on Equity and Access in Algorithms, Mechanisms, and Optimization (EAAMO '22)* (Article 6, pp. 1–8). Association for Computing Machinery. https://dl.acm.org/doi/10.1145/3551624.3555290

Bommasani, R., Zhang, D., Lee, T., & Liang, P. (2023). *Key takeaways improving transparency in AI language models: A holistic evaluation* (pp. 1–7). https://hai.stanford.edu/policy/improving-transparency-in-ai-language-models-a-holistic-evaluation

Buolamwini, J., & Gebru, T. (2018, January). Gender shades: Intersectional accuracy disparities in commercial gender classification. In *Conference on Fairness, Accountability and Transparency* (pp. 77–91). PMLR. https://proceedings.mlr.press/v81/buolamwini18a.html

CERN. (2025). *A short history of the Web.* https://home.cern/science/computing/birth-web/short-history-web

Chesterman, S. (2023). Good models borrow, great models steal: Intellectual property rights and generative AI. *SSRN Electronic Journal, 44*(February 2024), 23–37. https://doi.org/10.2139/ssrn.4590006

Cloete, F. (2024). Governing artificial intelligence (AI) and other technologies in the digital era. *Administratio Publica, 32*(1) https://hdl.handle.net/10520/ejc-adminpub_v32_n1_a3

Computer History Museum. (2025). *Timeline of computer history.* https://www.computerhistory.org/timeline/1990/

Daepp, M. I. G., & Counts, S. (2024). The emerging AI divide in the United States. *arXiv.* https://arxiv.org/abs/2404.11988

Daneliya, G., & Kurbanov, S. (2025, March 28). Development of AI regulations in Russia. *Asia Business Law Journal.* https://law.asia/russia-ai-regulations-legal-framework-ethics/

Davis, W. (2023, May 27). A lawyer used ChatGPT and now has to answer for its "bogus" citations. *The Verge.* https://www.theverge.com/2023/5/27/23739913/chatgpt-ai-lawsuit-avianca-airlines-chatbot-research

Department for Science, Innovation and Technology. (2023, March 29). *AI regulation: A pro-innovation approach* (CP 796). GOV.UK. https://www.gov.uk/government/publications/ai-regulation-a-pro-innovation-approach

Dimple, P. (2024). Impact of artificial intelligence on employment and workforce development: Risks, opportunities, and socioeconomic implications. https://papers.ssrn.com/sol3/papers.cfm?abstract_id=5057396

Ehsan, U., Liao, Q. V., Muller, M., Riedl, M. O., & Weisz, J. D. (2021). Expanding explainability: Towards social transparency in AI systems. *Conference on Human Factors in Computing Systems—Proceedings.* https://doi.org/10.1145/3411764.3445188

European Center for Not-for-Profit Law, Liberties, & European Civic Forum. (2024, April 3). *Packed with loopholes: Why the AI Act fails to protect civic space and the rule of law.* https://ecnl.org/news/packed-loopholes-why-ai-act-fails-protect-civic-space-and-rule-law

Fasken. (2023, August 29). *China's new rules for generative AI: An emerging regulatory framework.* Fasken Martineau DuMoulin LLP. https://www.fasken.com/en/knowledge/2023/08/chinas-new-rules-for-generative-ai

Fitzpatrick, G. (2018, September). A short history of human computer interaction: A people-centred perspective. In *Proceedings of the 2018 ACM SIGUCCS Annual Conference* (pp. 3-3). https://dl.acm.org/doi/10.1145/3235715.3242569

Giordano, G., Palomba, F., & Ferrucci, F. (2022). On the use of artificial intelligence to deal with privacy in IoT systems: A systematic literature review. *Journal of Systems and Software, 193*, 111475. https://doi.org/10.1016/j.jss.2022.111475

Government of Canada. (2023). *Artificial Intelligence and Data Act*. Innovation, Science and Economic Development Canada. https://ised-isde.canada.ca/site/innovation-better-canada/en/artificial-intelligence-and-data-act

Government of Canada. (2025). *The Artificial Intelligence and Data Act (AIDA) – Companion document*. Innovation, Science and Economic Development Canada. https://ised-isde.canada.ca/site/innovation-better-canada/en/artificial-intelligence-and-data-act-aida-companion-document

Gray, M., Samala, R., Liu, Q., Skiles, D., Xu, J., Tong, W., & Wu, L. (2024). Measurement and mitigation of bias in artificial intelligence: A narrative literature review for regulatory science. *Clinical Pharmacology & Therapeutics, 115*(4), 687–697. https://ascpt.onlinelibrary.wiley.com/doi/10.1002/cpt.3117

Halmos, P. R. (1973). The legend of John Von Neumann. *The American Mathematical Monthly, 80*(4), 382–394. https://gwern.net/doc/math/1973-halmos.pdf

Inside Higher Ed. (2024, April 15). *2024 Survey of College and University Chief Academic Officers*. https://www.insidehighered.com/reports/2024/04/15/2024-survey-college-and-university-chief-academic-officers

Johnson, T. (2000). Browsing back over a life on the Web. *Physics World, 13*(4), 47–48. https://doi.org/10.1088/2058-7058/13/4/27

Joshi, D. (2024). AI governance in India—Law, policy and political economy. *Communication Research and Practice, 10*(3), 328–339. https://doi.org/10.1080/22041451.2024.2346428

Kalligeropoulos, D., & Vasileiadou, S. (2008). The Homeric automata and their implementation. *Science and Technology in the Homeric Epics*. https://doi.org/10.1007/978-1-4020-8784-4_5

Kelley, J., Budington, B., & Cope, S. (2021). Proctoring tools and dragnet investigations rob students of due process. https://www.eff.org/deeplinks/2021/04/proctoring-tools-and-dragnet-investigations-rob-students-due-process

Khanal, S., Zhang, H., & Taeihagh, A. (2025). Development of new generation of artificial intelligence in China: When Beijing's global ambitions meet local realities. *Journal of Contemporary China, 34*(151), 19–42. https://doi.org/10.1080/10670564.2024.2333492

Khara, S., & Yadav, S. (2024). The legal liability of AI systems in India. *Alochana Journal, 13*(5), 446–449. https://alochana.org/wp-content/uploads/37-AJ2451.pdf=

Koike, R., Kaneko, M., & Okazaki, N. (2024). OUTFOX: LLM-generated essay detection through in-context learning with adversarially generated examples. *Proceedings of the AAAI Conference on Artificial Intelligence, 38*(19), 21258–21266. https://doi.org/10.1609/aaai.v38i19.30120

Liveley, G., & Thomas, S. (2020). Homer's intelligent machines: AI in antiquity. In *AI Narratives: Imaginative Thinking About Intelligent Machines* (pp. 25–48). Oxford Academic.

Lubello, V. (2025). Regulating the machine: Competing philosophies in U.S. federal AI governance. *DPCE Online, 12*(1), 1–18. https://www.dpceonline.it/index.php/dpceonline/article/download/2463/2681/3922

Martin, K. D., & Zimmermann, J. (2024). Artificial intelligence and its implications for data privacy. *Current Opinion in Psychology, 58*(June), 101829. https://doi.org/10.1016/j.copsyc.2024.101829

Martins, L. (2025, February 4). *Brazil's AI law faces uncertain future as big tech warms to Trump*. Tech Policy Press. https://www.techpolicy.press/brazils-ai-law-faces-uncertain-future-as-big-tech-warms-to-trump/

Mazarchuk, A. (2024). AI for war and peacetime: A Ukrainian perspective. *National Defense.*. https://www.nationaldefensemagazine.org/articles/2024/11/1/viewpoint-ai-for-war-and-peacetime-a-ukrainian-perspective

McCarthy, J., Minsky, M. L., Rochester, N., & Shannon, C. E. (1955). Automatic computers: How can a computer be programmed to use a language? http://jmc.stanford.edu/articles/dartmouth/dartmouth.pdf

McIntire, A., Calvert, I., & Ashcraft, J. (2024). Pressure to plagiarize and the choice to cheat: Toward a pragmatic reframing of the ethics of academic integrity. *Education Sciences, 14*(3), 244. https://doi.org/10.3390/educsci14030244

Nicks, C., Mitchell, E., Rafailov, R., Sharma, A., Manning, C., & Ermon, S. (2024). Large model detectors are easily optimized against. https://openreview.net/pdf?id=4eJDMjYZZG

Nishant, R., Kennedy, M., Corbett, J., Laval, U., & Prince, P. P. (2020). Artificial intelligence for sustainability: Challenges, opportunities, and a research agenda. *International Journal of Information Management, 53*(January), 102104. https://doi.org/10.1016/j.ijinfomgt.2020.102104

Nouraldeen, R. M. (2023). The impact of technology readiness and use perceptions on students' adoption of artificial intelligence: the moderating role of gender. *Development and Learning in Organizations, 37*(3), 7–10. https://doi.org/10.1108/DLO-07-2022-0133

Novet, J. (2024). Microsoft, BlackRock form group to raise $100 billion to invest in AI data centers and power. *CNBC News.*. https://www.cnbc.

com/2024/09/17/microsoft-blackrock-form-gaiip-to-invest-in-ai-data-centers-energy.html

Nussbaum, F. G. (2023). A comprehensive review of AI myths and misconceptions. https://doi.org/10.13140/RG.2.2.28098.15049

Obenza, B. N., Go, L. E., Francisco, J. A. M., Buit, E. E. T., Mariano, F. V. B., Cuizon, H. L., Jr., Cagabhion, A. J. D., & Agbulos, K. A. J. L. (2024). The nexus between cognitive absorption and AI literacy of college students as moderated by sex. *American Journal of Smart Technology and Solutions, 3*(1), 32–39. https://doi.org/10.54536/ajsts.v3i1.2603

Prickett, R. (2025, April 16). AI regulation: U.K. sits on regulatory fence between U.S. and E.U. Compliance Week. https://www.complianceweek.com/regulatory-policy/ai-regulation-uk-sits-on-regulatory-fence-between-us-and-eu/35937.article

Prins, C., Sheikh, H., & Schrijvers, E. (2023). Artificial intelligence: Definition and background. In J. E. J. Prins & F. W. A. Brom (Eds.), *Mission AI: Research for Policy* (pp. 15–39). Springer.

Putin, V. (2024, February 15). Decree No. 490 (as amended): On the development of artificial intelligence in the Russian Federation. https://base.garant.ru/72838946/

Ramos, G. (2022). Why we must act now to close the gender gap in AI. In *World Economic Forum.*. https://www.weforum.org/stories/2022/08/why-we-must-act-now-to-close-the-gender-gap-in-ai/

Regulation (EU) 2024/1689 of the European Parliament and of the Council of 13 March 2024 on laying down harmonised rules on artificial intelligence (Artificial Intelligence Act). *Official Journal of the European Union*. https://artificialintelligenceact.eu/the-act/

Reuters. (2024). How drone combat in Ukraine is changing warfare. https://www.reuters.com/graphics/UKRAINE-CRISIS/DRONES/dwpkeyjwkpm/

Sharma, A., Sharma, S. C., Soni, S. D., Agrawal, P., Mishra, P., & Mourya, G. (2025). Artificial intelligence in the Indian criminal justice system: Advancements, challenges, and ethical implications. *Journal of Lifestyle and SDGs Review, 5*(1), e04877–e04877.

Shelley, M. (2018). *Frankenstein*. Gutenberg.org. https://www.gutenberg.org/files/41445/41445-h/41445-h.htm

Spencer, T., & Singh, S. (2024). What the data centre and AI boom could mean for the energy sector. *International Energy Agency (IEA)*. https://www.iea.org/commentaries/what-the-data-centre-and-ai-boom-could-mean-for-the-energy-sector

Stevenson, D. (1994). *The Iliad*. Internet Classics Archive. https://classics.mit.edu/Homer/iliad.mb.txt

Tawalbeh, L. A., & Saldamli, G. (2021). Reconsidering big data security and privacy in cloud and mobile cloud systems. *Journal of King Saud University—*

Computer and Information Sciences, 33(7), 810–819. https://doi.org/10.1016/j.jksuci.2019.05.007

Tiedrich, L., Perset, K., Fialho Esposito, S., & Plonk, A. (2025). *Intellectual property issues in artificial intelligence trained on scraped data* (No. 33). OECD. https://www.oecd.org/content/dam/oecd/en/publications/reports/2025/02/intellectual-property-issues-in-artificial-intelligence-trained-on-scraped-data_a07f010b/d5241a23-en.pdf

Tonmoy, S. M., Zaman, S. M., Jain, V., Rani, A., Rawte, V., Chadha, A., & Das, A. (2024). A comprehensive survey of hallucination mitigation techniques in large language models. *arXiv Preprint*, arXiv:2401.01313. https://arxiv.org/abs/2401.01313

Toosi, A., Bottino, A. G., Saboury, B., Siegel, E., & Rahmim, A. (2021). A brief history of AI: How to prevent another winter (A critical review). *PET Clinics, 16*(4), 449–469. https://doi.org/10.1016/j.cpet.2021.07.001

Toy, T. (2023). Transparency in AI. *AI and Society*, 1–11. https://doi.org/10.1007/s00146-023-01786-y

Toynbee, A. (1956). *The Industrial Revolution*. Beacon Press. https://www.oecd.org/content/dam/oecd/en/publications/reports/2025/02/intellectual-property-issues-in-artificial-intelligence-trained-on-scraped-data_a07f010b/d5241a23-en.pdf

Trump, D. J. (2025a, January 14). *Executive Order No. 14141: Advancing United States leadership in artificial intelligence infrastructure*. Federal Register, 90(11), 5469–5476. https://www.federalregister.gov/documents/2025/01/17/2025-01395/advancing-united-states-leadership-in-artificial-intelligence-infrastructure

Trump, D. J. (2025b, January 25). *Executive Order No. 14142: Promoting innovation and competition in artificial intelligence*. Federal Register, 90(18), 7421–7425. https://www.federalregister.gov/documents/2025/01/26/2025-02172/promoting-innovation-and-competition-in-artificial-intelligence

Ulloa, R., Makhortykh, M., & Urman, A. (2022). Scaling up search engine audits: Practical insights for algorithm auditing. *Journal of Information Science, 50*(2). https://doi.org/10.1177/01655515221093029

UN Environment Programme. (2024). AI has an environmental problem: Here's what the world can do about that. https://www.unep.org/news-and-stories/story/ai-has-environmental-problem-heres-what-world-can-do-about

UNESCO. (2021). *Recommendation on the ethics of artificial intelligence*. https://www.unesco.org/en/legal-affairs/recommendation-ethics-artificial-intelligence

United Nations. (2019). Machines capable of taking lives without human involvement are unacceptable. *Secretary-General tells experts on autonomous weapons systems.*. https://press.un.org/en/2019/sgsm19512.doc.htm

United Nations. (2023). First Committee approves new resolution on lethal autonomous weapons, as speaker warns "An algorithm must not be in full control of decisions involving killing." https://press.un.org/en/2023/gadis3731.doc.htm

US Federal Trade Commission. (2024). A look behind the screens: Examining the data practices of social media and video streaming services. https://www.ftc.gov/reports/look-behind-screens-examining-data-practices-social-media-video-streaming-services

Vaughn, L. M., & Jacquez, F. (2020). Participatory research methods – Choice points in the research process. *Journal of Participatory Research Methods, 1*(1). https://doi.org/10.35844/001c.13244

von Neumann, J. (2017). In A. H. Taub (Ed.), *John von Neumann collected works: Volume V, Design of computers, theory of automata and numerical analysis.* Pergamon Press.

von Neumann, J. (2021). First draft of a report on EDVAC. In H. Lewis (Ed.), *Ideas that created the future: Classic papers of computer science.* https://doi.org/10.7551/mitpress/12274.001.0001

Warren, S., & Brandeis, L. (1890). The right to privacy. *Harvard Law Review, 4*(5), 193–220.

Wu, C. J., Raghavendra, R., Gupta, U., Acun, B., Ardalani, N., Maeng, K., et al. (2022). Sustainable AI: Environmental implications, challenges and opportunities. *Proceedings of Machine Learning and Systems, 4*, 795–813. https://proceedings.mlsys.org/paper_files/paper/2022

Wu, J., Yang, S., Zhan, R., Yuan, Y., Wong, D. F., & Chao, L. S. (2023). A survey on LLM-generated text detection: Necessity, methods, and future directions. *arXiv*. http://arxiv.org/abs/2310.14724

CHAPTER 4

Understanding AI Resistance and Adoption: A Theoretical Roadmap

Rebecca J. Allen

Introduction

Thinking back to graduate school days, I remember the mix of dread and confusion that came with trying to "find" a theory for a paper. In graduate education, faculty often begin teaching the research process by encouraging students to identify a real-world problem that matters to them. From there, students are guided to narrow the problem and locate a gap in the literature that can be explored through research. This "find-your-problem" approach has important strengths—researching something meaningful can be deeply motivating. However, challenges often arise when students are asked to align their problem with a theoretical framework.

As Gustafsson and Hagström (2018) point out, many graduate students have only a vague understanding of what a theory actually is. As a result, they often select a theory from a scattered set of lecture slides,

R. J. Allen (✉)
Center for IT Engagement (cITe), Mount St. Joseph University,
Cincinnati, OH, USA
e-mail: rebecca.allen@msj.edu

R. J. Allen, A. Nakonechnyi (eds.), *Using and Understanding AI in Higher Education*,
https://doi.org/10.1007/978-3-031-99754-9_4

missing the connections, relationships, and historical development of these frameworks—each one appearing in isolation, as though it exists on its own island rather than as part of an ongoing scholarly conversation. For the record, theory can be understood as a practice of naming, framing, and abstracting that helps scholars explain, interpret, or critique organizational phenomena (Cornelissen et al., 2021). A good theory helps us ask better questions: Why does this happen? What does it mean? How are these things related? What tools should we use to explore the problem? What assumptions are we making? And—perhaps most importantly—how might things be different?

In some ways, scholars studying AI education and human–computer interaction today face challenges similar to those of early graduate students. The terrain is still relatively new, and researchers are often unsure how best to frame or package the problems they are exploring. As discussed in the previous chapter, AI itself is not a new technology. What is new is the way the public now engages with AI—particularly through accessible, everyday tools like generative AI. As a result, subfields such as AI education, AI acceptance, and AI adoption are still emerging, and—like new scholars—are working to find their theoretical voices (Milička, 2024).

> The current quality of articles on this topic [generative AI] is often abysmal ... papers [are] on random observations about LLMs, devoid of any theoretical framework, written by individuals who confuse basic terminology and make avoidable mistakes (p. 1) ... we should start creating some comprehensive theories, stop carrying stones to a pile and start building a citadel together. (p. 16)

In this chapter, I attempt to do just that—to help stack some of those stones into something a bit more structured. My goal is to offer clear theoretical directions that can support both the empirical studies presented later in this book and the work of other scholars, especially graduate students, exploring AI in education.

Of course, I could not include every theory related to technology use. The choices we made reflect the arc of the book as a whole, which in turn reflects our own context as a higher education administrator and a university educator working with AI. One of the primary motivations for writing this book was to make sense of the widespread resistance to AI that we have observed, particularly among faculty. AI acceptance—an individual's willingness to engage with, adopt, or integrate artificial intelligence tools into their work, learning, or daily practices (Kelly et al., 2023)—is lacking across our higher educational institutions, particularly among faculty. While different institutions have different climates, the pattern of resistance appears quite consistent.

For example, a survey of 284 UK academics found that 48% were not using generative AI tools, even though 65% acknowledged that these tools were already changing their work, and 79% expected to use them more in the future. Faculty cited concerns about AI illiteracy, ethics, deskilling, dehumanization, and inaccuracy—concerns that reflect deeper anxieties about the erosion of scholarly identity and growing inequalities in academia (Watermeyer et al., 2024). Similarly, in a Hong Kong–based study by Chan and Colloton (2024), faculty voiced concerns about over-reliance, data privacy, academic integrity, job displacement, and the loss of human connection in teaching.

Teaching with AI clearly matters—but on many campuses, teaching may not be possible until resistance is addressed. Faculty embroiled in resistance are not going to teach AI. For instance, in the widely read ***Inside Higher Education***, in an article entitled "Burn it down: A license for AI resistance," Dusseau opines (2024):

> Now please open your newly generated hymnal, *How to Use but Not Abuse Artificial Intelligence*, to the chapter titled 'Faculty Embrace New Role as Handmaidens of Doom.' There is another way. To the silent, hopeless AI skeptics and Star Trek fans: resistance is not futile. We simply do not have to participate. Let Melville's Bartleby provide the brat slogan of our license to resist: "I would prefer not to."

In the context that higher education currently finds itself, this theoretical chapter focuses primarily on AI resistance, not pedagogy (for pedagogy see Chaps. 6, 10). This issue of AI resistance has two dimensions: understanding the causes of resistance and identifying potential pathways toward resolution. In this chapter, I focus on the first—conceptualizing AI resistance through a review of behavioral and adoption theories most commonly used in technology research. I will return to the second dimension in the book's conclusion, where I explore what might be required to shift attitudes and improve the broader environment for AI in higher education.

My aim here is not only to provide theoretical coherence for this book but also to support graduate students who may be encountering these ideas for the first time. Academic theory can often feel abstract, disconnected, or overly technical. But theory becomes much more approachable when it is presented in a clear context or developmental sequence, rather than as a disconnected list of models. Theories are, at their core, containers for ideas—and ideas build upon one another. Almost no great thinker worked in isolation; academic theories are shaped through ongoing dialogue and adaptation.

With that in mind, this chapter follows a chronological structure, tracing the evolution of major theories of technology adoption—from early diffusion models to more recent, hybrid frameworks. While the previous chapter traced the technical history of AI and how we arrived at today's ethical and policy debates, this chapter offers a parallel journey through the intellectual history of technology acceptance. Holding on to that sequence will help clarify how these frameworks emerged, how they relate to one another, and how they can be used to understand present-day concerns around AI resistance—Table 4.1 can be a useful roadmap. All of the theories discussed here are widely applied, but I also provide examples of how each has been used in the context of AI in higher education, offering a conceptual toolkit for researchers, educators, and graduate students alike.

And while Table 4.1 does in fact capture much of the past framing of technology adoption theory, we want to foreshadow what we explore at the end of this chapter—qualitative, participatory framings—how to help humans in real situations cope with technology adoption, is only beginning to be considered.

Diffusion of Innovation Theory (DIT)

In the early 1960s, sociologist Everett Rogers (1962) studied how farmers adopted new agricultural techniques. What puzzled him was not the availability of innovations—most were demonstrably better than older methods—but the inconsistent rates at which people embraced them. Some farmers eagerly tried new approaches; others resisted for years, even in the face of clear benefits. The innovations Rogers examined included hybrid seed corn, chemical fertilizers, pesticides, soil conservation practices, and mechanized equipment—technologies promising higher yields and greater efficiency. Yet adoption was uneven, shaped less by practical utility and more by communication, trust, social pressure, and timing.

These observations led Rogers to develop one of the most enduring frameworks in technology and communication studies: the Diffusion of

Table 4.1 Major technology resistance theories

Theory name (with Acronym)	*Author & Year*	*Core constructs (with Acronyms)*	*Distinguishing features*
Diffusion of Innovations (DIT)	Rogers, 1962	Relative Advantage (RA), Compatibility (C), Complexity (CX), Trialability (T), Observability (O)	Explains how innovations spread via communication and social systems; emphasizes role of opinion leaders
Theory of Reasoned Action (TRA)	Ajzen & Fishbein, 1980	Attitude Toward the Behavior (ATT), Subjective Norm (SN), Behavioral Intention (BI)	Early model focused on volitional behavior and behavioral intention
Social Cognitive Theory (SCT)	Bandura, 1989; 2001	Self-Efficacy (SE), Vicarious Learning (VL), Self-Regulation (SR), Personal/Proxy/Collective Agency (PA, PrA, CA)	Emphasizes human agency and social modeling; includes individual and collective action
Technology Acceptance Model (TAM)	Davis, 1985	Perceived Usefulness (PU), Perceived Ease of Use (PEOU), Behavioral Intention (BI)	Rational model focused on perceived utility and effort; widely adopted in tech studies
Model of Personal Computing Utilization (PCU)	Thompson et al., 1991	Perceived Difficulty of Use (PDU), Long-Term Consequences (LTC), Affect Toward Use (AFT), Social Factors (SF), Facilitating Conditions (FC), Habit (HAB)	Focuses on actual use rather than just intention; incorporates emotion, routine, and social context
Theory of Planned Behavior (TPB)	Ajzen, 1991	Attitude Toward the Behavior (ATT), Subjective Norm (SN), Perceived Behavioral Control (PBC), Actual Behavioral Control (ABC), Past Behavior (PB)	Expands TRA by including perceived and actual control; supports behavior under constraints
Motivational Model (MM)	Davis et al., 1992	Intrinsic Motivation (IM), Extrinsic Motivation (EM), PU, PEOU, BI	Builds on TAM by adding motivation and enjoyment; blends cognition and emotion
Unified Theory of Acceptance and Use of Technology (UTAUT)	Venkatesh et al., 2003	Performance Expectancy (PE), Effort Expectancy (EE), Social Influence (SI), Facilitating Conditions (FC); Moderators: Age, Gender, Experience, Voluntariness	Synthesizes 8 earlier models; includes demographic moderators

Innovations Theory (DIT). DIT suggests that an innovation's likelihood of adoption is influenced by five characteristics: relative advantage (RA), compatibility (C), complexity (CX), trialability (T), and observability (O). Today, DIT remains foundational in fields as diverse as marketing, public health, education, and information technology. In DIT, individuals adopt innovations at different rates, categorized as innovators, early adopters, early majority, late majority, and laggards. Rogers later expanded his theory beyond agriculture to areas like family planning, HIV prevention, and educational technologies—highlighting how interpersonal networks and opinion leaders often shape adoption more than scientific evidence alone. Although it originated in rural development, DIT now informs understandings of phenomena from online learning platforms to the rise of generative AI.

Examples of AI Research Drawing on DIT

Though first published in the 1960s, Rogers continued refining DIT until 2003, and it remains highly relevant. Recent research by Jin et al. (2025) demonstrates how DIT is being applied to study AI adoption in higher education. To examine institutional responses to generative AI, Jin et al analyzed official policy documents from 40 universities across Africa, Asia, Europe, Latin America, North America, and Oceania. Selected based on QS World University Rankings, these universities were expected to act as trendsetters. Researchers manually collected policies, guidelines, and statements, translated them into English, and analyzed them using a thematic approach grounded in DIT. Their analysis focused on how institutions addressed innovation characteristics like compatibility, trialability, and observability; the communication channels used; and the roles assigned to faculty, students, and administrators in facilitating adoption.

The study also revealed critical challenges. According to DIT, adoption success depends not only on an innovation's qualities but also on communication practices, institutional culture, and broader social systems. While most universities acknowledged the relative advantage of generative AI—especially its potential to support teaching, learning, and workforce preparation—factors like trialability and observability were often neglected. Few institutions created clear mechanisms for piloting AI tools or evaluating their impact. Communication strategies were similarly inconsistent; fewer than half the universities used collaborative channels to engage stakeholders. Additionally, universities in the Global South faced greater barriers to equitable access and were less likely to define clear stakeholder roles. These findings reinforce that adoption is not merely about access to new technologies; it is a fundamentally social process, shaped by trust, transparency, and institutional alignment.

Theory of Reasoned Action

The Theory of Reasoned Action (TRA), developed by Ajzen and Fishbein (1980), provides a foundational framework for understanding human behavior. It suggests that a person's actions are primarily guided by their behavioral intentions, which are shaped by two key factors: their attitude toward the behavior (how positively or negatively they view it) and subjective norms (the perceived social pressure to perform or not perform the behavior). For example, someone who believes that recycling is good for the environment (positive attitude) and thinks that their community expects them to recycle (subjective norm) is more likely to intend to recycle—and, consequently, more likely to do so (Fig. 4.1).

Ajzen (2020, p. 316) himself, however,quickly began to see that while his theory was useful in certain respects, it suffered from some limitations:

After working with the theory of reasoned action for several years, I realized that the assumption of perfect volitional control placed severe limitations on the theory's ability to deal with behaviors that pose difficulty of execution (see Ajzen, 1987). Clearly, people can face problems or be prevented from acting on intentions to perform even such a mundane behavior as attending a concert if, for example, the person's car breaks down on the way to the venue or tickets have run out. In fact,

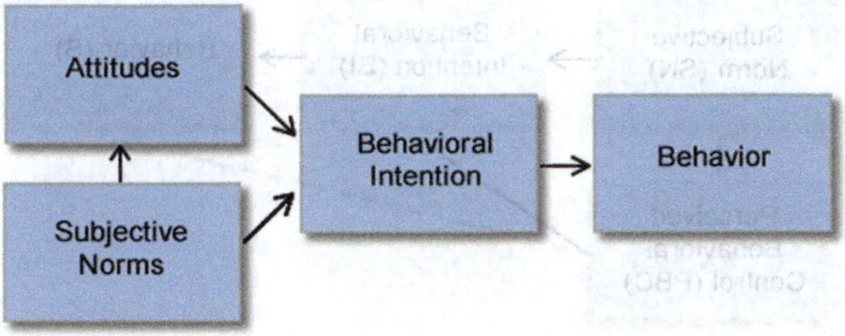

Fig. 4.1 Theory of reasoned action

performance of many behaviors entails possession of certain skills and knowledge or requires cooperation by other people; and it may demand the ability to overcome such barriers as lack of money, time, or other resources. For this reason, I added the construct of control, calling the revised model the TPB [Theory of Planned Behavior].

Theory of Planned Behavior

Seeing a need, Ajzen (1991) expanded the Theory of Reasoned Action (TRA) into the Theory of Planned Behavior (TPB) to better explain behaviors that are not entirely under a person's control. At its core, TPB proposes that the most immediate predictor of behavior is a person's behavioral intention (BI)—their motivation or plan to carry out a specific action. This intention is shaped by three key constructs: attitude toward the behavior (ATT), subjective norm (SN), and perceived behavioral control (PBC) (Fig. 4.2).

ATT refers to the individual's overall evaluation of the behavior as favorable or unfavorable, based on their beliefs about its likely outcomes. For example, a person might believe that wearing a heart monitor could help detect heart arrhythmia (a positive outcome) or might find it uncomfortable and inconvenient (a negative experience); both beliefs would contribute to their attitude. SN reflects the perceived social pressure to engage

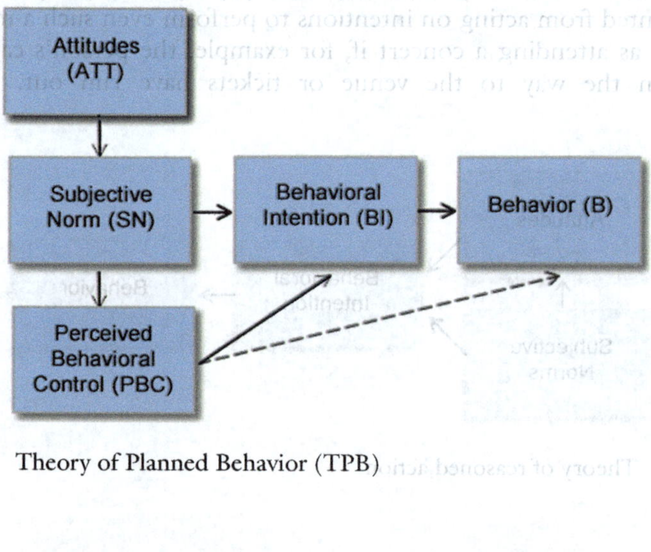

Fig. 4.2 Theory of Planned Behavior (TPB)

in or avoid the behavior and includes two types of normative beliefs: injunctive (what important others think one should do) and descriptive (what those others actually do). A person may believe that their physician or coworkers approve of wearing a heart monitor (injunctive norm) or that many people in their social circle already use one (descriptive norm).

PBC involves a person's perceived ease or difficulty in performing the behavior, shaped by beliefs about facilitating or hindering factors such as time, money, knowledge, or support. For instance, someone might want to use a health-monitoring device but feel uncertain about how to set it up or whether they can afford it—leading to lower perceived control. In addition to perceived control, TPB also accounts for actual behavioral control (ABC)—whether the individual truly has the resources and ability to perform the behavior. A person might believe they are capable of completing a task but face external barriers like malfunctioning equipment or lack of access, which can prevent them from following through despite strong intentions.

Many applications of TPB also incorporate past behavior (PB), recognizing that previous experiences shape future beliefs and intentions. Ajzen (2020) offers an example of someone who initially plans to work out before work but discovers that traffic, fatigue, and a lack of encouragement from coworkers make the behavior more difficult than expected. These experiences may reduce the person's attitude, sense of control, and social support, ultimately changing their future intentions.

To enhance predictive accuracy, TPB emphasizes that behaviors must be clearly defined along four dimensions: target, action, context, and time (TACT). For instance, "when studying technology acceptance, a researcher might define the behavior at a specific level of detail—such as 'installing (action) a webcam monitor (target) at home (context) in the next three months (time frame)'" (Ajzen, 2020, pp. 314–315). This precision ensures that all related beliefs and intentions are aligned with the behavior being studied.

Example of AI Research Drawing on TPB

Wang et al. (2024) provide a clear example of how the Theory of Planned Behavior (TPB) can be applied to study technology acceptance in higher education, specifically in the context of generative AI tools such as ChatGPT and Sora. Their study focuses on university students in China and investigates the relationships among TPB's core constructs: attitude toward the behavior (ATT), subjective norm (SN), and perceived behavioral control (PBC).

To test these relationships, the researchers used Structural Equation Modeling (SEM), a common method in TPB research that allows for the simultaneous analysis of multiple variables and pathways, including mediating effects. Their findings show that students' attitudes significantly predicted behavioral intention to use generative AI and that both AI literacy and subjective norms influenced students' attitudes and PBC. Notably, attitude served as a full mediator between both AI literacy and SN and the students' intention to use AI, with the model explaining 59.3% of the variance in behavioral intention.These results reinforce the value of TPB for understanding technology adoption: efforts to promote meaningful AI use in education may be most effective when they focus on shaping positive attitudes and building students' confidence and skills, rather than relying solely on external expectations or mandates.

Technology Acceptance Model

Moving forward in time, the Technology Acceptance Model (TAM) was originally conceived as part of Fred Davis' dissertation project (1985). Before beginning his Ph.D., Davis completed a Bachelor of Science in Industrial Engineering and pursued a minor in Computer Science. While still studying, he worked at a healthcare financial consulting firm, where he designed and implemented information systems for budgeting and financial modeling. He had seen firsthand that users were sometimes reluctant to adopt systems that could benefit their work processes—a common observation at the time. Difficulties in end-user acceptance were widely documented in the 1970s and 1980s; in fact, Davis's model builds upon earlier social psychology theories, particularly the Theory of Reasoned Action (TRA) and the Theory of Planned Behavior (TPB), both of which he cites in his dissertation.

Nevertheless, at the time, user acceptance was seen as an unsolvable and unpredictable problem, often attributed to resistance to change or broader political dynamics (Davis & Granić, 2024). Davis' dissertation proposal to tackle user acceptance was initially downplayed by faculty, who questioned why he would succeed where many had failed. Davis argued that emergent behavioral theories and increasingly robust psychometric measurement techniques were needed.

Davis' (1985) resultant Technology Acceptance Model (TAM) postulates that two main factors influence whether someone decides to use a technology: perceived usefulness (PU)—how much users believe the technology will improve their performance or make tasks easier—and perceived ease of use (PEOU), or how simple and effort-free the technology appears. These two perceptions shape users' attitudes toward the technology, which then impact their behavioral intention (BI)—their reported likelihood or willingness to use the system in the future. BI is a core construct in TAM and serves as the immediate predictor of actual system use: the stronger a user's intention to engage with a technology, the more likely they are to follow through and adopt it in practice (Fig. 4.3).

In many applications of TAM, PU is found to have a stronger influence on BI than PEOU, especially in performance-driven contexts where efficiency and productivity are valued. However, PEOU still plays an important role, both directly (by influencing BI) and indirectly (by shaping PU—technologies that are easier to use are often also seen as more useful). TAM assumes a rational, utility-based decision process in which users weigh effort against benefit, and it has been widely applied across domains such as workplace technologies, mobile apps, online learning, and AI-driven systems. Over time, scholars have extended the model to include additional predictors of BI—such as social influence, trust, enjoyment, and intrinsic motivation—to better account for the emotional, contextual, and interpersonal dynamics involved in technology adoption.

Example of AI Research Drawing on TAM

Karan and Chakma (2025) offer an empirical example of TAM applied to artificial intelligence (AI) in higher education. Their study investigates how university students' perceptions influence their acceptance of AI-supported learning tools. Drawing on responses from 405

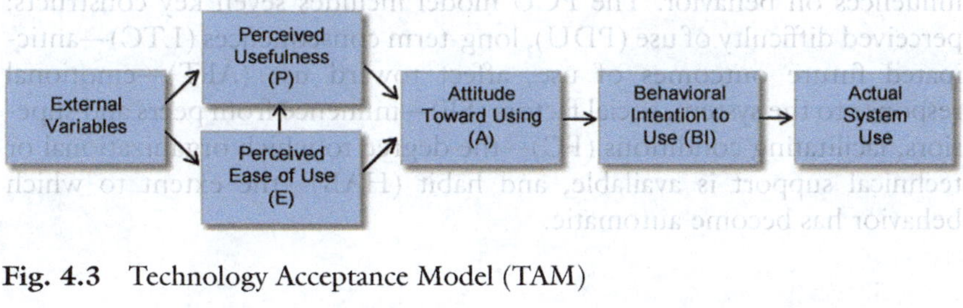

Fig. 4.3 Technology Acceptance Model (TAM)

undergraduate and postgraduate students at a university in Bangladesh, the authors used a survey to measure key TAM constructs: perceived usefulness, perceived ease of use, and behavioral intention to use AI. To analyze the data, they applied structural equation modeling (SEM), a statistical technique that tests relationships between latent variables and assesses how well a theoretical model fits the observed data. SEM allowed them to simultaneously evaluate the influence of perceived ease of use on perceived usefulness and the impact of both on students' intention to adopt AI in their studies.

Their results showed strong model fit and confirmed that perceived usefulness was the most significant predictor of behavioral intention, while perceived ease of use played a smaller but still meaningful role. This study affirms TAM's relevance as a theoretical framework for understanding student acceptance of AI in contemporary educational settings and demonstrates the value of SEM in validating technology acceptance models in empirical research.

Model of Personal Computing Utilization (PCU)

The advent of the personal computer in the 1980s and 1990s elicited sharp public reactions, much like generative AI has today. Resistance to computers was not just about the machines themselves—it was deeply tied to confidence, identity, prior experience, and social context. It mirrors today's AI anxiety in many ways: people feel excluded, overwhelmed, or unsure how to start, even though the tools are increasingly accessible (Powell, 2013).

Thompson et al. (1991) proposed the Model of Personal Computing Utilization (PCU) to explain the factors influencing actual computer use in workplace settings. While Thompson et al. cite Davis and Ajzen, their focus is not on directly building from those models but rather on identifying a broader set of constructs that capture both individual and contextual influences on behavior. The PCU model includes seven key constructs: perceived difficulty of use (PDU), long-term consequences (LTC)—anticipated future outcomes of use, affect toward use (AFT)—emotional response to the system, social factors (SF)—influence from peers and superiors, facilitating conditions (FC)—the degree to which organizational or technical support is available, and habit (HAB)—the extent to which behavior has become automatic.

By emphasizing actual system use—rather than just behavioral intention—the model brings attention to how routine, emotion, and the workplace environment can directly shape technology adoption. In doing so, it expands the conversation beyond individual cognition to include the social and institutional conditions that make technology use more or less likely.

The advent of the personal computer in the 1980s and 1990s elicited sharp public reactions, much like generative AI has today. Resistance to computers was not just about the machines themselves—it was deeply tied to confidence, identity, prior experience, and social context. It mirrors today's AI anxiety in many ways: people feel excluded, overwhelmed, or unsure how to start, even though the tools are increasingly accessible (Powell, 2013).

Thompson et al. (1991) proposed the Model of Personal Computing Utilization (PCU) to explain the factors influencing actual computer use in workplace settings. While Thompson et al. cite Davis and Ajzen, their focus is not on directly building from those models but rather on identifying a broader set of constructs that capture both individual and contextual influences on behavior. The PCU model includes seven key constructs: perceived difficulty of use (PDU), long-term consequences (LTC)—anticipated future outcomes of use, affect toward use (AFT)—emotional response to the system, social factors (SF)—influence from peers and superiors, facilitating conditions (FC)—the degree to which organizational or technical support is available, and habit (HAB)—the extent to which behavior has become automatic.

By emphasizing actual system use—rather than just behavioral intention—the model brings attention to how routine, emotion, and the workplace environment can directly shape technology adoption. In doing so, it expands the conversation beyond individual cognition to include the social and institutional conditions that make technology use more or less likely.

Motivational Model

Not unlike the Model of Personal Computing Utilization (PCU), the Motivational Model (MM) acknowledges that subjective perceptions can shape behaviors. MM was developed by Davis et al. (1992)—it is worth noting that this Davis is the same Fred Davis who originally conceived of the Technology Acceptance Model (TAM).

The Motivational Model builds directly from TAM by retaining its emphasis on how users' beliefs about a system's usefulness and ease of use influence their intention to adopt it. However, it adds an important layer by introducing a distinction between two types of motivation: extrinsic motivation (EM) and intrinsic motivation (IM). EM refers to using a system because it serves a practical purpose or is required (for example, using a tool to complete work tasks efficiently), while IM refers to using it because the experience is enjoyable or satisfying in itself (such as liking a program because it is intuitive or visually engaging). The model also shows that systems perceived as easier to use are more likely to be seen as both useful and enjoyable. In doing so, the MM offers a richer understanding of technology adoption by accounting not only for rational judgments but also for emotional and experiential factors.

Although Fred Davis developed both the Technology Acceptance Model (TAM) and the Motivational Model (MM), MM has not gained as much usage as TAM. Nevertheless, it has been influential in explaining why people adopt technology. While TAM emphasizes cognitive evaluations of usefulness and ease of use, MM focuses on intrinsic and extrinsic motivation—highlighting the affective and psychological drivers behind technology use. When navigating the literature and writing, it is helpful to note that TAM and MM are frequently paired in applied studies, particularly in educational technology contexts.

Example of a Study Employing MM

In their study of ChatGPT adoption among undergraduates, Lai et al. (2023) integrated the Technology Acceptance Model (TAM) with the Motivational Model (MM) and self-determination theory to better understand what drives students to use AI tools for active learning. Conducted in Hong Kong, the study surveyed 473 undergraduate students from eight universities, making it one of the earliest large-scale empirical investigations of ChatGPT in higher education.

While TAM traditionally emphasizes perceived usefulness (PU), perceived ease of use (PEOU), and behavioral intention (BI), this study extends the model by adding intrinsic motivation (IM) as a central factor. Using structural equation modeling, the researchers found that IM—students' internal interest, enjoyment, and curiosity—was the strongest predictor of their intention to use ChatGPT, surpassing even perceived usefulness. In contrast, PEOU had no significant impact, suggesting that when it comes to generative AI, how enjoyable and engaging students find the tool may matter more than how easy it is to use. By weaving motivational constructs into a TAM-based framework, this study highlights the importance of considering both cognitive and affective dimensions when seeking to understand how and why students adopt new AI-powered learning technologies.

Social Cognitive Theory and Agency

While Davis's Motivational Model (MM) focuses on what motivates technology use—typically emphasizing extrinsic motivation (e.g., usefulness) and intrinsic motivation (e.g., enjoyment)—Bandura moves beyond motivation alone and introduces the concept of agency: the idea that people are active shapers of their actions and environments, not merely responders to rewards or outcomes.

In his seminal 1989 work, Bandura emphasized that humans are not passive responders to stimuli but active agents who learn by observing others (vicarious learning), think ahead about outcomes (forethought), regulate their actions according to goals and standards (self-regulation), and reflect on their performance (self-reflection). In 2001, he expanded this framework by identifying four core features of agency—intentionality, forethought, self-reactiveness, and self-reflectiveness—and introduced three modes of agency: personal agency (acting on one's own), proxy agency (relying on others to act on one's behalf), and collective agency (working together to achieve shared goals) (Bandura, 1989, 2001).

Subsequently, in an increasingly interconnected world, Bandura argued that the ability of groups to act with shared purpose—collective efficacy—is essential for addressing complex societal challenges.

Example of a Study Using SCT

Shata and Hartley (2025) conducted a survey of full-time faculty members at two mid-sized public universities in the United States to examine the factors influencing faculty adoption of generative AI (GenAI) tools in academic settings. Using a quantitative approach grounded in Structural Equation Modeling (SEM), their study drew on both Social Cognitive Theory (SCT) and the Technology Acceptance Model (TAM) to explore how social context and personal perceptions shape technology adoption.

SCT provided a lens to examine the influence of trust, social reinforcement, and self-efficacy, while TAM focused on perceived usefulness (PU) and perceived ease of use (PEOU). The findings showed that trust in

GenAI—viewing it as appropriate, ethical, and dependable—and social reinforcement from peers and institutional culture were strong predictors of adoption. In contrast, self-efficacy had little impact. TAM constructs also played a significant role, with perceived usefulness emerging as the most influential factor in shaping both attitudes and behavioral intention to adopt GenAI. While perceived ease of use mattered, its effect was smaller.

Overall, the study demonstrated that GenAI adoption is not just a matter of perceived value or usability, but also deeply influenced by the social and institutional environment in which faculty operate.

Unified Theory of Acceptance and Use of Technology

A more recent development in the study of technology adoption is the Unified Theory of Acceptance and Use of Technology (UTAUT), proposed by Venkatesh, Morris, Gordon Davis, and Fred Davis in 2003. Notably, Fred Davis was also the originator of the Technology Acceptance Model (TAM) and co-developer of the Motivational Model, making UTAUT both a continuation and consolidation of his earlier contributions to the field. The model was designed to address a common challenge in the literature: the fragmentation caused by numerous overlapping theories, each with slightly different constructs and assumptions.

To construct the unified model, the authors analyzed and empirically compared eight of the most influential frameworks in technology acceptance research: Innovation Diffusion Theory (Rogers, 1962), Social Cognitive Theory (Bandura, 1989), the Theory of Reasoned Action (Ajzen & Fishbein, 1980), the Technology Acceptance Model (Davis, 1985), the Theory of Planned Behavior (Ajzen, 1991), the Model of PC Utilization (Thompson et al., 1991), and the Motivational Model (Davis et al., 1992). Rather than simply combining all these models, the authors tested their predictive power in multiple organizational settings using three workplace technologies. Through this process, they identified the constructs that most consistently and effectively predicted user behavior.

The resulting framework includes four core constructs: performance expectancy, or the belief that using a system will improve job performance; effort expectancy, or the perceived ease of system use; social influence, or the perception that others believe one should use the system; and facilitating conditions, referring to the extent to which infrastructure and support are available to assist with system use. In addition, the model introduced four key moderating variables—age, gender, experience, and voluntariness of use—to explain variation in how these core constructs influence behavioral intention and actual usage across different user groups.

What makes UTAUT especially influential is not just its theoretical scope, but its empirical strength. In a series of longitudinal field studies, the model explained up to 77 percent of the variance in behavioral intention and 52 percent of the variance in actual system use (Venkatesh et al., 2003)—a significant increase over earlier models like TAM, which typically explained around 40 percent. These findings helped confirm UTAUT's value in both academic and applied research on technology use.

Example of a Study Using UTAUT

In their 2021 study, Andrews et al. (2021) used the Unified Theory of Acceptance and Use of Technology (UTAUT) to explore how academic and public librarians in North America perceive and intend to adopt AI and related technologies. The study was motivated by the growing presence of AI in library contexts and the need to understand which factors most influence librarians' willingness to adopt these emerging tools.

The authors adopted UTAUT as a guiding framework, drawing on its core constructs—performance expectancy, effort expectancy, social influence, and facilitating conditions—to develop their survey instrument. Notably, they also incorporated attitude toward use as a fifth construct, a variable originally included but later removed in the original UTAUT model by Venkatesh et al. (2003). In this context, the authors argued that attitudes may be particularly relevant given ongoing debates and uncertainty around AI's role in professional practice.

To test their model, the authors distributed a survey to public and academic librarians across various professional listservs in the U.S. and Canada, yielding 236 valid responses. They used structural equation modeling (SEM) to analyze the relationships among UTAUT constructs and determine which ones significantly predicted the intention to adopt AI technologies. Their findings indicated that performance expectancy and attitude toward use significantly influenced librarians' intention to adopt AI and related technologies. In contrast, effort expectancy and social influence did not show significant effects. The model explained 72 percent of the variance in intention to adopt, suggesting a strong fit. Additionally, moderating variables such as gender, library type (public vs. academic), and current AI usage were tested through multigroup SEM analysis but did not significantly alter the main relationships.

The Lack of Qualitative Research in the Field

As we have reviewed the major theories used to study AI acceptance, a notable absence emerges: none are grounded in constructivist, participatory, or emancipatory research paradigms. These approaches—which emphasize meaning-making, lived experience, and the co-construction of knowledge—are common in fields like education and critical social science but are almost entirely missing from the AI acceptance literature. The literature remains overwhelmingly quantitative in nature. In a 2023 systematic review, Kelly, Kaye, and Oviedo-Trespalacios found that 50 of the 60 studies on AI acceptance used survey-based methods, with only seven relying on qualitative interviews and two adopting mixed methods. This heavy reliance on structured surveys limits the field's ability to capture the nuances of lived experience, social dynamics, and power relations that shape technology use.

This lack of qualitative and participatory inquiry is a major issue. If we want to understand not only whether users accept AI but how they make sense of it, resist it, or reimagine its role in their lives and institutions, we need more research that invites dialogue, centers user voice, and treats theory not only as a tool for prediction but also as a lens for reflection and change.

Directions for Future Research

The first half of this chapter reviewed foundational models of technology adoption, emphasizing individual attitudes and behavioral intentions. However, to fully understand the complexities of AI integration in education, we must also attend to what these models leave out. The following section shifts the focus from prediction to critique, examining how complexity, structural barriers, cultural narratives, and unequal access complicate the story of adoption. Rather than assuming that adoption is always desirable or feasible, this section explores when—and for whom—adoption is contested, constrained, or reimagined.

When Adoption Is Not Neutral: Power, Hype, and Resistance

While models like the Technology Acceptance Model (TAM) frame resistance primarily as a failure of individual attitudes—emphasizing perceived usefulness or ease of use—Selwyn (2013) offers a more structurally aware critique. In a time before the advent of publically available generative AI, he argues that educational technology is not merely adopted or resisted in a vacuum of rational choice, but is discursively constructed within systems of power, profit, and institutional control. From this perspective, the concept of *disruption* is far from neutral; it functions as a rhetorical device used to normalize neoliberal reforms under the appealing guise of innovation and modernization. The language surrounding technological adoption, in Selwyn's view, serves to align education with market logics and entrepreneurial individualism while obscuring alternative values such as equity, democratic participation, or collective agency. In short, Selwyn challenges the assumption that technology adoption is a universal or inherently desirable goal, urging educators and researchers to interrogate *why* technologies are being promoted, *whose interests* they serve, and *what kinds of educational futures* they foreclose. Promotion of technology for technology's sake should not be a goal.

This critique of unexamined technology adoption highlights a critical need in AI research: to move beyond binary measures of acceptance and consider how people actually make sense of, negotiate, and reshape AI in real-world contexts. If adoption is not inherently good, then understanding how AI is integrated—or resisted—in practice becomes all the more important. This calls for approaches that do more than predict behavior; it requires methods that reveal meaning, power, and lived experience.

When Adoption Is Anxiety Provoking: Creative Displacement Anxiety

While Selwyn has raised important concerns about the mercantile drivers behind technology adoption, Caporusso (2023) brings much-needed attention to the psychological complexities associated specifically with generative AI. He argues that the unprecedented capacity of these systems to produce text, images, and other forms of creative content once considered uniquely human can give rise to a range of psychological challenges. These may include anxiety, impostor syndrome, loss of identity, depression, resentment, and feelings of alienation. In response to such emotional and cognitive strain, individuals may choose to disengage from AI entirely, avoiding tools they perceive as threatening their creative relevance.

When Adoption Is Not Feasible: Access Is Not Universal

Selwyn challenges the notion that technology adoption is inherently good, and Caporusso points out that technology can make humans anxious. But we may do well to take a further step back and realize that for much of the world, AI adoption is something done perhaps around them, but not something attainable for them personally. Discussions of AI adoption often center on its rapid growth, less attention is paid to the nearly 3 billion people worldwide who remain offline—highlighting the foundational issue of digital exclusion. According to the World Economic Forum (2023), only 35% of people in developing nations had internet access as of 2022, compared to over 80% in wealthier countries. Even within developed nations like the United States, access remains unequal: one in four Americans over 65 has never been online, and 14% of those with only a high school education report being offline. Rural residents are also less connected than their urban and suburban counterparts. The World Economic Forum further notes that in the European Union, 7.6% of people at risk of poverty cannot afford internet access. In Sub-Saharan Africa, only 29% of the population uses mobile internet, and 210 million people live in areas without any coverage at all. These disparities underscore that access to AI-powered tools and services presupposes basic digital infrastructure—reliable internet, a device, and digital literacy—which remains out of reach for many. If people lack access or are grappling with more immediate concerns such as food, housing, or healthcare, AI becomes irrelevant or even alienating. Arguably, technology adoption theories are skewed toward developed nations with stable infrastructure and access to the actual technologies under discussion.

When AI Adoption Is Complex: AI as a Wicked Problem

Even when access to technological infrastucture is stable, reasons for AI adoption or resistance can be complex and varied. Krause (2012) describes wicked problems as those that are difficult to define, lack clear solutions, and involve overlapping and often conflicting values among stakeholders.

Such problems resist technical fixes and instead require iterative, context-sensitive multi-faceted responses. AI adoption and education bear many of these characteristics. Chapters 1–3 highlight the emotional and cognitive load that many learners experience when approaching AI: confusion about what it is, uncertainty about where to begin, and a deep-seated fear that AI is a tool meant for others, not for them. When viewed through Krause's lens, AI adoption becomes not just a question of skills training or infrastructure, but a complex social challenge that must be addressed through culturally responsive, participatory, and empowering approaches. Addressing fear and building trust, as the earlier chapters argue, is not optional—it is the necessary starting point.

Reimagining AI Engagement: From Prediction to Participation

The research on AI acceptance is beginning to move beyond solely survey instruments and predictive models to include qualitative and participatory approaches that illuminate how people actually engage with AI in context—but participatory AI is still very much in the process of finding its voice (Delgado et al., 2024). Methodologically, approaches like interviews, focus groups, ethnography, and action research can surface the lived experiences, interpretations, and social dynamics that influence how AI is understood, adopted, or resisted.

Also, working directly with educators, students, or staff to co-develop research questions or pilot tools can reveal how institutional norms, prior experience, or concerns about relevance and control shape everyday interactions with AI. These approaches do not just generate richer data—they open up space for reflection, feedback, and adaptation. Yet, as Delgado et al. (2024) note, participatory AI remains largely consultative in practice, with most projects limiting stakeholder input to surface-level decisions like interface design. Very few efforts empower participants to shape deeper questions—such as how models function, what problems AI should solve, or whether AI should be used at all.

Rather than asking only "Will you use this tool?" we should also be asking "How might it be adapted to better support your goals?" Expanding the methodological range in this way would strengthen the field by grounding it more firmly in the realities of practice and the voices of those most affected.

Finally, it is important not only to study AI acceptance as a current state, but also to explore how best to teach and foster it. The chapters that follow begin to examine how students, faculty, and staff want to learn about AI, highlighting the kinds of resources and support they find most meaningful. The final chapter builds on this conversation, advocating for more accessible AI education and opening the door to a broader discussion about how we can meet the growing demand for thoughtful, practical learning opportunities.

Try It Out: A Social Media Post for the AI-Resistant

Many faculty on university campuses express anxiety, skepticism, or outright resistance to AI in higher education. Rather than respond with a sales pitch or ignore the discomfort, you want to open a conversation—gently, thoughtfully, and publicly—on LinkedIn, a blog, or another professional platform.

In terms of effective science communication, it seems wise to bear in mind the history of AI that was outlined in Chap. 2. Hype has stalled AI development before and brought about so-called AI winters. Unbriddled hype may not be effective nor age well.

Your Task:

Draft a 150- to 300-word social media post or short blog entry that:
Acknowledges the real concerns behind AI resistance (e.g., ethics, deskilling, job security, pedagogy, or loss of scholarly identity).

Shares a constructive insight or personal reflection grounded in one or more of the theories discussed in this chapter (e.g., TPB, TAM, SCT, DIT, UTAUT, or a critical framework like Selwyn's).

Encourages *AI literacy* rather than uncritical adoption—focus on understanding, exploration, and responsible engagement, not evangelism.

Ends with a genuine, open-ended question or invitation for dialogue from colleagues.

***Nuance Required*:**

Your goal is not to convince everyone to adopt AI, but to model thoughtful engagement. This means showing how theory can inform respectful disagreement, curiosity, and shared inquiry. Avoid either/or framing—resistance and reflection can coexist.

Post-Write Reflection:

After writing, jot down a short reflection (2–3 sentences):
How did the theory or theories in this chapter shape your message, tone, or framing?

What assumptions about AI or academic identity were you trying to challenge or honor?

Questions for Reflection and Discussion

Which of the classic models discussed in this chapter (e.g., TAM, TPB, UTAUT) made the most sense to you—and which felt limited or outdated? Why?

This chapter argues that traditional adoption models often ignore factors like culture, identity, and power. Can you think of an example from your own experience or institution where these overlooked factors shaped how people responded to a new technology?

Reflect on a time when you adopted or resisted a new technology (AI or otherwise). What influenced your decision—was it ease of use, peer influence, personal values, or something else? How does your experience line up with the theories described in the chapter?

The chapter critiques the idea that resistance to AI is simply due to "lack of training." What other reasons might educators or students have for resisting AI, especially in academic settings?

If you were to design a strategy for introducing AI at your university, workplace, or community, how would you go beyond traditional adoption models? What additional factors would you need to consider?

References

Ajzen, I. (1991). The theory of planned behavior. *Organizational Behavior and Human Decision Processes, 50*(2), 179–211.

Ajzen, I. (2020). The theory of planned behavior: Frequently asked questions. *Human Behavior and Emerging Technologies, 2*(4), 314–324. https://doi.org/10.1002/hbe2.195

Ajzen, I., & Fishbein, M. (1980). *Understanding attitude and predicting social behavior*. Prentice-Hall.

Andrews, J. E., Ward, H., & Yoon, J. (2021). UTAUT as a model for understanding intention to adopt AI and related technologies among librarians. *The*

Journal of Academic Librarianship, 47(6), 102437. https://doi.org/10.1016/j.acalib.2021.102437

Bandura, A. (1989). Social cognitive theory. In R. Vasta (Ed.), *Annals of child development* (Vol. 6, pp. 1–60). JAI Press.

Bandura, A. (2001). Social cognitive theory: An agentic perspective. *Annual Review of Psychology, 52*, 1–26. https://doi.org/10.1146/annurev.psych.52.1.1

Caporusso, N. (2023). Generative artificial intelligence and the emergence of creative displacement anxiety. *Research Directs in Psychology and Behavior, 3*(1), 1–12. https://doi.org/10.53520/rdpb2023.10795

Chan, C. K. Y., & Colloton, T. (2024). *Generative AI in higher education: The ChatGPT effect*. Routledge. https://doi.org/10.4324/9781003459026

Cornelissen, J., Höllerer, M. A., & Seidl, D. (2021). What theory is and can be: Forms of theorizing in organizational scholarship. *Organization Theory, 2*(3), 1–18. https://doi.org/10.1177/26317877211020328

Davis, F. (1985). *A technology acceptance model for empirically testing new end-user information systems: Theory and results* [Doctoral dissertation, Massachusetts Institute of Technology].

Davis, F., & Granić, A. (2024). *The technology acceptance model: 30 years of TAM*. Springer. https://doi.org/10.1007/978-3-030-45274-2

Davis, F. D., Bagozzi, R. P., & Warshaw, P. R. (1992). Extrinsic and intrinsic motivation to use computers in the workplace 1. *Journal of Applied Social Psychology, 22*(14), 1111–1132.

Delgado, F., Yang, S., Madaio, M., & Yang, Q. (2024). The participatory turn in AI design: Theoretical foundations and the current state of practice. *Proceedings of the 2023 ACM Conference on Fairness, Accountability, and Transparency (FAccT)*. https://doi.org/10.1145/3617694.3623261

Dusseau, M. (2024, November 12). Burn it down: A license for AI resistance. *Inside Higher Ed.*. https://www.insidehighered.com/opinion/views/2024/11/12/burn-it-down-license-ai-resistance-opinion

Gustafsson, K., & Hagström, L. (2018). What is the point? Teaching graduate students how to construct political science research puzzles. *European Political Science, 17*(4), 634–648. https://doi.org/10.1057/s41304-017-0130-y

Karan, B., & Chakma, C. (2025). Influence of higher education students' perceived behaviour on their artificial intelligence acceptance: An empirical investigation using Technology Acceptance Model. *Journal of Applied Research in Higher Education*. https://doi.org/10.1108/JARHE-11-2023-0535

Kelly, S., Kaye, S. A., & Oviedo-Trespalacios, O. (2023). What factors contribute to the acceptance of artificial intelligence? A systematic review. *Telematics and Informatics, 77*, 101925. https://doi.org/10.1016/j.tele.2022.101925

Krause, K. L. (2012). Addressing the wicked problem of quality in higher education: Theoretical approaches and implications. *Higher Education Research & Development, 31*(3), 285–297.

Lai, C. Y., Cheung, K. Y., & Chan, C. S. (2023). Exploring the role of intrinsic motivation in ChatGPT adoption to support active learning: An extension of the technology acceptance model. *Computers and Education: Artificial Intelligence, 5*, 100178. https://doi.org/10.1016/j.caeai.2023.100178

Milička, J. (2024). Theoretical and methodological framework for studying texts produced by large language models. *arXiv preprint*. http://arxiv.org/abs/2408.16740

Powell, A. L. (2013). Computer anxiety: Comparison of research from the 1990s and 2000s. *Computers in Human Behavior, 29*(6), 2337–2381. https://doi.org/10.1016/j.chb.2013.05.012

Rogers, E. M. (1962). *Diffusion of innovations*. Free Press of Glencoe.

Selwyn, N. (2013). Discourses of digital "disruption" in education: A critical analysis. In *Fifth International Roundtable on Discourse Analysis, City University Hong Kong, May 23–25, 2013* (pp. 1–28).

Shata, A., & Hartley, K. (2025). Artificial intelligence and communication technologies in academia: Faculty perceptions and the adoption of generative AI. *International Journal of Educational Technology in Higher Education, 22*(1), Article 11. https://doi.org/10.1186/s41239-025-00511-7

Thompson, R. L., Higgins, C. A., & Howell, J. M. (1991). Personal computing: Toward a conceptual model of utilization. *MIS Quarterly, 15*(1), 125–142. https://doi.org/10.2307/249443

Venkatesh, V., Morris, M. G., Davis, G. B., & Davis, F. D. (2003). User Acceptance of Information Technology: Toward a Unified View. *MIS Quarterly*, 27(3), 425–478. https://doi.org/10.2307/30036540

Wang, C., Wang, H., Li, Y., Dai, J., Gu, X., & Yu, T. (2024). Factors influencing university students' behavioral intention to use generative artificial intelligence: Integrating the theory of planned behavior and AI literacy. *International Journal of Human-Computer Interaction, 40*(5), 1–23. https://doi.org/10.1080/10447318.2024.2383033

Watermeyer, R., Lanclos, D., Phipps, L., Shapiro, H., Guizzo, D., & Knight, C. (2024). Academics' weak(ening) resistance to generative AI: The cause and cost of prestige? *Postdigital Science and Education*. https://doi.org/10.1007/s42438-024-00524-x

World Economic Forum. (2023, September 5). *These are the places in the world where internet access is still an issue—And why*. https://www.weforum.org/stories/2023/09/broadband-no-luxury-basic-necessity/

CHAPTER 5

Listening First: A University Campus-Based Participatory Survey of Generative AI Literacy Needs

Rebecca J. Allen and Jermaine Poynter

Introduction

Most experts agree that generative AI is here to stay. In higher education, instructor acceptance is rising but still lags behind student adoption. According to a national *Cengage* survey (2025) of over 950 instructors, use of generative AI among faculty nearly doubled in a single year—from 24% in 2023 to 45% in 2024. Positive sentiment also rose, with 49% of instructors expressing a favorable view in 2024 compared to 28% the previous year. Yet even as acceptance grows, challenges remain: 82% of instructors continue to express concerns about academic integrity, and nearly 90% believe generative AI poses moderate to severe risks for education.

R. J. Allen (✉) • J. Poynter
Center for IT Engagement (cITe), Mount St. Joseph University, Cincinnati, OH, USA
e-mail: rebecca.allen@msj.edu; Jermaine.Poynter@msj.edu

R. J. Allen, A. Nakonechnyi (eds.), *Using and Understanding AI in Higher Education*,
https://doi.org/10.1007/978-3-031-99754-9_5

Meanwhile, students have embraced AI tools at a much faster pace—often informally and without structured support. A 2024 *Student Voice* survey cited in the same *Cengage* report found that 31% of students were unsure how or when to use AI appropriately for coursework, highlighting a gap between access and literacy. As faculty scramble to respond, many turn to unreliable AI detection tools and must navigate ambiguous institutional policies, ultimately stigmatizing AI use and pushing it underground, out of sight but certainly not out of mind (Ardito, 2024). Faculty members often find themselves caught in a cat-and-mouse game that may be unwinnable. In workshops I lead, one of the most frequent questions is, "How do I catch students who cheat by generating text with AI?" Yet detecting AI-generated text fairly and reliably remains an unresolved challenge (Wu et al., 2023). Unlike traditional plagiarism which involves a direct copy from a particular source, generative AI produces original output with each prompt, making it difficult to trace or match definitively.

These early findings raise an urgent question: **How can higher education institutions move beyond reactive measures and instead foster responsible, equitable, and critical conversations about engagement with generative AI?** To address this question, this paper first examines the limitations of traditional technology acceptance models for explaining AI engagement in education. It then presents results from a campus-wide survey and interview study on faculty, staff, and student perceptions of generative AI. Finally, it describes the design and initial outcomes of a student-led initiative, the AI Café, which aims to build grassroots AI literacy through participatory, culturally relevant approaches. By integrating theory, empirical research, and practical intervention, this study seeks to illuminate how institutions can support thoughtful AI adoption that strengthens rather than undermines educational and ethical commitments.

Theory

In the previous chapter, the book outlined the theoretical frameworks that have historically shaped technology acceptance research, including Diffusion of Innovations (DIT), Theory of Reasoned Action (TRA), Theory of Planned Behavior (TPB), Technology Acceptance Model (TAM), Model of Personal Computing Utilization (PCU), Motivational Model (MM), Social Cognitive Theory (SCT), and Unified Theory of Acceptance and Use of Technology (UTAUT) (see Venkatesh et al., 2003). While each offers a valuable lens for understanding AI acceptance, these models share underlying assumptions that limit their collective scopes. Rooted primarily in cognitive psychology and rational behavior theory, they have brought methodological rigor to the study of technology use—but at a cost.

Although some frameworks, such as SCT and PCU, acknowledge the role of context and agency, they still largely portray human actors as predictable agents responding to perceived utility or social pressures, rather than as complex individuals embedded in institutional, cultural, and epistemic systems. What remains largely absent from the literature is a deeper commitment to understanding the *why* of AI resistance—not merely as a matter of attitudes or perceived control, but as a reflection of meaning, power, and identity. Researchers would also be well advised to hold space for the idea that AI adoption for adoption's sake is not a goal—there are pros and cons to any technology as we discussed practically and theoretically in the previous Chaps. 3 and 4. While not all faculty may choose to adopt AI for all things, what we do want to promote is literacy and informed choices.

Moreover, the dominance of survey-only based methods that often go along with the prevalining frameworks has constrained the field's capacity to engage deeper questions: What does AI mean to different stakeholders? How does it intersect with concerns around labor, surveillance, equity, and professionalism? And, most importantly: Why does any of this matter, and what can we do about it? Surveys may be a good start, but following up with qualitative research and action-based interventions is much needed.

Methods

We chose to employ Rothman's (1997) action evalation because it offers a structured, participatory approach to navigating the deep anxieties surfacing around AI on campus. Action evaluation has its roots in solving issues in rapidly evolving conflicts around the globe. Generative AI is certainly rapidly evolving, and while it generally does not impose a physical threat, many faculty, students, and staff perceive AI as a threat to their roles, identities, and professional futures, creating tensions that are not merely technical; these tensions can be deeply personal. In this context, action evaluation provides a way to surface those fears and values early, using open-ended surveys followed by interviews to elicit what matters most to participants. These insights are then translated into shared, evolving goals that guide the project over time (Ross, 2001; Rothman, 1997).

Development of the Survey and Interview Questions

The survey used in this study was developed by the authors, drawing on both the empirical literature highlighted earlier and the theoretical frameworks presented in earlier chapters of this book. To ensure clarity and relevance, we pilot-tested the instrument with a group of ten students. These pilot responses were excluded from the final dataset, but the feedback was instrumental in refining the survey. Based on the pilot, we made minor language adjustments to improve clarity and ensure the questions were accessible to participants from a range of academic backgrounds. The final survey included both quantitative and open-ended items.

The interview questions were developed based on emergent trends identified in the survey data. We sought to deepen our understanding of these trends through follow-up conversations. Importantly, the interviews were conducted by a trained undergraduate researcher and coauthor of this study. His peer status may have helped reduce the power dynamics often present in researcher-participant relationships, making interviewees—particularly students—feel more at ease when sharing their experiences and concerns about generative AI. All interviews were recorded and transcribed for analysis, expect for those in which interviewees expressed a preference for notetaking.

Setting and Participants

The study took place at a small, private Catholic institution located in the Midwest region of the United States. Serving approximately 2000 undergraduate and graduate students, the university offers a range of professional and liberal arts programs within a values-based framework rooted in its religious and regional heritage.

In the U.S. context, these institutions, despite the relatively small size of each one, are highly significant in the aggregate. Primarily undergraduate institutions (PUIs)—often concompassing private non-profit colleges and community colleges—collectively educate a substantial portion of the U.S. college population. As of Fall 2023, 4.1 million students were enrolled at private non-profit institutions and 5.3 million at public two-year colleges, compared to 7.7 million students at typically larger public four-year institutions (National Student Clearinghouse, 2024). Despite often being overlooked in national research agendas, clearly many students choose these typically smaller schools. Moreover, smaller institutions produce more future STEM PhDs relative to their student body size than R1 institutions, making them powerful yet under-recognized contributors to the STEM pipeline (Gordon et al., 2022; The Council of Independent Colleges, 2014). Their close-knit, student-centered environments are particularly well-suited to fostering inclusive, community-engaged pathways into fields like human-computer interaction and AI.

Findings

Participants

The survey included a total of 151 respondents affiliated with the university. The sample consisted of undergraduate students (n = 108; 71.5%), followed by faculty members (n = 28; 18.5%) and staff (n = 15; 9.9%)—faculty and staff were grouped together in the analysis. As the university is a liberal arts institution offering degrees in a wide variety of disciplines, the participants identified themselves as being in a wide variety of fields (see Fig. 5.1).

Eight participants were subsequently interviewed to give more explanation to the findings and also aid in directions for future AI supports.

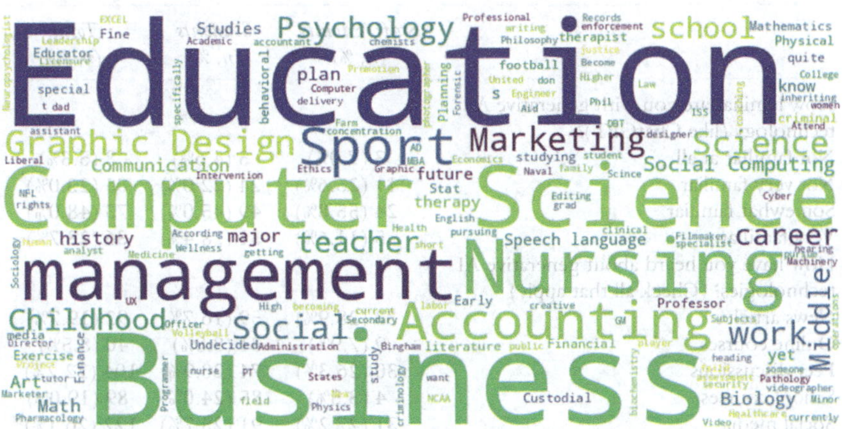

Fig. 5.1 The disciplines of the participants varied widely; frequency is represented by size of words in the word cloud

Familiarity with Generative AI

We first wanted to get a sense of the campus' familiarity with generative AI (see Table 5.1).

Table 5.1 presents data on participants' self-reported familiarity with generative AI technologies, such as ChatGPT, as well as the ways they first encountered these tools. Across both students and faculty/staff, nearly half of respondents (48.0%) indicated that they were "somewhat familiar" with generative AI, and approximately one in four (23.7%) reported being "very familiar." However, familiarity levels differed significantly by role. While a majority of both groups selected "somewhat familiar," students were much more likely than faculty/staff to rate themselves as "very familiar" (28.4% of students vs. 11.6% of faculty/staff; $p = .047$), highlighting a generational or professional gap in AI engagement.

Qualitative data from the survey offer insight into how participants interpret and describe their familiarity. One faculty member reflected on their cautious but open-minded stance: "Personally, I want to know how to caution students from using AI instead of their own minds, but I think that AI could prove useful as a grammar assistant or to help students settle on the best word choices or to articulate difficult ideas." This ambivalence was echoed in the interviews, where one staff participant said simply, "Not

Table 5.1 Staff, faculty and student familiarity with generative AI

	Staff/Faculty (n, %)	*Students (n, %)*	*Total (n, %)*
How familiar are you with generative AI technology (like ChatGPT)?			
Not familiar at all	3 (7.0%)	5 (4.6%)	8 (5.3%)
Not very familiar	11 (25.6%)	24 (22.0%)	35 (23.0%)
Somewhat familiar	24 (55.8%)	49 (45.0%)	73 (48.0%)
Very familiar	5 (11.6%)	31 (28.4%)	36 (23.7%)
How have you heard about generative AI technologies? (Check all that apply)			
News articles	33 (28.9%)	59 (16.7%)	92 (19.7%)
Online courses	9 (7.9%)	31 (8.8%)	40 (8.5%)
Peer discussions	30 (26.3%)	74 (20.9%)	104 (22.2%)
School courses	4 (3.5%)	85 (24.0%)	89 (19.0%)
Social media	31 (27.2%)	91 (25.7%)	122 (26.1%)
Nowhere	2 (1.8%)	1 (0.3%)	3 (0.6%)
Other	5 (4.4%)	13 (3.7%)	18 (3.8%)

at all," when asked about their familiarity with AI on campus, while another stated, "I have a son that's a tech guy. I know what it is, but I don't think the majority of people here know what it is." In contrast, students described more regular and casual interactions with generative AI. One student wrote in the survey that they use ChatGPT to "help with creative writing … it can give you prompts to practice your writing or help you get some ideas to finish plot points." Another said, "I use it here where I have it summarize something for me so I can send it … it's more just kind of cleaning up things and streamlining stuff." These responses suggest that students are more likely to experiment with AI across a variety of academic and everyday tasks, even if they do not identify as experts.

Information Sources About Generative AI

In terms of how participants first heard about generative AI, informal channels dominated. The most common sources were social media (26.1%), peer discussions (22.2%), and news articles (19.7%). These findings reinforce the role of peer networks and media in shaping perceptions and awareness of AI technologies (Table 5.2).

Perceived Benefits of Generative AI

Table 5.3 summarizes participants' perceptions of where generative AI could be most beneficial, including enhancing creativity and art, accelerating scientific research, and improving productivity in work or studies.

Across all domains, participants rated improving work or studies (productivity) as the most promising application. Over half of respondents (52%) rated this benefit as either "very" or "extremely" beneficial. One staff member explained how they already use AI to save time: "I used ChatGPT just to clean up emails or find cohesive times of things … it's more just kind of cleaning up things and streamlining stuff where you're not overthinking it" (faculty/staff interview). Another noted, "If AI can help me streamline things and open up an hour or two a week for other stuff, that would be ideal" (faculty interview).In the open-ended survey data, several students also emphasized productivity, with one sharing: "I think it would help my field of study or future career [by] making tasks much faster and easier."

The second-highest rated area was accelerating scientific research, with 45.4% of participants rating this use as "very" or "extremely" beneficial.

Table 5.2 How staff, faculty, and students perceive potential generative AI benefits on tasks

	Staff/Faculty (n, %)	*Students (n, %)*	*Total (n, %)*
How do you feel about these potential benefits of generative AI? [Enhancing creativity and art			
1. Not very beneficial	7 (16.7%)	22 (20.0%)	29 (19.1%)
2. Slightly beneficial	10 (23.8%)	15 (13.6%)	25 (16.4%)
3. Somewhat beneficial	15 (35.7%)	44 (40.0%)	59 (38.8%)
4. Very beneficial	7 (16.7%)	19 (17.3%)	26 (17.1%)
5. Extremely beneficial	3 (7.1%)	10 (9.1%)	13 (8.6%)
How do you feel about these potential benefits of generative AI? [Accelerating scientific research]			
1. Not very beneficial	1 (2.4%)	13 (11.8%)	14 (9.2%)
2. Slightly beneficial	6 (14.3%)	15 (13.6%)	21 (13.8%)
3. Somewhat beneficial	15 (35.7%)	33 (30.0%)	48 (31.6%)
4. Very beneficial	13 (31.0%)	27 (24.5%)	40 (26.3%)
5. Extremely beneficial	7 (16.7%)	22 (20.0%)	29 (19.1%)
How do you feel about these potential benefits of generative AI? [Improving work or studies]			
1. Not very beneficial	1 (2.4%)	11 (10.0%)	12 (7.9%)
2. Slightly beneficial	2 (4.8%)	16 (14.5%)	18 (11.8%)
3. Somewhat beneficial	16 (38.1%)	27 (24.5%)	43 (28.3%)
4. Very beneficial	12 (28.6%)	31 (28.2%)	43 (28.3%)
5. Extremely beneficial	11 (26.2%)	25 (22.7%)	36 (23.7%)

Several faculty respondents highlighted the value of AI in analyzing large datasets or generating hypotheses, though they also noted caveats. One said, "Perhaps hypothesis generation or data modeling could eventually be helpful in the sciences? However, I am extremely skeptical of AI's effectiveness, rigor, and reproducibility." Another staff member reflected on their interest in learning how AI could "influence what we do in a positive way to be a better return on investment for the university."

AI's use for enhancing creativity and art received more mixed responses. While 38.8% of participants rated it as "somewhat beneficial," only 25.7% said it was "very" or "extremely" beneficial. Concerns were particularly pronounced among students in creative fields. One student survey respondent explained, "I am also in the art community and dislike the future that

Table 5.3 Perceived benefits of generative AI

	Staff/Faculty (n, %)	*Students (n, %)*	*Total (n, %)*
How do you feel about these potential benefits of generative AI? [Enhancing creativity and art			
1. Not very beneficial	7 (16.7%)	22 (20.0%)	29 (19.1%)
2. Slightly beneficial	10 (23.8%)	15 (13.6%)	25 (16.4%)
3. Somewhat beneficial	15 (35.7%)	44 (40.0%)	59 (38.8%)
4. Very beneficial	7 (16.7%)	19 (17.3%)	26 (17.1%)
5. Extremely beneficial	3 (7.1%)	10 (9.1%)	13 (8.6%)
How do you feel about these potential benefits of generative AI? [Accelerating scientific research]			
1. Not very beneficial	1 (2.4%)	13 (11.8%)	14 (9.2%)
2. Slightly beneficial	6 (14.3%)	15 (13.6%)	21 (13.8%)
3. Somewhat beneficial	15 (35.7%)	33 (30.0%)	48 (31.6%)
4. Very beneficial	13 (31.0%)	27 (24.5%)	40 (26.3%)
5. Extremely beneficial	7 (16.7%)	22 (20.0%)	29 (19.1%)
How do you feel about these potential benefits of generative AI? [Improving work or studies]			
1. Not very beneficial	1 (2.4%)	11 (10.0%)	12 (7.9%)
2. Slightly beneficial	2 (4.8%)	16 (14.5%)	18 (11.8%)
3. Somewhat beneficial	16 (38.1%)	27 (24.5%)	43 (28.3%)
4. Very beneficial	12 (28.6%)	31 (28.2%)	43 (28.3%)
5. Extremely beneficial	11 (26.2%)	25 (22.7%)	36 (23.7%)

[AI] might be used instead of human planning and design." Another worried that generative tools like Midjourney are "trained on thousands of art pieces, and in many cases no consent of the original artist was given." Despite these concerns, some participants were excited about creative applications. One student wrote, "I want to use AI to generate text for characters in a video game and create life-like interactions."

Fears of Generative AI

Table 5.4 presents participants' biggest fears about generative AI across five areas: job displacement, misinformation, loss of privacy, bias and discrimination in algorithms, and student cheating.

Table 5.4 Fears of generative AI among staff, faculty, and students

	Staff/Faculty (n, %)	*Students (n, %)*	*Total (n, %)*
What are your biggest fears concerning generative AI? [Job displacement]			
1. Not at all fearful	11 (26.2%)	6 (5.5%)	17 (11.3%)
2. Slightly fearful	10 (23.8%)	24 (22.0%)	34 (22.5%)
3. Somewhat fearful	8 (19.0%)	29 (26.6%)	37 (24.5%)
4. Very fearful	6 (14.3%)	28 (25.7%)	34 (22.5%)
5. Extremely fearful	7 (16.7%)	22 (20.2%)	29 (19.2%)
What are your biggest fears concerning generative AI? [Misinformation and fake content]			
1. Not at all fearful	2 (4.8%)	3 (2.7%)	5 (3.3%)
2. Slightly fearful	0 (0.0%)	2 (1.8%)	2 (1.3%)
3. Somewhat fearful	9 (21.4%)	22 (20.0%)	31 (20.4%)
4. Very fearful	6 (14.3%)	34 (30.9%)	40 (26.3%)
5. Extremely fearful	25 (59.5%)	49 (44.5%)	74 (48.7%)
What are your biggest fears concerning generative AI? [Loss of privacy]			
1. Not at all fearful	2 (4.8%)	9 (8.3%)	11 (7.3%)
2. Slightly fearful	4 (9.5%)	16 (14.7%)	20 (13.2%)
3. Somewhat fearful	12 (28.6%)	21 (19.3%)	33 (21.9%)
4. Very fearful	10 (23.8%)	26 (23.9%)	36 (23.8%)
5. Extremely fearful	14 (33.3%)	37 (33.9%)	51 (33.8%)
What are your biggest fears concerning generative AI? [Bias and discrimination in AI algorithms]			
1. Not at all fearful	4 (9.5%)	5 (4.6%)	9 (6.0%)
2. Slightly fearful	1 (2.4%)	21 (19.3%)	22 (14.6%)
3. Somewhat fearful	8 (19.0%)	28 (25.7%)	36 (23.8%)
4. Very fearful	12 (28.6%)	26 (23.9%)	38 (25.2%)
5. Extremely fearful	17 (40.5%)	29 (26.6%)	46 (30.5%)
What are your biggest fears concerning generative AI? [Student cheating]			
1. Not at all fearful	3 (7.1%)	13 (12.0%)	16 (10.7%)
2. Slightly fearful	0 (0.0%)	22 (20.4%)	22 (14.7%)
3. Somewhat fearful	9 (21.4%)	28 (25.9%)	37 (24.7%)
4. Very fearful	6 (14.3%)	19 (17.6%)	25 (16.7%)
5. Extremely fearful	24 (57.1%)	26 (24.1%)	50 (33.3%)

The most significant concern was misinformation and fake content, with nearly half of participants (48.7%) rating themselves as "extremely fearful." One student warned that AI "can literally show someone doing something they have never done and make it look like real life," calling that potential "terrifying." Faculty shared similar concerns: one described students trusting AI "a little too much," adding, "you don't think that artificial intelligence could just guess, but it can."

Loss of privacy also stood out, with 33.8% of participants rating themselves as "extremely fearful," and 23.8% as "very fearful." That means more than half of respondents had high levels of concern. Several participants connected this anxiety to academic or healthcare environments. A faculty interviewee remarked, "I work with student grades … and I think about that. Then I take it back to the medical field too. How much can they grab and use?" Another stated more generally, "We're being used for profit … I know it's oversimplified, but it's real."

Fears of bias and discrimination in AI algorithms were also common. About 30.5% of participants were "extremely fearful," with significant differences between groups: 40.5% of faculty selected this response versus 26.6% of students ($\chi^2 = 9.63$, $p = .042$). These fears often centered on the fairness and reliability of algorithmic outputs, particularly in research and hiring contexts.

Concerns about student cheating were especially pronounced among faculty. While 33.3% of all participants said they were "extremely fearful," this figure was much higher for faculty (57.1%) than students (24.1%)—a statistically significant difference ($\chi^2 = 19.49$, $p = .001$). One instructor warned that students may simply "copy-paste a three-page paper" without understanding the material, adding, "They don't realize it doesn't sound like them." Another student echoed the tension around detection: "I hesitate to use it in schoolwork because I don't want to get docked points if [AI detectors] think I used it—even if I didn't."

Preferences About Regulation of Generative AI

Table 5.5 shows staff, faculty and students' opinions regarding whether AI should be regulated.

A clear majority of staff/faculty (72.1%) believed generative AI should be regulated, compared to only half of students (50.0%). This difference was statistically significant ($p = .012$), suggesting that faculty may feel a greater urgency or responsibility in addressing the societal impacts of

Table 5.5 Beliefs about necessity and feasibility of regulation of generative AI

	Staff/Faculty (n, %)	*Students (n, %)*	*Total (n, %)*
Do you believe generative AI should be regulated?			
Yes	31 (72.1%)	55 (50.0%)	86 (56.2%)
No	1 (2.3%)	13 (11.8%)	14 (9.2%)
Unsure	11 (25.6%)	42 (38.2%)	53 (34.6%)
How confident are you in the ability of policymakers to regulate generative AI effectively?			
Response Option	Staff/Faculty (n, %)	Student (n, %)	
1. Not at all confident	25 (61.0%)	23 (21.3%)	48 (32.2%)
2. Slightly confident	16 (39.0%)	52 (48.1%)	68 (45.6%)
3. Moderately confident	0 (0.0%)	29 (26.9%)	29 (19.5%)
4. Very confident	0 (0.0%)	4 (3.7%)	4 (2.7%)
5. Extremely confident	0 (0.0%)	0 (0.0%)	0 (0.0%)

AI. One faculty member expressed concern that "some generative AIs are using training data sets that violate copyright law," emphasizing that "malicious applications should be illegal—for example, fake videos to harm the public image of an individual." Another noted that art-generating tools like Midjourney raise concerns about intellectual property and consent, arguing that "there needs to be more regulation of how the models are trained."

Students also voiced support for certain regulatory boundaries, particularly around identity and misinformation. One student called for stricter limits on generative AI's ability to imitate people, writing that "the mimicry and recreation of real-life people needs to be restricted," including "voice cloning."

Despite these calls for oversight, respondents across both groups expressed notably low levels of confidence in policymakers' ability to regulate AI effectively. While skepticism was widespread, the distribution of responses differed significantly between roles ($\chi^2(3, N = 153) = 24.39$, $p < .001$). Faculty were overwhelmingly concentrated in the "not at all confident" category (61.0%), reflecting deep doubt about the readiness of institutions to respond. As one faculty interviewee put it, "I don't even really know what policies are in place—and I don't think they do either." Students, while somewhat more optimistic, were still cautious, with only

26.9% expressing moderate or higher confidence. Some expressed concern that regulation might come too late or be too reactive, while others worried that it might limit beneficial uses. One student reflected, "If we regulate it, it might make it harder for people with good intentions to utilize it—but it'll still be developed criminally. It'd be a net loss."

Willingness to Have Generative AI Training

Finally, as can be seen in Table 5.6, we explored participants' needs for training and willingness to attend possible trainings.

In terms of skills that are needed for AI usage, respondents selected a broad range of competencies, with research skills and information literacy (25.7%), ethics (25.1%), technical skills such as coding (23.4%), and creativity and innovation (23.2%) receiving comparable levels of endorsement. This even distribution suggests a shared understanding that AI preparation requires more than just technical proficiency—it also includes ethical awareness, creative thinking, and the ability to critically engage with information.This idea of a need for broad skills was echoed in participant comments. One faculty interviewee described the need for more accessible tools to build practical knowledge: "If someone was to train me

Table 5.6 AI training needs and willingness to attend

	Staff/Faculty (n, %)	*Students (n, %)*	*Total (n, %)*
What skills or knowledge do you think are necessary to prepare for a future with widespread use of generative AI? (Check all that apply)			
Creativity and innovation	28 (21.4%)	81 (23.9%)	109 (23.2%)
Ethics	38 (29.0%)	80 (23.6%)	118 (25.1%)
Research skills and information literacy	36 (27.5%)	85 (25.1%)	121 (25.7%)
Technical skills (like coding)	26 (19.8%)	84 (24.8%)	110 (23.4%)
Other	3 (2.3%)	9 (2.7%)	12 (2.6%)
Would you be interested in taking a course and/or workshop on generative AI?			
Response Option	Staff/Faculty (n, %)	Student (n, %)	Total (n, %)
Yes	24 (58.5%)	36 (33.0%)	60 (40.0%)
No	5 (12.2%)	29 (26.6%)	34 (22.7%)
Maybe	12 (29.3%)	44 (40.4%)	56 (37.3%)

and say, here's a handout or something on the website that tells you how to maximize AI in your area, I'd be very, very willing to look at that." Similarly, a student emphasized the importance of foundational skills across disciplines: "Technical skills, ethics, information literacy … it's not just about coding. You have to know how to ask the right questions."

Despite this agreement on necessary skills, interest in formal training differed significantly by role ($\chi^2(2, N = 150) = 8.58, p = .014$). While 58.5% of faculty said they would be interested in taking a course or workshop on generative AI, only 33.0% of students said the same. Students were more likely than faculty to select "maybe" (40.4%) or "no" (26.6%). Participants highlighted a preference for more interactive or applied formats. As one staff interviewee explained, "Don't give me a video. Show me one-on-one or in a small group. That's how I'd learn it best." This emphasis on hands-on, accessible formats was echoed by students, who said they would be more likely to engage if the learning environment was collaborative or embedded in real-life use cases.

Discussion

Our campus-wide survey and interviews revealed shared enthusiasm among students, staff, and faculty for using generative AI to boost productivity in work and study. While both groups see practical value in the technology, their approaches differ. Students tend to experiment more freely and prefer peer-led learning formats, while faculty take a more cautious, risk-aware stance and favor hands-on, guided workshops. Faculty also expressed greater concern about issues like academic integrity and called for clearer policies and regulation. These findings highlight the importance of tailoring AI support and education to the distinct needs and perspectives of each group. Table 5.7 gives an overall summary (Fig. 5.2).

Despite the gaps in needs, experiences and perception, our findings point to a promising willingness to engage: 87.8% of faculty and staff, and 73.4% of students, indicated they would be open to participating in AI-related training. This widespread openness provides a valuable starting point for institutional strategies focused not only on technology adoption, but also on responsible and informed AI literacy.

Table 5.7 Comparison of staff/faculty and student approaches to AI

Aspect	*Staff/Faculty*	*Students*
Familiarity with AI	Generally somewhat familiar; fewer very familiar (11.6%).	More very familiar (28.4%); regular informal use across tasks.
Primary Use Cases	Productivity (e.g., streamlining emails, administrative work).	Productivity (e.g., writing, brainstorming, summarizing)
Key Fears	High concern about academic integrity, misinformation, bias.	Concern about misinformation, privacy, and being unfairly penalized.
Fear of Student Cheating	Very high (57.1% extremely fearful).	Lower (24.1% extremely fearful); worry about false accusations.
Attitudes Toward Regulation	72.1% believe AI should be regulated; skeptical of policymakers' ability.	50% believe AI should be regulated; slightly more optimistic but cautious.
Confidence in Regulation	61% not confident at all in policymakers.	Only 21.3% not confident at all; more "slightly confident" responses.
Interest in AI Training	58.5% interested in taking a course or workshop.	33% interested; 40.4% "maybe."
Preferred Training Style	Small-group, hands-on workshops; personalized help.	Peer-led, applied, relatable examples (e.g., AI Café videos).
Overall Approach to AI	Risk management-focused; cautious integration.	Creative experimentation; faster adoption with less formal guidance.
Role in Campus AI Initiatives	Seek more guidance, policies, and ethical frameworks.	Serve as early adopters and peer leaders (e.g., AI Café project).

Responding to What We Found Out

One key priority of the project from the beginning was not just that the research be a theoretical exploration of attitudes. We wanted to act to meet needs. In response to identified needs on campus the computer science department launched the AI Café project—an undergraduate student-led initiative aimed at gathering additional data, deepening student learning, and providing accessible AI training and resources.

To start off with, I (Rebecca) shared the preliminary analysis of these survey resuts with students. However, rather than simply telling students what had already been done, I wanted to create space for students to also engage directly with the complexities of AI literacy on campus. Therefore, undergraduate researchers conducted eight additional interviews with campus stakeholders. They collaboratively analyzed transcripts (Best et al.,

Fig. 5.2 Staff/Faculty and students have both overlapping and distinct needs and opinions about generative AI. This image was generated with DALL-E (AI) and more information about how to generate images like this is foundi in the Try it Out Section

2022) and identified three recurring needs: general awareness and help getting started with AI, support for citation and formatting, and strategies for using AI to enhance academic productivity (e.g., organizing thoughts, meetings, or notes). This data, along with the data contained in this article, informated our next steps.

The undergraduate researchers spent a semester making AI videos and a webmiste centered on the needs of the campus community. Our goal was not just to create more tutorials but rather to create local, trustworthy examples. The project was never about producing content for content's sake—it was about reframing AI as approachable and culturally relevant. In the coming fall, we will be eager to see if having identifiable peers using AI helps to promote AI literacy and learning on our campus.

The videos provide a starting point for more varied learning opprotunities.We aim to continue working with undegraduates to provide AI café learning opprotunies for our campus community. Positioning this work within undergraduate research amplifies its developmental value. Studies show undergraduate research experiences promote critical thinking, identity formation, and stronger pathways to graduate school (Lopatto, 2010). By inviting students to act as co-creators and facilitators of AI literacy, we foster deeper engagement, leadership, and real-world skill development. Importantly, this also challenges traditional hierarchies in higher education. Rethinking who "teaches" and who "learns" is essential to building inclusive, participatory approaches to ethical technology adoption. Students are often more nimble and confident users of AI than faculty. As primary stakeholders in their education, students have valuable insights into how AI can support learning. Although it may seem counterintuitive to position undergraduates as guides to faculty, this mirrors real-world expectations for graduates entering a workforce increasingly shaped by rapid technological change. Framing students as local AI mentors not only meets institutional needs—it also builds their leadership skills and professional readiness.

One challenge we have seen with our undergraduate research model is the star-stop nature of undergraduate research. While participatory and action research frameworks often prioritize long-term engagement (Bradbury Huang, 2010), undergraduate research presents a challenge: student availability is limited and often inconsistent due to academic schedules (Lopatto, 2010). To address this, we designed research roles with clearly defined start and stop points, embedding leadership and reflection opportunities throughout the process. One unique aspect of our computer science program is that we offer a research methods coruse that is a first year requirement (see Chap. 6 for more information about this program)—the idea is that IT products needs to be centered in human needs. For The launch of the AI Café by happenstance, mostly fourth year students participated. Moving forward, there is a need to tap into the affordance of recruiting trained students earlier in their academic careers.

The AI Café's videos ar just a starting point. Looking ahead, we plan to expand our offerings in several directions. One is integrating trained near-peer tutors—computer science students who can provide real-time AI support. We also envision "stand-up AI trainings": brief, mobile sessions offered around campus to meet learners where they are. Finally, we aim to develop project-based opportunities for students to serve as "AI consultants," helping campus partners explore prompt engineering and tool selection as part of their coursework or capstone experiences.

Conclusion

Our findings revealed a notable gap between student adoption and faculty readiness, with students using AI tools frequently and informally, while faculty remained more cautious—often citing concerns about academic integrity, misinformation, and institutional ambiguity. At the same time, strong interest in training from both groups points to a shared willingness to learn.

Ultimately, the goal of this work is not to mandate how educators should use generative AI, but to foster conditions where thoughtful, informed conversations can take place. As our findings suggest, students are already engaging with these tools—often creatively, but also without sufficient guidance. Faculty concerns about ethics, pedagogy, and academic integrity are real and valid, yet disengagement risks ceding this moment of transformation to misunderstanding or mistrust.

AI literacy—understood as the ability to critically, ethically, and effectively use and evaluate AI tools—is not just a technical skill set; it is a prerequisite for productive dialogue. The more we teach our students about how these tools work, their limitations, and their risks, the more critically engaged and careful consumers of AI they can become.

When educators are empowered to explore these technologies on their own terms, they are better positioned to shape institutional values, support student learning, and guide the development of policies that reflect shared goals. Moving forward, it is not expertise alone that will matter, but a willingness to stay in the conversation.

Acknowledgment Open AI's Dall-E was used to create Fig. 5.2.

Ethics Approval The protocol for this study (Reference IRB Protocol S124-26: Course Undergraduate Research Experience (CURE): Fears and Hopes about AI on Campus) was approved by Mount St. Joseph University's Institutional Research Board (IRB) on January 3, 2024.

Try It Out: Visualize Your Group's AI Needs and Concerns (with DALL·E)

In this chapter, Fig. 5.2, for example, was created with DALL·E to portray the emotional and practical divide between faculty/staff and student reactions to generative AI. While the faculty group expresses concern about cheating and surveillance, the student group is navigating creativity, uncertainty, and judgment. This type of image can reveal tensions, needs, or blind spots that written descriptions alone might overlook.

When individuals or groups create images using generative AI, they are prompted to clarify their feelings, values, and fears in ways that are both expressive and accessible. An image can act as a shared artifact—something that invites conversation across roles and disciplines, even when people are hesitant to speak up. In participatory research and inclusive design, visual methods are powerful tools for democratizing expression, especially for those who may feel sidelined in technical conversations. Let us walk through how you can use generative AI to communicate with through visuals.

Step 1: Reflect on Your Group's Perspective

Think about a group you belong to or work with—students, faculty, staff, healthcare professionals, librarians, artists, etc.

Write down responses to these questions:
What is your group curious about or hoping for when it comes to AI?

What anxieties, barriers, or institutional challenges exist?

What's misunderstood about your group's relationship with AI?

What values or priorities guide your group's decisions about technology?

Summarize your group's AI "story" in a few phrases or key themes.

Step 2: Write a Prompt for DALL·E

Turn your group's story into a visual scene using a detailed, descriptive prompt.

Before submitting any prompt:
Remove personal names, identifiable data, or specific institutional references.

If drawing from real experiences or conversations, obtain consent from participants first.

Make sure to fictionalize or generaleizing sensitive elements to protect privacy.

DALL·E works best when prompts include:

Subjects: Who is present? (e.g., "a group of students," "two teachers and a librarian")

Setting: Where is the scene taking place? (e.g., "a faculty meeting," "a digital library," "a rural health clinic")

Mood: What emotions or tensions are visible? (e.g., "hesitant," "energized," "conflicted," "left behind")

Symbols or metaphors: What visual elements could represent AI concerns or hopes? (e.g., "a glowing lock," "a data cloud that some can't access," "a bridge made of circuit boards")

Style (optional): Do you want the image to look like a photograph, painting, sketch, comic panel, or abstract concept?

Sample prompts:

> "A group of community college students standing in a hallway labeled 'Future Careers,' looking at glowing screens that say 'AI tools.' Some look excited, some look overwhelmed. A teacher is watching from behind, unsure."

> "In a faculty meeting room, professors are gathered around a table made of old books and rulebooks, while a student presents a digital artwork titled 'AI creativity.' The room is split between shadow and light."

Take your time crafting a prompt that reflects your group's tone and reality. If you are not quite sure of what sort of imagery would reflect your themes, be sure to brainstorm with your tool by asking for ideas.

You can choose to further refine your images by continuing to prompt. Canva.com also offers a Magic Design ™ tool where you may edit aspects of your image, such as its text (i.e. change mispelled words).

Step 3: Reflect and (Optionally) Share

After you generate the image, reflect on:

What aspects of your group's experience does the image capture well?

What feels oversimplified or missing?

How might this image be used to start a meaningful conversation in your group or institution?

You may choose to share your image anonymously as part of a class, workshop, or discussion group.

Questions for Reflection and Discussion

What surprised you most about the similarities and differences between faculty and student perspectives on GenAI reported in the survey? What do you think accounts for these gaps or alignments?

This chapter emphasizes that students are already using GenAI tools, often without formal guidance. What are the risks and benefits of this informal, independent exploration of AI tools?

What role should student voices play in shaping GenAI-related campus policies and instructional practices? What mechanisms could be used to ensure meaningful student participation?

Based on the survey findings, what kinds of support structures (e.g., faculty development, student workshops, updated academic integrity policies) might be most urgent or helpful on your own campus?

The chapter points to uneven awareness and access to GenAI tools. What forms of AI literacy should be prioritized for students, faculty, and staff? Who should be responsible for that education?

How might these survey findings be used to initiate campus-wide dialogue and collaborative planning around GenAI? What follow-up actions would make the survey meaningful beyond reporting the results?

References

Ardito, C. G. (2024). Generative AI detection in higher education assessments. *New Directions for Teaching and Learning, 2024*(1), 1–18. https://doi.org/10.1002/tl.20624

Best, P., Badham, J., McConnell, T., & Hunter, R. F. (2022). Participatory theme elicitation: Open card sorting for user-led qualitative data analysis. *International Journal of Social Research Methodology, 25*(2), 213–231. https://doi.org/10.1080/13645579.2021.1876616

Bradbury Huang, H. (2010). What is good action research? Why the resurgent interest? *Action Research, 8*(1), 93–109. https://doi.org/10.1177/1476750310362435

Cengage. (2025). *At the trailhead: The state and future of AI in higher education.* https://cp.cengage.com/genai-research-higher-ed_wp_3454380

Gordon, J., Einaudi, P., & Kang, K. (2022). *Baccalaureate origins of U.S. research doctorate recipients* (NSF 22-321). National Science Foundation. https://ncses.nsf.gov/pubs/nsf22321

Lopatto, D. (2010). Undergraduate research as a high-impact student experience. *Peer Review, 12*(2), 27–30.

National Student Clearinghouse. (2024). *Current term enrollment estimates: Fall 2023.* https://nscresearchcenter.org/current-term-enrollment-estimates/

Ross, M. (2001). Action evaluation in the theory and practice of conflict resolution. *Peace and Conflict Studies, 8*(1), 1–16. https://doi.org/10.46743/1082-7307/2001.1011

Rothman, J. (1997). Action evaluation and conflict resolution training: Theory, method and case study. *International Negotiation, 2*(3), 451–470.

The Council of Independent Colleges. (2014). http://www.cic.edu/Research-and-Data/Research-Studies/Pages/STEM-Report.aspx

Venkatesh, V., Morris, M. G., Davis, G. B., & Davis, F. D. (2003). User acceptance of information technology: Toward a unified view. *MIS Quarterly, 27*(3), 425–478. https://www.jstor.org/stable/30036540

Wu, J., Yang, S., Zhan, R., Yuan, Y., Wong, D. F., & Chao, L. S. (2023). A survey on LLM-generated text detection: Necessity, methods, and future directions. *arXiv*. http://arxiv.org/abs/2310.14724

CHAPTER 6

Developing Researcher and Writer Identities in the Age of AI: A Case Study of a University Undergraduate Research Program

Brook K. Batch and Mark A. Sulzer

Introduction

The benefits of undergraduate research experiences are well documented in the literature, with numerous studies highlighting its role in fostering deeper learning, enhancing academic success, and increasing student engagement and retention—particularly for students from marginalized and underrepresented backgrounds (Bowman & Holmes, 2018; Council on Undergraduate Research, n.d.; Haeger et al., 2024; Sell et al., 2018). Research participation is thought to not only strengthen students' critical thinking, communication, and writing abilities but also support their identity formation as emerging scholars (Adedokun et al., 2013; Kuh, 2008; Lopatto, 2010; Seifan et al., 2022). Additionally, these experiences can

B. K. Batch (✉) • M. A. Sulzer
School of Education, University of Cincinnati, Cincinnati, OH, USA
e-mail: batchbk@mail.uc.edu; mark.sulzer@uc.edu

R. J. Allen, A. Nakonechnyi (eds.), *Using and Understanding AI in Higher Education*,
https://doi.org/10.1007/978-3-031-99754-9_6

encourage undergraduate students to pursue graduate studies and research-based careers (Council on Undergraduate Research, n.d.; Hanson et al., 2016; Kilgo & Pascarella, 2016).

Despite the well-documented benefits of undergraduate research, many students—particularly those new to the research process—may encounter challenges as they navigate research and academic writing. Research tasks like developing research questions, identifying and evaluating scholarly sources, designing data collection instruments, conducting research, and sharing findings through written reports and presentations can be overwhelming for beginning researchers, especially if they feel underprepared or uncertain about where to start (Cooper et al., 2023). The unfamiliarity of these tasks paired with the pressure of balancing research tasks with academic and personal responsibilities and fears of failure can create apprehension and lead to disengagement in the course (Ceyhan & Tillotson, 2020; Cooper et al., 2023).

Within the past couple of years, generative artificial intelligence (GenAI) has emerged as a potential tool for academic writers, educators, students, and researchers. Defined as "computational techniques that are capable of generating seemingly new, meaningful content such as text, images, or audio from training data" (Feuerriegel et al., 2024, p. 111), GenAI goes beyond traditional AI-based grammar and spell-checkers to create new content in response to a user's prompting. In their GenAI usage guide, the Cornell Task Force (2023) distinguishes between AI-based spellcheckers and grammar tools versus GenAI tools by focusing on the intent behind their use. Put simply, an AI tool is considered a GenAI tool when it "produces outputs that contain concepts and interpretations that the researcher or author did not supply" (Cornell University Task Force, 2023, p. 6).

Research suggests many young people are open to using GenAI tools, experimenting with and adopting different use cases of GenAI. A recent Common Sense report found that about 70% of surveyed 13- to 18-year-olds have used GenAI, primarily through AI-based search engine summaries, chatbots, and text generators (e.g. ChatGPT or My AI on SnapChat), with over half using these tools for school-related tasks like summarizing educational content, brainstorming, and drafting written content, among others (Madden et al., 2024). When it comes to higher education, GenAI tools may offer opportunities to address some of the challenges undergraduate students may face while navigating research and academic writing experiences. These tools can be useful for helping beginning researchers navigate unfamiliar academic disciplines and ways of communicating within those spaces by clarifying complex concepts that can be challenging to understand (Barros et al., 2023). GenAI tools can also help ward off symptoms of writer's block (Colby, 2025). Several studies found students may use GenAI tools like ChatGPT to brainstorm topic ideas, create outlines, and even start the drafting process (Barrett & Pack, 2023; Chan & Hu, 2023). GenAI tools can also give students almost human-like feedback on their writing, critiquing arguments and offering suggestions on how to bring their writing to the next level (Ruwe & Mayweg-Paus, 2023).

While GenAI can serve as a source of support for students, concerns about academic integrity, authorship, biases, ownership, overreliance, and privacy are well documented within the literature. The swift rise and growing prevalence of GenAI tools and what can and should be done to address potential ethical issues has sparked debates to "levels comparable to only a few other technological innovations such as genetics or nuclear power" (Prem, 2023, p. 699). A prevalent question raised with GenAI use is if and how these tools could be used ethically within research and writing. Some GenAI tools claim to produce writing that is undetectable by AI generation checkers, which is cause for concern for many educators (Fyfe, 2023). However, it is known that GenAI-produced text can be challenging for instructors to identify and GenAI text detection platforms are not always accurate (Plate et al., 2025; Wu et al., 2025). While many students have adopted GenAI tools, some have expressed concerns that GenAI might not be transparent about its information sources, resulting in plagiarism (Barrett & Pack, 2023; Chan & Hu, 2023; Gasaymeh et al., 2024). Additionally, students may be hesitant to use AI if they see it as a form of cheating (Golding et al., 2024). Some researchers have also questioned if students will develop an overreliance on AI systems like ChatGPT or Gemini, automatically accepting what these systems produce as truth without questioning accuracy, potentially reducing critical thinking and decision-making skills (Buçinca et al., 2021; Zhai et al., 2024). Overreliance on GenAI is a concern students themselves have also identified (Chan & Hu, 2023).

The unique tensions that exist between GenAI being a source of support and a potential challenge spotlights the importance of providing students with various strategies for using GenAI as a source of support rather than a replacement for their critical thinking. Rather than banning GenAI tools, some researchers argue that educators ought to integrate these tools into their classes and teach students how to use them ethically and efficiently (Barros et al., 2023; Johnson, 2023). Another push for integrating GenAI tools within higher education stems from the idea that students may need to develop AI literacy to be prepared to enter the workforce (Golding et al., 2024). A recent survey conducted by the Pew Research Center found around 16% of survey-takers have used AI tools as part of their work, with another 2% sharing that they AI tools to complete all or the majority of their work (Lin & Parker, 2024).

Despite the rapidly increasing presence of GenAI within educational environments, little research has explored their impact on the development of first-year undergraduate students' research and writing identities—that is, how students perceive and describe themselves as researchers and writers. While existing research explores AI's role within higher education writing spaces, this work often focuses on GenAI's technical capabilities or student and instructor perceptions rather than GenAI's potential influence on students' researcher and writer identities (Barrett & Pack, 2023; Barros et al., 2023; Cummings et al., 2024; Kim et al., 2024; A. Williams, 2024a). Moreover, undergraduate students may be among the individuals most impacted by policies determining how, if at all, GenAI can be used within higher education; however, student voices are often absent in conversations about GenAI integration in writing-intensive classrooms. Including student voices in conversations about GenAI may be beneficial because policy decisions about its use directly affect their learning and educational experiences. Additionally, these identified gaps stress the need for research that explores not only how GenAI may shape students' perceptions of themselves as researchers and writers but also how they can take a more active role in discussions about AI-driven teaching practices.

This chapter explores students' needs and perspectives on research and academic writing in the age of GenAI. The chapter also provides practical tools and strategies for integrating GenAI into undergraduate research writing instruction. To frame this discussion, the chapter considers the challenges and opportunities students face when using GenAI in academic writing contexts. Three key questions guide this work:

How can AI tools be used within undergraduate research and academic writing instruction?

What are undergraduate students' perceptions of using AI for academic research and writing purposes?

How does using AI influence undergraduate students' perceptions of themselves as writers?Drawing on data from exit tickets, Group Level Assessment (GLA) sessions, semi-structured interviews, and teaching reflections, we explore students' perceptions of GenAI and its role in their academic work as well as share reflections on various learning activities that invite students to engage with GenAI tools and AI-generated content in meaningful ways. In addition, we discuss various ways to promote students' participation and stakeholder buy-in, both of which are important in keeping university courses relevant and responsive to continuously evolving educational landscapes.

Literature Review

Teaching with GenAI: Uses in Writing and Research Instruction

Understandably, the rapid insurgence of GenAI tools has left many educators grappling with the pedagogical, ethical, and practical implications of navigating the inclusion or exclusion of GenAI in writing and research instruction. That said several studies serve as examples of how GenAI tools can be integrated into writing-intensive courses. Cummings et al. (2024) designed first-year writing composition coursework that prompted students to deliberately engage with GenAI tools. Throughout their class, students used these platforms to help create research questions, identify potential counterarguments to their claims, and revise their writing (Cummings et al., 2024). While most students were generally receptive of the GenAI tools and appreciated the scaffolding they provided, others noted reviewing GenAI-provided feedback felt time-consuming or shared they felt anxious that using GenAI would cause them to lose their unique writing voices or would lead to accidental plagiarism (Cummings et al., 2024). Similarly, Su et al. (2023) propose using ChatGPT in writing classrooms to offer guiding feedback to students, especially those with lower levels of writing self-efficacy, as they brainstorm topic ideas, develop and evaluate paper outlines, as well as edit and proofread their papers. For the final project in a multidisciplinary, writing-intensive seminar on critical data literacy, Fyfe (2023) introduced a final project that asked students to use GenAI to co-write their essays. When they submitted their final papers, students also shared a version of the paper that shared what content was

AI-generated along with a reflection on their experiences integrating AI-generated text into their work. Reflecting, some students shared that the process of co-writing with GenAI helped them overcome writer's block, while others shared they encountered hallucinations and misinformation, struggled with knowing how to properly cite AI-generated texts, and were surprised by how well the GenAI tool adopted their writing styles (Fyfe, 2023).

Much of the literature exploring the role GenAI can and should play in writing-centered courses stresses the importance of providing sufficient scaffolding to support learners. Some researchers advocate for modeling prompt engineering, that is, showing students how they can create effective prompts that guide GenAI tools toward a particular output (Colby, 2025; Mabrito, 2024). For example, in Mabrito's (2024) classroom, students learned the fundamentals of prompt engineering while creating chatbots. Within writing-intensive classrooms, many educators have embraced holding open dialogues with students in regard to the ethical challenges associated with GenAI tool use as well as the risks of hallucinations (Colby, 2025).

Student Attitudes and Perceptions of GenAI Tools

Research suggests students' attitudes and perceptions of GenAI tools are often complex. While many students seem open to using GenAI tools in their writing processes, many have concerns revolving around academic integrity (Cummings et al., 2024; Fyfe, 2023). Many of students' GenAI-related concerns seem to revolve around being afraid of committing unintentional ethical violations. In their work, Barrett and Pack (2023), Gasaymeh et al. (2024), Higgs and Stornaiuolo (2024), and many others all found that some students may worry that co-writing with GenAI tools could result in accidental plagiarism or that writing with GenAI in itself might be unethical. Despite concerns about plagiarism, many students are open to using GenAI tools to help with their writing. Many students report feeling comfortable using GenAI tools to help brainstorm, outline, and revise their academic writing (Barrett & Pack, 2023; Chan & Hu, 2023). GenAI tools' abilities to offer personalized writing feedback and be available 24/7 have not gone unnoticed by students (Chan & Hu, 2023). This research suggests it may be important for educators to consider that students may be harboring mixed feelings toward GenAI, weighing both the potential benefits and risks of GenAI use.

GenAI, Identity, and Writing Self-Efficacy

As GenAI tools continue to be folded into academic research and writing practices, the use of these tools raises questions about authorship, identity, and writing self-efficacy. When it comes to authorship, both researchers and students have expressed some hesitation to use GenAI tools because they are concerned that co-writing with GenAI could cause them to lose their voice (Cummings et al., 2024; Lingard, 2023). Additionally, the act of co-writing with GenAI can cause some students to feel like their role shifts from being a writer to that of a curator or an editor, which may feel more comfortable for some students than others (Fyfe, 2023). However, for some students, GenAI can help build confidence. If students are struggling with writer's block or adjusting to academic writing conventions, engaging with GenAI as a writing partner can offer students quick, detailed feedback, potentially reducing feelings of anxiety and giving students a starting point (Chan & Hu, 2023). The scaffolding that GenAI can offer students during the initial writing stages, such as brainstorming can support students who feel overwhelmed or unsure of where to start (Barrett & Pack, 2023). However, while GenAI tools can offer students additional, personalized support, instructor guidance and support is still needed (R. Williams, 2024b)

Conceptual Framework

This project draws on three major frameworks to explore how GenAI tools can be integrated into a writing-intensive research methods course sequence for undergraduate students as well as how students are using GenAI within their writing practices. These guiding frameworks include: the Substitution, Argumentation, Modification, and Redefinition (SAMR) model, the Unified Theory of Acceptance and Use of Technology, and self-efficacy.

SAMR Model

Within this work, we utilized key principles of the Substitution, Augmentation, Modification, Redefinition (SAMR) model, which offers guidance on integrating technology into educational practices using a ladder-like, four-level approach that goes from enhancing to transforming learning (Hamilton et al., 2016; Puentedura, 2006). At the substitution level, digital technologies take the place of analog tools, but the core purpose of the task remains the same (Puentedura, 2014). With augmentation, technology still replaces traditional tools, but improves the functionality of the task (Hamilton et al., 2016). Educators enter the modification level of SAMR when utilizing technology requires major redesigns to the activity (Puentedura, 2006). The fourth level, the redefinition level, is the point in which integrating technology enables educators and students to do a completely new task or activity (Hamilton et al., 2016; Puentedura, 2014). When using the SAMR model to look at GenAI integration, it is generally thought that these tools fit within the substitution and augmentation levels (Haroud & Saqri, 2025).

The Unified Theory of Acceptance and Use of Technology

This study also taps into the Unified Theory of Acceptance and Use of Technology (UTAUT) (Venkatesh et al., 2003) to understand how key constructs—such as how useful students feel the tool is, how easy the tools are to use, and perceived social pressures to use or not use a GenAI tool—impact their adoption of these tools.

Writing Self-Efficacy and AI

AI may also help increase students' writing self-efficacy. Self-efficacy theory holds a person's attitudes and actions are influenced by their belief in their ability to successfully perform a behavior needed to accomplish a specific task (Bandura, 1977). Students' levels of self-efficacy toward research and writing are influenced by their prior experiences with research and writing tasks, their experiences observing others doing these tasks, positive and/or negative feedback from others, and both affective and cognitive processing (Bandura, 1977). The degree to which someone does or does not believe in their ability to complete a specific task—such as identifying keywords for journal searchers, reading and understanding academic journal articles, and writing one's findings section—can impact how much effort they will put forth to push through challenges and complete the task at hand. GenAI tools could support students' research and writing self-efficacy by easing them into the research and writing process, especially for those with lower initial levels of self-efficacy. If GenAI tools can facilitate a more positive and guided experience, then these tools may gradually help increase students' self-efficacy toward writing and research tasks over time (Bandura, 1977). Recent research suggests that using GenAI tools has the potential to encourage undergraduate students' self-efficacy growth. For example, Pellas (2023) suggests GenAI tools used for digital storytelling and writing tools helped many students feel more capable when it came to writing.

Methods

This quality improvement project is rooted in action research (AR) approaches. AR focuses on bringing about positive, lasting change in a community through cycles of planning, acting, observing, and reflecting (Baum et al., 2006; Greenwood & Levin, 2007). This project drew on principles of practitioner action research (Anderson et al., 2007), where insiders—those who conduct research within their communities—strive to better understand their environments and bring about lasting change. Through this lens, we used practitioner action research to explore how students responded to the integration of GenAI tools, both within Brook's research methods courses and within their own research and writing practices.

Context

This project took place within a multidisciplinary computer science program at a small, private liberal arts college in the Midwestern United States. The program enrolls approximately 50 students per cohort and highlights the importance of user-centered design and development approaches. During their first year, students engage in a two-part writing-intensive research methods course sequence where they first conduct a literature review—collecting, evaluating, and synthesizing academic literature—and then carry out a small-scale research project of their own. Throughout the course sequence, students shared their work through academic research papers as well as poster and oral presentations.

With the release of OpenAI's ChatGPT in 2022 (OpenAI, 2022) and the rise in the number of GenAI tools, our program recognized the need to explore how we could incorporate and discuss GenAI tools within the context of our research methods courses. Rather than taking a restrictive or punitive approach to GenAI, we wanted to show students how GenAI could be used as a tool to enhance their efforts and have open conversations with students about GenAI use in the classroom (Barros et al.,

2023). We began incorporating AI into our research methods courses through various in-class activities, demonstrations, and discussions. Throughout this process, we aimed to create opportunities for students to share their needs, thoughts, and experiences, allowing their input to shape the directions we were taking in the research methods courses. Our experience suggested while there were some initial feelings of GenAI-related apprehension, many students were curious about these tools and were willing to share their learning needs and experiences using GenAI both within and outside of the classroom. By involving students in the decision-making process, we sought to ensure that their voices and perspectives play a central role in keeping our courses relevant to their needs while remaining adaptable to the rapidly evolving educational and AI landscape.

Participants, Data Collection, and Analysis

Participants in this project included students who were currently enrolled in or had previously taken the program's first-year research methods course sequence. This project draws on multiple sources of institutional data, including exit tickets, Group Level Assessment (GLA) sessions, semi-structured interviews, and teaching reflections to offer real-time feedback and deeper reflections on GenAI's role in research writing instruction and students' research writing practices.

Exit Tickets

Exit tickets (Danley et al., 2016) served as a way to gather real-time feedback on students' learning experiences, helping to identify immediate challenges and areas where they needed more support as well as give input on the types of activities they felt were beneficial. The program implemented exit tickets into our research methods course sequence because we did not want to rely solely on end-of-semester course evaluations to understand students' experiences. These exit tickets allowed us to gather anonymous feedback throughout the semester, helping us gauge students' understanding of course material, identify activities they found most engaging, and determine where additional support was needed (Danley et al., 2016). Beyond asking students to reflect on their learning, these exit tickets also provided insight into students' attitudes toward research, writing, and GenAI, allowing instructors to offer encouragement and targeted support when necessary.

We created these anonymous, weekly exit tickets using Google Forms and shared them through our school's learning management system. Completing the exit tickets was optional and did not tie to students' grades in any way. Despite responses being optional, many students consistently filled out the exit tickets. For this chapter, I (Brook) reviewed two years' worth of exit ticket responses from seven research methods training courses with the program, totaling 82 exit tickets. During this timeframe, 164 students were enrolled in the courses, with an average class size consisting of 23 students. Response rates varied across courses, ranging from approximately 48% to 83%, with an average response rate of about 67%. Of the 82 exit tickets collected from the course, 23 exit tickets (approximately 28% of the total dataset) included questions or responses related to GenAI—these 23 exit tickets were the focus of the analysis for this chapter. The exit tickets typically contained between four and eight questions, averaging around five questions per survey, and each survey took approximately five minutes or less to complete.

Exit Ticket Analysis. While course instructors analyzed the exit ticket throughout their courses, I (Brook) used a combination of descriptive statistics and thematic analysis to highlight key pain points and learning moments for this chapter.

Group Level Assessment

This project also drew on two Group level assessment (GLA) sessions (Vaughn & Lohmueller, 2014), which sought to help us better understand students' perceptions of using GenAI for research writing. The GLA sessions also provided a platform for students to engage in decision-making about GenAI's role in research writing, brainstorming action plans to better support their learning needs in the research-writing classroom. The GLA sessions involve seven steps: (1) climate setting, (2) generating, (3) appreciating, (4) reflecting, (5) understanding, (6) selecting, and (7) action (Vaughn & Lohmueller, 2014). During the climate setting stage, I (Brook) provided an overview of the session schedule, explaining why we chose a GLA session as a data collection and analysis approach and how the process works; I also led an icebreaker activity to help students get to know one another before getting started (Vaughn & DeJonckheere, 2019). In the generating stage, students walked around the room, responding to a series of open-ended, close-ended, and creative prompts on large sticky pads posted around the room with colored markers (Vaughn

& DeJonckheere, 2019). In the appreciating stage, students read the responses, sometimes adding checkmarks or stars next to statements that resonated with them (Vaughn & DeJonckheere, 2019). During the reflection stage, students walked around the room once more, reflecting on the responses (Vaughn & DeJonckheere, 2019). Next, in the understanding stage, small groups of students worked together to analyze the responses, identify emerging themes, and report their findings to the larger group (Vaughn & DeJonckheere, 2019). In the selecting stage, we reviewed each group's initial themes, consolidating them as needed, and students voted on the themes they found most important (Vaughn & DeJonckheere, 2019). After this, we met for the action stage, where students brainstormed actionable steps that we could implement to address the needs they identified. The major outcome of this effort was the creation of a custom GPT, developed with input from a group of students—some who had completed the research methods course sequence and a small number of others who were currently enrolled—who helped brainstorm the GPT's functions and test the tool before we implemented it.

Semi-Structured Interviews

In addition to exit tickets and GLA sessions, nine students participated in semi-structured interviews (DiCicco-Bloom & Crabtree, 2006) to gain additional insights on their perceptions of GenAI as well as if and how they saw GenAI playing a role in shaping how they saw themselves as beginning researchers and academic writers. The interviews were conducted in person and recorded, then the first author transcribed them using Temi, an audio transcription service (Temi, 2020).

Interview Data Analysis. The first author and a team of five student co-researchers analyzed the interview data using a modified participatory theme analysis approach (Best et al., 2022; Jackson, 2008), in which we reviewed the transcripts, working together to highlight key quotes and ideas. Throughout this process, we talked about aspects of the interviews that stood out to us and reflected on why they captured our attention. These informal discussions hinted at potential emerging themes, which we expanded on during our follow-up brainstorming session to sort the data and generate initial grouping themes, which included: 1) student knowledge/wariness of AI, 2) AI uses, 3) writing improvement, and 4) research support. Once we identified these initial grouping themes, we went through each pile, reading each quote one-by-one, and discussed how well they fit within the existing themes. As we worked through the data, we identified areas where themes overlapped or where subthemes emerged, prompting us to refine our categories. Some themes were combined, collapsed, or renamed to capture the nuances in participants' responses. By the end of this process, we ended with the following themes: 1) AI as an assistant, not a replacement, 2) understanding research, 3) proofreading, 4) generating ideas and direction, and 5) resource finding.

Findings and Discussion

To make sense of students' experiences engaging with GenAI in their research and writing, we have organized the findings thematically. Drawing on institutional data, including teacher reflections on classroom activities, exit tickets, GLA sessions, and student interviews, these themes offer a snapshot of how students perceive and engage with GenAI tools. Rather than examining each data source in isolation, we chose to look at them collectively to see the distinct roles GenAI played in the classroom and students' writing practices. The findings are organized around three central themes: GenAI as a course guide, GenAI as a writing coach, and GenAI as a research partner. Together, these themes highlight the ways students use, or did not use, GenAI in their research and writing practices, their perceptions of its benefits and limitations, and how, if at all, these tools impacted their identities as writers and researchers. Please see Table 6.1 for a summary of students' reported uses of GenAI for research and writing.

GenAI as a Course Guide

Within the context of our program's research and academic writing classroom, one of the ways I (Brook) used GenAI—specifically a custom GPT affectionately named after the university's mascot—was to serve as an interactive, course navigation and resource tool. During the GLA action planning session, many students talked about their use of and familiarity with ChatGPT, OpenAI's large language model (LLM)-driven chatbot (OpenAI, 2022). When thinking about what could help future students navigate our research methods courses, they decided that we should create a custom GPT for the course that could help keep students on track and help them get started with assignments. OpenAI's GPTs (2023) allow users to create customized versions of ChatGPT without requiring any

Table 6.1 Students' Reported uses of GenAI for research and writing

Category	*Specific use*	*Example*
Course Navigation	Clarifying course policies and deadlines	A student shared they used the custom GPT to ask about extension policies and assignment due dates.
	Course planning and scheduling	The class asked the custom GPT what assignments were due that week.
Writing Support	Brainstorming	Students shared they used GenAI to generate ideas.
	Creating outlines	Students used GenAI to create outlines for their literature review and findings sections.
	Drafting initial sections	Students reported using GenAI to help create first drafts that they later revised.
	Proofreading and revisions	Students used GenAI to improve grammar, sentence structure, and style.
	Clarifying and organizing ideas	One student shared how she used GenAI to organize her ideas.
	Peer review	Another student shared they used GenAI like a peer review partner.
Research Support	Summarizing academic sources	Students used GenAI tools to help make academic journal articles easier to understand.
	Finding quotes in uploaded documents	Students reported using GenAI tools to find specific quotes and ideas in their articles.
	Refining research questions	Students used GenAI to brainstorm or revise research questions.
	Developing keywords for literature searches	Students used GenAI to generate search terms for their literature searches.
	Locating journal articles and position papers	Students used GenAI to suggest organizations that conduct research on their topics.
	Formatting APA citations and references	Students reported using GenAI to format APA-style citations.

coding; instead, users can configure the model by providing prompts, guidance, and uploaded reference documents (OpenAI, n.d.).

In response to students' recommendations, I built a custom GPT for the course and uploaded the syllabus, course calendar, lecture notes and resources, and assignment instructions, training the GPT through prompting. I tested the custom GPT with several students, correcting any bugs they found and implementing new ideas they shared. After the pilot GPT was complete, we shared it with a section of our introduction to primary research course through a link posted on our course's home page along with a message that our custom GPT is "still learning—it is not perfect and may make mistakes sometimes." In the post, I encouraged students to verify important deadlines against those posted on the learning management system and reach out to me if they had any questions or suspected hallucinations.

When the class GPT launched, over 86% of students shared positive sentiments toward the platform on that week's exit ticket, with many students sharing they thought it was a "cool idea" and "useful to guide me during the semester." One student shared they created a custom GPT themselves with a similar purpose to help navigate another course.

Throughout the semester, we used the custom GPT to review what lecture activities and assignments were coming up in the course. I would also demonstrate specific use cases of the custom GPT to students such as prompting it to provide summaries of assignment instructions and upcoming deadlines. Most students seemed receptive to the custom GPT. While I trained the custom GPT to specifically draw on the materials that were uploaded and repeatedly tested our GPT before sharing it with students, I wanted to hold open discussions with students about the potential for hallucinations. Students were reminded to critically examine the content generated by the GPT and share if felt it hallucinated. To date, no students have reported feeling like the GPT provided inaccurate information.

When it comes to use cases beyond our classroom demonstrations, one student shared she used our custom GPT to create an outline for her research paper's literature review section, serving as a way to brainstorm potential angles she could take and expand on. Other students share they used it to help them create outlines for their findings sections, providing an outline of their main themes and asking the GPT to generate an initial section structure they could build off and customize. Students have also reported using the custom GPT to navigate course policy information, like how to request additional time to complete assignments.

Although the original purpose behind the custom GPT was to help students navigate the course, I did not anticipate its development would spark a sense of ownership and pride in the students who conceptualized and refined it during our action planning and pilot sessions. One student shared, "We got like some really good ideas...we made a ChatGPT for the class to like help." This insight suggests that providing students with opportunities to discuss their experiences, brainstorm ideas of how challenges could be addressed, and bring about change through the creation of custom GPTs, or similar course tools, could do more than serve a practical purpose; it can also provide students with meaningful opportunities to contribute something tangible to their learning community.

I (Brook) find it worth noting that the custom GPT was a newer addition to the course, piloted in one section of the primary research methods course. Based on the enthusiasm students showed during our in-class demonstrations—and the positive impact the brainstorming and debugging process seemed to have on students who helped develop the tool—I am inclined to continue using and modifying the custom GPT in future course sections. Additionally, I am interested in finding ways to involve students more directly in the creation of custom GPTs, not only to demonstrate how to build custom GPTs but also to give students more ownership over the resources we use. It is also worth noting that custom GPTs can be used in a number of educational settings. For example, in an inquiry project about GenAI essay grading on the Ohio State Test, Ohio middle school students demonstrated how GenAI evaluations prioritize structural dimensions of writing over the substance of ideas, raising critical questions about how AI may cultivate young writers toward narrow conceptions of writing (Hufford et al., 2025).

GenAI as a Writing Coach

One of the most frequent ways students engaged with GenAI was as a writing coach, using it to generate ideas, overcome writer's block, draft initial sections, and revise grammatical and stylistic aspects of their work.

Brainstorming and Overcoming Writer's Block

Students commonly reported using GenAI to support brainstorming and early drafting. In one exit ticket, about 77% of students reported using GenAI tools to help brainstorm ideas for their papers or research projects, and approximately 29% of students used GenAI to help create outlines. Students frequently described GenAI tools as helpful for organizing their thoughts, starting paragraphs, and working through moments of writer's block.

In an interview, one student shared:

> It helped me create more like outlines, um, just for individual paragraphs or sections of the paper…and sometimes I would ask it to like, write something for me, and then I would go through it and read it and see kind of like what

> it had pulled, and then I would rewrite it…so it was good for like prompting me to begin writing. It helped me kind of transition into the activity. (Student 2)

Students also described ways they have integrated GenAI tools into their drafting process. In his interview, one student described how he would prompt ChatGPT or Gemini by providing topic ideas and would ask the platform to "Expand on the idea and gimme ideas, and I'd look at it, but then I personally would look into it, and if I get stuck, that's when I'd go back and use AI for assistance" (Student 4). Reflecting on her writing process, another student shared "If I was stuck in like a writing block, it [ChatGPT] would help me generate ideas and like, okay, that would be a good idea to look into. And then finding that research and going into it" (Student 9). These insights seem to suggest that students may turn to GenAI to help them get started with tasks they might find challenging. Research suggests that students may feel less anxious about research and writing if they have an idea of what is needed to complete an academic research writing task (Cooper et al., 2023). For some students, GenAI could serve as another source of support for students who might be looking for additional guidance.

Refining and Revising Writing

In addition to generating ideas, students used GenAI tools to help support their editing and proofreading processes. In an exit ticket, about 53% of students reported using GenAI tools to improve grammar and sentence structure, while 6% had used it to find synonyms to add more variety to their language use. During interviews, students described moments in their writing processes when they used GenAI to help organize their ideas or clarify their arguments. Speaking on her experience with ChatGPT, one student shared:

> It can help you revise and…organize your ideas. I feel like you can kind of word dump. Like sometimes I've done this like word dump for a couple minutes into it, like everything that you need to do and it can kind of like break it down. Like, "here's what you should do about this"…Like you have a bunch of ideas…having ChatGPT look at it and being like, "oh you can do this with this" or, I don't know. It's just like a really helpful like tool that can help you visualize things more…It's like dumping your mind out and then, ChatGPT clearing it up. (Student 6)

Like many writing-focused courses, our research methods sequence incorporates peer review activities, where students provide feedback on each other's work using a set of guiding questions and prompts. In addition to this traditional peer review process, several students independently used GenAI tools as a peer review partner, prompting the platform to evaluate their writing and offer suggestions for strengthening arguments or improving paragraph structures. During an interview, one student explained:

> The biggest use that AI can do is that you can plug in a paper and you can say "if you're an academic writer, is this gonna be any good?" And it is very honest with you. It will say, "it's well written", you know, it'll say "it's well written, this stuff, but this doesn't make much sense. I think you could revise this section"…then you look back at it and you're just like, "okay, you know, that's just fair enough." (Student 1)

Others echoed this use of GenAI as a proofreading tool. Another student explained she used GenAI for grammar support, sharing that ChatGPT "gives a very good review…of what you wrote…It helped me a lot to correct grammatical issues because when I'm trying to express an opinion, I usually think more about the idea than about grammar. And then sentences become…strange" (Student 7).

While students' use of GenAI tools for writing feedback is not new, their independent use of these platforms for peer review may present an opportunity for instructors to provide guidance on how to prompt GenAI, interpret its feedback, and revise with this feedback in mind effectively. One way to do this could be through modeling how to prompt GenAI to provide quality feedback or through reflection prompts that ask students to compare GenAI feedback with that of their peers or instructors.

The practice of using GenAI as a peer review partner may warrant further research. One study found students were more likely to trust the quality of writing feedback provided by GenAI over that of their peers, or even their instructors (Ruwe & Mayweg-Paus, 2023). This is not to suggest that GenAI should replace traditional forms of peer and instructor feedback—which offer valuable opportunities to build relationships and foster dialogue within the classroom—but rather point toward another potential source of support that could scaffold students' writing development.

GenAI as a Research Partner

Students noted several different ways they used GenAI to support their research efforts, especially when it came to secondary research-related tasks such as identifying keywords, developing research questions, and understanding research articles. In an exit ticket, approximately 71% of students reported using GenAI to summarize articles or research papers. Around 35% of students shared they have used these tools to format citations and references, and another 35% used them to locate journal articles and position papers. Additionally, about 29% of students used GenAI to identify keywords, while 29% also used it to help draft research questions.

Summarizing and Understanding Research Articles

One of the major ways students used GenAI during the research process was to help summarize research papers. Learning how to read and understand academic research can take some time. For some students, GenAI tools served as a way to make disciplinary-specific language more accessible. Reflecting on her experience learning how to read academic research and later communicate her ideas in an academic writing style, one senior shared she felt that researchers are:

> Experts who already know their topic and they talk about it in a way that only really they or other experts can understand. But, the idea is that you need to make it accessible for everyone. So, I think that's something ChatGPT is incredible at (Student 7).

Another student highlighted how she used GenAI to find key ideas and quotes in the articles she found. She shared she used Sharley AI—an GPT-4-powered platform that summarizes and allows users to chat with uploaded documents (Sharly AI, n.d.)—to summarize articles for her. She noted that this tool was helpful because "sometimes they're [articles] so long and hard to read all of it. So, that was a really good tool with reading through those and then finding quotes specific to what you need" (Student 9). Another student shared she used Google's Notebook LM—a platform built on Gemini 2.0 and marketed as "a personalized AI expert in the information that matters most to you" that allows users to upload information sources and identifies connections across those documents, generating summaries that users can interact with through a chat-based interface (Google, n.d., para. 2). After collecting and reading her sources, the student shared she used Notebook LM "to find specific quotes ...I can just be like, 'where is quotes from it [the article] about this' instead of trying to search a whole article when I've already skimmed it" (Student 5).

While some students seemed eager to utilize GenAI tools to distill research and locate key quotes, others expressed concerns with the accuracy of GenAI's summary abilities. For one student, GenAI could serve as a starting point, but human oversight is needed. He shared:

You still have to look through it yourself. You definitely have to look at it. I mean, it's not going to put it in a way where you're gonna be able to use it on your own. It'll give you an idea that then you can go look into deeper (Student 1).

These findings are consistent with prior research, which suggests that many students find that GenAI tools can help make academic language more accessible (Barros et al., 2023). However, Student 1's comment hints at the importance of instructors stressing the need to critically evaluate GenAI-produced content and discuss how GenAI can be integrated into students drafting and proofreading practices (Barrett & Pack, 2023; Johnson, 2023).

Developing Keywords and Refining Search Terms

Students also reported using GenAI tools to help collect academic literature for their literature reviews. In an exit ticket, about 35% of students shared they used GenAI tools to locate journal articles and position papers, with approximately 29% students specifically mentioning they used GenAI to identify keywords they could use for their article searches.

During the first section of the research methods sequence, the instructor guide students through a series of activities designed to help them develop keyword search terms. To begin, the instructor demonstrates how to start with a research question and generate a list of keywords, along with alternative terms (Central Michigan University Libraries, n.d.). After that, the instructor models how to ChatGPT to expand on these keywords as well as efficiently format them as Boolean search terms. This activity seems to resonate with students across class sections, with more than 72% during the 2023–24 academic year listing the ChatGPT-driven keyword search activity as one of their key learning highlights from that class session. Students shared about their experiences developing keywords and searching for articles beyond the classroom in their interviews. Weighing the potential benefits and shortcomings of using ChatGPT for article searches, one student shared they have used ChatGPT for "finding keywords. I would not recommend it for finding sources. Like just asking it for sources, I don't think it works" (Student 5). In that, the student points toward a known challenge that ChatGPT sometimes reports false information or invents sources (Lingard, 2023), an issue that is repeatedly discussed in the research methods sequence. GenAI tools can and sometimes do hallucinate—that is, present false information with unabashed confidence, so, it may be important for instructors teaching research and writing-intensive courses to openly discuss potential shortcomings regardless if they intend to integrate GenAI into their pedagogy (Colby, 2025).

Critiquing GenAI-Created Survey Questions

We also used GenAI to facilitate discussions about creating high-quality data collection instruments. To begin, we review key principles of good survey question design—such as using clear language and avoiding asking leading questions (Creswell, 2014). After this, students are divided into groups, with each group being tasked with critiquing a set of GenAI-created survey questions. I ask students to read through the questions, noting which, if any, questions seem problematic and offering solutions as needed. This activity seems to resonate with students, as each time I (Brook) have used it, both small group and whole classroom discussions are lively. Many students, it seems, are eager to openly critique their question sets. The challenge of figuring out how to break up a double-barreled question or balance using close-ended and open-ended questions seems to serve as a starting point for critical and creative questions within students' small groups. In our whole-class discussions, we worked through the questions and students' suggestions, often addressing the potential limitations of GenAI-produced texts, the importance of high quality prompting, and the need for human oversight. This activity helps demonstrate the importance of prompt engineering that is, providing a GenAI tool with clear, direct instructions or statements to improve the chances of receiving a relevant output and reduce chances of hallucination (Tonmoy et al., 2024). While GenAI can be a useful tool, students may not know how to use it effectively (Johnson, 2023). As such, it may be important for instructors to model how to develop and refine high-quality prompts when working with GenAI tools.

Formatting APA Reference Citations

Students also used GenAI tools to format APA citations and reference lists. On an exit ticket, about 35% of students shared they have used GenAI to guide them in navigating APA style citations and references. One interviewed student shared he found ChatGPT helpful for managing references and generating citations. After uploading a paper to ChatGPT, he shared he would ask ChatGPT to "give me the APA citation for it. And it does" (Student 1). However, he also stressed the need to double-check the citation and reference because "most of the time it pulls from the right information…[but] sometimes it gets itself a little confused" (Student 1). The use of GenAI tools to format APA citations and generate reference lists appears to be a less common use case of GenAI (Deschenes & McMahon, 2024). However, considering the increasing prevalence of GenAI tools and their perceived ease of use, it may be important for instructors to include discussions centered on GenAI, source credibility, and citation accuracy during conversations about searching for, working with, and citing sources. Incorporating an activity where students use GenAI to draft an essay, including in-text citations and a reference list, and evaluate the accuracy and completeness of the generated citations could be one way to prompt discussions about verifying GenAI-produced outputs (van Niekerk et al., 2025).

Conclusion

In this chapter, we explored how students engaged with generative AI (GenAI) tools during their academic research and writing journeys both within the context of a writing-intensive research methods course and across their own writing practices. The findings suggest that GenAI can be used to help students navigate course policies and assignment expectations, offer additional scaffolding throughout the writing process, and provide support as students work through research tasks that could feel potentially challenging or anxiety inducting. When it came to GenAI donning the role of course guide, the custom GPT helped students navigate course materials, brainstorm outlines for specific paper sections based on assignment instructions, and understand course policies. In addition to the practical source of support this custom GPT offered, supporting the development of the custom GPT seemed to serve as a source of empowerment for the students involved. As a writing coach, students shared how they used GenAI to brainstorm topics and outlines, draft, and revise their work. As a research partner, GenAI supported students in understanding challenging academic texts, identifying keyword for their literature searches, developing and refining research questions and data collection instruments, and formatting APA citations and references. While students' experiences pointed toward several potentially beneficially uses of GenAI, many students also stressed the need to evaluate its outputs critically, especially when it came to locating and summarizing sources.

This project offers several practical takeaways for instructors teaching research and writing-intensive courses. To begin, it seems that modeling specific examples of how students could use GenAI for research and writing purposes can be beneficial both for their learning and for facilitating classroom discussions on acceptable use cases and the need to evaluate GenAI outputs. Additionally, creating space for students to share their experiences and brainstorm ideas for course-level actions could encourage a sense of engagement and ownership.

This work contributes to the conversations about the role GenAI can and should play within higher education, especially in research and writing intensive courses. While the findings of this work may not be generalizable, the participatory aspects of the project, that is collaborating with students to understand better their experiences and empowering them to contribute to pedagogical changes, could be adapted in other teaching contexts.

While this work offers insights into how GenAI can be folded into a research and writing intensive course, there are some limitations to note. This work took place at a small, private liberal arts college within a computer science program, where class sizes are relatively small and a high level of instructor involvement. These factors may make it more feasible to develop and implement custom GPT tools than in large, lecture-based courses.

Future research might explore how students' uses and perceptions of GenAI change over time or across different disciplines. Researchers and educators may also consider, as able, involving their classes in creating custom GPT tools or creating specific GenAI use guides for the course.

Ethics Approval The University of Cincinnati Institutional Research Board (IRB) reviewed and approved the research protocol (MOD01_2024-0238) on August 9, 2024.

Try It Out: Critiquing Survey and Interview Questions with GenAI

As mentioned in Chap. 6, providing students with opportunities to engage with generative AI tools in a structured, low-stakes way can help build foundational skills while also creating a space for meaningful dialogue about the potential affordances and limitations of AI-assisted research. This activity encourages students to evaluate GenAI-generated questions, apply research design principles, and reflect on the ethical and practical dimensions of co-authoring with AI.

This activity can be further supported with prompting strategies over-viewed in *ChatGPT in Scientific Research and Writing: A Beginner's Guide* (a highly recommended book, reviewed in the Appendix list of Additional AI learning Resources).

Step 1: Introduce Key Principles of Question Design
Begin by reviewing essential criteria for effective survey or interview questions, such as clarity, neutrality, specificity, and appropriate format.

Step 2: Generate Initial Question Sets Using GenAI
Use a generative AI tool (such as ChatGPT or Gemini) to create sample questions related to a research topic chosen by the instructor or students. To demonstrate how prompt quality impacts output: begin with a vague or underdeveloped prompt., then show how more specific prompts result in clearer, more relevant questions.

Step 3: Critique and Revise Questions in Small Groups
Assign each small group a subset of the GenAI-generated questions. Ask students to:

- Identify unclear wording, bias, jargon, double-barreled items, or flawed response options.
- Suggest improvements and revise questions using their checklist or with the assistance of GenAI.
- Optionally, have students pilot the revised questions on each other by responding to them and discussing whether the intended meaning and clarity are maintained.

Step 4: Facilitate Whole-Class Discussion
Bring the class together to share observations. Discuss:

Common issues identified across question sets.
The role of prompt quality in shaping GenAI output.
The strengths and weaknesses of GenAI as a co-author of research tools.
Insights gained from peer piloting, including which revisions improved clarity or effectiveness.

Step 5: Refine and Reflect
Demonstrate how to further revise the original list using student feedback. Then invite students to reflect—either in writing or discussion—on the following:

What did they learn about designing clear and effective research questions?
When might GenAI be a helpful brainstorming tool, and when is human oversight essential?
What ethical or practical considerations emerged from using GenAI in this context?

Questions for Reflection and Discussion

Here are some questions to guide your reflection and discussions:

1. How can custom GenAI tools be used to help students navigate courses?
2. What, if any, are the potential risks involved with relying on GenAI tools to support course navigation?
3. How, if at all, could students' input be incorporated into course-specific GenAI tool development, creation, and refinement? Should students be involved in these decisions? Why or why not?
4. What are the ethical implications of using GenAI to support one's writing practice, especially when writers are using GenAI as a starting point?

References

Adedokun, O. A., Bessenbacher, A. B., Parker, L. C., Kirkham, L. L., & Burgess, W. D. (2013). Research skills and STEM undergraduate research students' aspirations for research careers: Mediating effects of research self-efficacy. *Journal of Research in Science Teaching, 50*(8), 940–951.

Anderson, G. L., Herr, K., & Nihlen, A. S. (2007). *Studying your own school: An educator's guide to practitioner action research*. Corwin Press.

Bandura, A. (1977). Self-efficacy: Toward a unifying theory of behavioral change. *Psychological Review, 84*(2), 191–215. https://doi.org/10.1037/0033-295X.84.2.191

Barrett, A., & Pack, A. (2023). Not quite eye to A.I.: Student and teacher perspectives on the use of generative artificial intelligence in the writing process. *International Journal of Educational Technology in Higher Education, 20*(59), 1–24. https://doi.org/10.1186/s41239-023-00427-0

Barros, A., Prasad, A., & Śliwa, M. (2023). Generative artificial intelligence and academia: Implication for research, teaching and service. *Management Learning, 54*(5), 597–604. https://doi.org/10.1177/13505076231201445

Baum, F., MacDougall, C., & Smith, D. (2006). Participatory action research. *Journal of Epidemiology & Community Health, 60*(10), 854–857.

Best, P., Badham, J., McConnell, T., & Hunter, R. F. (2022). Participatory theme elicitation: Open card sorting for user led qualitative data analysis. *International Journal of Social Research Methodology, 25*(2), 213–231. https://doi.org/10.1080/13645579.2021.1876616

Bowman, N. A., & Holmes, J. M. (2018). Getting off to a good start? First-year undergraduate research experiences and student outcomes. *Higher Education, 76*, 17–33. https://doi.org/10.1007/s10734-017-0191-4

Buçinca, Z., Malaya, M. B., & Gajos, K. Z. (2021). To trust or to think: Cognitive forcing functions can reduce overreliance on AI in AI-assisted decision-making. *Proceedings of the ACM on Human-Computer Interaction, 5*(CSCW1), 1–21. https://doi.org/10.1145/3449287

Central Michigan University Libraries. (n.d.). *How to conduct a literature review: Search strategy.* https://libguides.cmich.edu/lit_review/LR_searchstrategy

Ceyhan, G. D., & Tillotson, J. W. (2020). Early year undergraduate researchers' reflections on the values and perceived costs of their research experience. *International Journal of STEM Education, 7*, 1–19. https://doi.org/10.1186/s40594-020-00248-x

Chan, C. K. Y., & Hu, W. (2023). Students' voices on generative AI: Perceptions, benefits, and challenges in higher education. *International Journal of Educational Technology in Higher Education, 20*(43), 1–18. https://doi.org/10.1186/s41239-023-00411-8

Colby, R. S. (2025). Playing the digital dialectic game: Writing pedagogy with generative AI. *Computers and Composition, 75*, 102915. https://doi.org/10.1016/j.compcom.2025.102915

Cooper, K. M., Eddy, S. L., & Brownell, S. E. (2023). Research anxiety predicts undergraduates' intentions to pursue scientific research careers. *CBE—Life Sciences Education, 22*(1), ar11. https://doi.org/10.1187/cbe.22-02-0022

Cornell University Task Force. (2023). *Generative AI in academic research: Perspectives and cultural norms.* Cornell University. https://it.cornell.edu/sites/default/files/itc-drupal10-files/Generative%20AI%20in%20Research_%20Cornell%20Task%20Force%20Report-Dec2023.pdf

Council on Undergraduate Research. (n.d.). *Mission and vision*. https://www.cur.org/who/organization/mission_and_vision/

Creswell, J. (2014). *Research design: Qualitative, quantitative, and mixed methods approaches*. Sage Publications.

Cummings, R. E., Monroe, S. M., & Watkins, M. (2024). Generative AI in first-year writing: An early analysis of affordances, limitations, and a framework for the future. *Computers and Composition, 71*, 102827. https://doi.org/10.1016/j.compcom.2024.102827

Danley, A., McCoy, A., & Weed, R. (2016). Exit tickets open the door to university learning. *InSight: A Journal of Scholarly Teaching, 11*(1), 48–58. https://files.eric.ed.gov/fulltext/EJ1110134.pdf

Deschenes, A., & McMahon, M. (2024). A survey on student use of generative AI chatbots for academic research. *Evidence Based Library and Information Practice, 19*(2), 2–22. https://doi.org/10.18438/eblip30512

DiCicco-Bloom, B., & Crabtree, B. F. (2006). The qualitative research interview. *Medical Education, 40*(4), 314–321.

Feuerriegel, S., Hartmann, J., Janiesch, C., & Zschech, P. (2024). Generative AI. *Business & Information Systems Engineering, 66*(1), 111–126. https://doi.org/10.1007/s12599-023-00834-7

Fyfe, P. (2023). How to cheat on your final paper: Assigning AI for student writing. *AI & Society, 38*(4), 1395–1405. https://doi.org/10.1007/s00146-022-01397-z

Gasaymeh, A.-M. M., Beirat, M. A., & Abu Qbeita, A. A. (2024). University students' insights of generative artificial intelligence (AI) writing tools. *Education Sciences, 14*(10), 1062. https://doi.org/10.3390/educsci14101062

Golding, J. M., Lippert, A., Neuschatz, J. S., Salomon, I., & Burke, K. (2024). Generative AI and college students: Use and perceptions. *Teaching of Psychology*. https://doi.org/10.1177/00986283241280350

Google. (n.d.). *NotebookLM*. https://notebooklm.google/

Greenwood, D. J., & Levin, M. (2007). *Introduction to action research: Social research for social change* (2nd ed.). SAGE Publications, Inc.

Haeger, H., Bueno, E. H., & Sedlacek, Q. (2024). Participation in undergraduate research reduces equity gaps in STEM graduation rates. *CBE—Life Sciences Education, 23*(1), ar11. https://doi.org/10.1187/cbe.22-03-0061

Hamilton, E. R., Rosenberg, J. M., & Akcaoglu, M. (2016). The substitution augmentation modification redefinition (SAMR) model: A critical review and suggestions for its use. *TechTrends, 60*(5), 433–441. https://doi.org/10.1007/s11528-016-0091-y

Hanson, J. M., Paulsen, M. B., & Pascarella, E. T. (2016). Understanding graduate school aspirations: The effect of good teaching practices. *Higher Education, 71*(5), 735–752. https://doi.org/10.1007/s10734-015-9934-2

Haroud, S., & Saqri, N. (2025). Generative AI in higher education: Teachers' and students' perspectives on support, replacement, and digital literacy. *Education Sciences, 15*(4), 396. https://doi.org/10.1007/s10734-015-9934-2

Higgs, J. M., & Stornaiuolo, A. (2024). Being human in the age of generative AI: Young people's ethical concerns about writing and living with machines. *Reading Research Quarterly, 59*(4), 632–650. https://doi.org/10.1002/rrq.552

Hufford, M., Lyons, W., Elswick, A., Capaldo, A., Queen, G., Carper, J., Hinkle, R., Hines, K., Miller, J., Ehas, S., Mosley, A., Johns, W., & Rapp, J. (2025). Authentic dialogue in a digital world: Student research in AI in writing assessment [Conference presentation]. *Ohio Council of English Language Arts Conference, 2025.*

Jackson, S. F. (2008). A participatory group process to analyze qualitative data progress. *Progress in Community Health Partnerships: Research, Education, and Action, 2*(2), 161–170. 10.1353/cpr.0.0010

Johnson, G. P. (2023). Don't act like you forgot: Approaching another literacy "crisis" by (re)considering what we know about teaching writing with and through technologies. *Composition Studies, 51*(1), 169–175.

Kilgo, C. A., & Pascarella, E. T. (2016). Does independent research with a faculty member enhance four-year graduation and graduate/professional degree plans? Convergent results with different analytical methods. *Higher Education, 71*, 575–592. https://doi.org/10.1007/s10734-015-9925-3

Kim, J., Yu, S., Detrick, R., & Li, N. (2024). Exploring students' perspectives on generative AI-assisted academic writing. *Education and Information Technologies, 1–36*. https://doi.org/10.1007/s10639-024-12878-7

Kuh, G. D. (2008). *High-impact educational practices: What they are, who has access to them, and why they matter.* Association of American Colleges and Universities.

Lin, L., & Parker, K. (2024). *U.S. workers are more worried than hopeful about future AI use in the workplace* (pp. 1–33). Pew Research Center. https://www.pewresearch.org/wp-content/uploads/sites/20/2025/02/ST_2025.2.25_AI-Workers_REPORT.pdf

Lingard, L. (2023). Writing with ChatGPT: An illustration of its capacity, limitations & implications for academic writers. *Perspectives on Medical Education, 12*(1), 261–270. https://doi.org/10.5334/pme.1072

Lopatto, D. (2010). Undergraduate research as a high-impact student experience. *Peer Review, 12*(2), 27–31.

Mabrito, M. (2024). Artificial intelligence in the classroom: Conversation design and prompt engineering for English majors. *International Journal of Technologies in Learning, 31*(2), 129–142. https://doi.org/10.18848/2327-0144/CGP/v31i02/129-142

Madden, M., Calvin, A., Hasse, A., & Lenhart, A. (2024). *The dawn of the AI era: Teens, parents, and the adoption of generative AI at home and school* (pp. 1–56). Common Sense. https://www.commonsensemedia.org/sites/default/files/research/report/2024-the-dawn-of-the-ai-era_final-release-for-web.pdf

OpenAI. (2022). *Introducing ChatGPT.* https://openai.com/index/chatgpt/

OpenAI. (2023). *Introducing GPTs.* https://openai.com/index/introducing-gpts/

OpenAI. (n.d.). *Creating a GPT.* Retrieved February 11, 2024, from https://help.openai.com/en/articles/8554397-creating-a-gpt

Pellas, N. (2023). The effects of generative AI platforms on undergraduates' narrative intelligence and writing self-efficacy. *Education Sciences, 13*(11), 1155. https://doi.org/10.3390/educsci13111155

Plate, D., Melick, E., Hutson, J., & Edele, S. (2025). *Generative AI in the English composition classroom: Practical and adaptable strategies* (1st ed.). https://doi.org/10.4324/9781003507949

Prem, E. (2023). From ethical AI frameworks to tools: A review of approaches. *AI and Ethics, 3*, 699–716. https://doi.org/10.1007/s43681-023-00258-9

Puentedura, R. (2006). *Transformation, technology, and education.* Hippasus. http://hippasus.com/resources/tte/puentedura_tte.pdf

Puentedura, R. (2014). *Building transformation: An introduction to the SAMR Model.* Hippasus. http://www.hippasus.com/rrpweblog/archives/2014/08/22/BuildingTransformation_AnIntroductionToSAMR.pdf

Ruwe, T., & Mayweg-Paus, E. (2023). "Your argumentation is good," says the AI vs humans—The role of feedback providers and personalised language for feedback effectiveness. *Computers and Education: Artificial Intelligence, 5*, 100189. https://doi.org/10.1016/j.caeai.2023.100189

Seifan, M., Lal, N., & Berenjian, A. (2022). Effect of undergraduate research on students' learning and engagement. *International Journal of Mechanical Engineering Education, 50*(2), 326–348. https://doi.org/10.1177/0306419021988962

Sell, A. J., Naginey, A., & Stanton, C. A. (2018). The impact of undergraduate research on academic success. *Scholarship and Practice of Undergraduate Research, 1*(3), 19–29. https://doi.org/10.18833/spur/1/3/8

Sharly AI. (n.d.). *Sharly: Your AI research assistant.* https://sharly.ai/

Su, Y., Lin, Y., & Lai, C. (2023). Collaborating with ChatGPT in argumentative writing classrooms. *Assessing Writing, 57*, 100752. https://doi.org/10.1016/j.asw.2023.100752

Temi. (2020). *Temi homepage.* www.temi.com

Tonmoy, S. M., Zaman, S. M., Jain, V., Rani, A., Rawte, V., Chadha, A., & Das, A. (2024). A comprehensive survey of hallucination mitigation techniques in large language models. *arXiv Preprint*, arXiv:2401.01313. https://arxiv.org/abs/2401.01313

van Niekerk, J., Delport, P. M. J., & Sutherland, I. (2025). Addressing the use of generative AI in academic writing. *Computers and Education: Artificial Intelligence, 8*, 100342. https://doi.org/10.1016/j.caeai.2024.100342

Vaughn, L. M., & DeJonckheere, M. (2019). Methodological progress note: Group level assessment. *Journal of Hospital Medicine, 14*(10), 627–629. https://doi.org/10.12788/jhm.3289

Vaughn, L. M., & Lohmueller, M. (2014). Calling all stakeholders: Group-Level Assessment (GLA)—A qualitative and participatory method for large groups. *Evaluation Review, 38*(4), 336–355. https://doi.org/10.1177/0193841x14544903

Venkatesh, V., Morris, M. G., Davis, G. B., & Davis, F. D. (2003). User acceptance of information technology: Toward a unified view. *MIS Quarterly, 27*(3), 425–478.

Williams, A. (2024a). Comparison of generative AI performance on undergraduate and postgraduate written assessments in the biomedical sciences. *International Journal of Educational Technology in Higher Education, 21*(1), 52. https://doi.org/10.1186/s41239-024-00485-y

Williams, R. (2024b). The ethical implications of using generative chatbots in higher education. *Frontiers in Education, 8*, 1331607. https://doi.org/10.3389/feduc.2023.1331607

Wu, J., Yang, S., Zhan, R., Yuan, Y., Chao, L. S., & Wong, D. F. (2025). A survey on LLM-generated text detection: Necessity, methods, and future directions. *Computational Linguistics, 1–64*. https://doi.org/10.1162/coli_a_00549

Zhai, C., Wibowo, S., & Li, L. D. (2024). The effects of over-reliance on AI dialogue systems on students' cognitive abilities: A systematic review. *Smart Learning Environments, 11*, 28. https://doi.org/10.1186/s40561-024-00316-7

CHAPTER 7

Researchers' Perspectives on AI in Higher Education: A Focus Group Study

Maria Chiara De Angelis

Introduction

The genesis of artificial intelligence (AI) has brought about a significant transformation in higher education, reshaping academic organizational structures and driving both ideological and practical changes across teaching, research, and services (Ghnemat et al., 2022; Barros et al., 2023). Academic literature highlights that digital transformation—particularly through generative artificial intelligence (GAI)—has a wide-ranging impact on teaching methods, improving quality, saving time, enhancing data analysis, and refining student assessment and feedback processes (Abbasi et al., 2025). AI tools enable personalized learning by identifying knowledge gaps, offering tailored insights, and providing targeted feedback. These capabilities help students overcome academic challenges and support peer interaction, fostering more dynamic and responsive educational environments (Kok et al., 2024).

M. C. De Angelis (✉)
Department of Human Sciences, Link Campus University, Rome, Italy
e-mail: mc.deangelis@unilink.it

R. J. Allen, A. Nakonechnyi (eds.), *Using and Understanding AI in Higher Education*,
https://doi.org/10.1007/978-3-031-99754-9_7

Extending beyond its impact on teaching and learning, artificial intelligence is also reshaping other dimensions of higher education, including student support services and the research enterprise. AI-driven chatbots and virtual assistants offer just in time assistance by answering frequently asked questions, providing course-related information, and supporting career guidance (Zaman, 2023). These tools also contribute to inclusive educational environments by addressing diverse learner needs and reducing barriers to access (Šumak et al., 2024; Wayahdi & Zaki, 2025). In parallel, AI is increasingly influencing the planning, execution, and dissemination of scientific research by supporting the generation of knowledge, facilitates access to and sharing of research data, and enhances engagement with external stakeholders (De Angelis, 2024; De Angelis & Velardi, 2024).

As artificial intelligence (AI) continues to reshape higher education, universities are responding through a variety of strategies: developing institutional guidelines, hosting workshops for faculty and students, and addressing the ethical challenges posed by AI integration (Chan, 2023). Recognizing that digital innovation carries significant social and ethical implications for both research and teaching, this chapter examines how AI is transforming the work, instructional practices, and scholarly activities of academics in higher education.

Our objective is to encourage critical reflection on AI knowledge and its application within the educational community, while also providing guidance for university policies and strategies that respond to these ongoing changes. To do so, we investigate how digitalization is transforming academic methods, identify key implications for research, and recognize the role of researchers' subjectivity in shaping this transition.

To explore how AI is reshaping academic life, this chapter is guided by the following core research question: How are researchers and lecturers in higher education experiencing the challenges, risks, and opportunities of artificial intelligence, and how are the skills required for academic work shifting in response? To investigate this question, we conducted a qualitative multilevel study based on two international exploratory focus groups with participants from six countries. Braun and Clarke's (2008) six-stage thematic analysis was used to identify and interpret key patterns in the data—ranging from objective setting and coding to theme development and narrative construction. The findings are organized around seven central themes that map directly onto the core elements of our inquiry: institutional responses to AI, integration into teaching and assessment, perceived risks and benefits, ethical considerations, and the evolving skill-sets required of both educators and researchers. Rather than offering definitive conclusions, this chapter presents insights grounded in the lived experiences of scholars actively navigating AI's integration into academic practice. These findings aim to support critical reflection and inform more adaptive, inclusive institutional strategies for higher education's digital future.

Literature Review

The Evolution of Artificial Intelligence and Its Impact on Education

Artificial intelligence has a rich history that extends back to the 1960s. Its roots can be found in the work of the English mathematician Alan M. Turing, who contemplated whether machines could think. The term "artificial intelligence" was first introduced in 1956 at the Dartmouth Conference by John McCarthy, Marvin Minsky, Nathaniel Rochester, and Claude Shannon, formalizing AI as a recognized field of research (Berente et al., 2021; McCarthy et al., 2006). However, it was during the 1970s that a significant acceleration was observed when the Japanese researcher Kunihiko Fukushima established the foundational principles for developing multilayer neural networks. These networks currently underpin the definition of deep learning, based on the concept of the network as self-organizing, which allows it to "learn without a teacher" (Fukushima, 1980).

In recent years, there has been a swift and disruptive acceleration in AI advancements, driven by major improvements in data availability, computing capacities, and machine learning techniques. The affirmation of Artificial Intelligence in Education (AIED) as an emerging field—focused on enhancing and personalizing teaching and learning through AI technologies—has gained momentum, particularly following OpenAI's public release of the generative AI tool ChatGPT (Su & Yang, 2023). This milestone has spurred a significant proliferation of customized chatbots for diverse applications, profoundly affecting various aspects of human life, especially in higher education and scientific research, while simultaneously introducing new opportunities and challenges. These technologies have reached a high level of complexity, enabling AI systems to understand human language, engage in learning processes, and perform sophisticated tasks such as logical reasoning, image recognition, natural language processing, and independent decision-making. As a result, AI offers unique opportunities for academic creativity and growth—expanding access, boosting productivity for scholars and staff, promoting inclusivity, and enhancing both the quality and quantity of academic output (ERC, 2023; Lin & Chen, 2024).

The Impact of AI in Higher Education

Generative AI (GenAI) tools are significantly enhancing learning, teaching, and research processes within higher education. When used thoughtfully, features such as intelligent tutoring systems, adaptive learning methodologies, automated assessment capabilities, chatbots, learning analytics dashboards, and interactive robots can support and enrich educational practices (Udeh, 2025). Recent studies highlight GenAI's wide-ranging capabilities, including outperforming average students in writing, synthesizing literature reviews, translating content (Michel-Villarreal et al., 2023; Grassini, 2023), offering detailed feedback, enhancing multimedia learning (Javaid et al., 2023; Yu, 2023), and customizing educational materials to meet individual student needs (Baidoo-Anu & Ansah, 2023; Alam, 2023).

A study by Jin et al. (2025), grounded in the Diffusion of Innovations Theory (DIT) (see Chap. 4, for more information about DIT), analyzed AI policy adoption across 40 universities in six global regions and found that many institutions are generally embracing GenAI, integrating it with traditional pedagogical methods to improve teaching effectiveness. However, to remain competitive and innovative in the face of technological disruption, higher education institutions must invest in teacher professionalization. Educators are now required to critically evaluate AI-generated content, adapt it to their learners' needs, and address concerns related to data protection, ethics, and privacy (Chan & Tsi, 2023). This complexity calls for enhanced AI and data literacy among educators, students, and administrators—not only in terms of technical skills, but also regarding the social, ethical, and environmental implications of data usage (Galih & Barát, 2024; Van Audenhove et al., 2024).

Despite these advancements, concerns have been raised about the widening digital divide. Unequal access to GenAI technologies may intensify existing educational disparities (Al-Zahrani, 2024). Moreover, there is growing apprehension about students' overreliance on generative AI, which could negatively impact their critical thinking, creativity, and academic independence (Zhai et al., 2024). Research shows that students often accept AI-generated responses uncritically, a behavior reinforced by cognitive biases and reliance on heuristics (Gao et al., 2023). Zhang et al. (2024) found a correlation between AI dependency and increased academic stress, highlighting the psychological impact of these tools. Overdependence may also affect students' self-efficacy and performance expectations.

These behavioral shifts have significant implications for academic integrity. Scholars have warned that misuse of AI tools can contribute to plagiarism, fabrication, and violations of data and intellectual property rights (McGuire, 2023; Perkins, 2023; Leong & Zhang, 2025; Lund et al., 2025; Sozon et al., 2024). More broadly, the growing interaction between humans and AI systems raises ethical concerns—ranging from cognitive offloading and bias reinforcement to the erosion of human dignity and deepening of social inequalities (Abbass, 2019). Krause et al. (2025) note that while GenAI offers personalized instruction and around-the-clock support, these benefits must be balanced with robust ethical guidance to prevent academic dishonesty and the weakening of students' self-regulation.

To mitigate these risks, scholars stress the importance of cultivating critical AI literacy and fostering a reflective approach to tool usage. Cotton et al. (2024) recommend institutional policies that promote ethical engagement, including AI-recognition technologies and curriculum-integrated ethics education. Tripathi and Thakar (2024) caution against treating AI as a miraculous fix, urging instead for its mindful adoption. Ultimately, educators play a crucial role in guiding ethical use, reinforcing student integrity, and modeling responsible AI engagement within broader frameworks of social and emotional learning.

Methodology

Research Design

Building on prior research, this study offers an in-depth exploration of the opportunities and challenges that artificial intelligence poses within higher education and the broader scientific community. Adopting a multifaceted lens, it assesses current practices, anticipates future developments, and critically reflects on key issues from the perspective of academic researchers.

The methodology operates at both the meso and micro levels, examining institutional policies, curricular integration, and individual educational and research experiences related to AI. It also considers the development of new competencies needed to navigate these evolving demands.

To guide this analysis, I draw on Jussi Välimaa's (1998, 2008) cultural perspective, which views universities as socially embedded cultural institutions responsible for shaping societal values. This exploratory study employs a qualitative, inductive framework, allowing theories to emerge organically from the data rather than imposing predefined models (Strauss & Corbin, 2008). Data were collected through focus group discussions and analyzed using Braun and Clarke's (2008) six-phase approach to thematic analysis—a widely used and adaptable method for identifying, analyzing, and reporting patterns within qualitative data.

Population and Sampling

This study explores the role of artificial intelligence in higher education from a transnational perspective. Researchers and lecturers from six countries—Italy, Portugal, Morocco, China, Lithuania, and Spain—participated in the study. Participants were self-selected in response to an open call distributed through academic networks and social media platforms (e.g., ResearchGate, LinkedIn), as well as the DITES RC mailing list. Selection criteria included availability, willingness to engage in the focus group discussions, and relevant subject-matter expertise (Silverman, 2013).

Two online focus groups were conducted during the second semester of the 2024–2025 academic year, with five participants in each group. All sessions were recorded and carried out in accordance with ethical research standards, ensuring participant anonymity and data confidentiality.

The data collection process consisted of two online focus groups, during which participants responded to identical questions. Following established qualitative protocols (Corrao, 2000), the groups were intentionally kept homogeneous—comprising only researchers and lecturers—to promote open dialogue among peers. A moderator facilitated each session using a structured interview guide, beginning with opening and transition questions before leading into key thematic areas. At the conclusion of each session, the moderator summarized the main points and invited participants to offer final reflections. Each online focus group generally lasted approximately two hours. The questions asked in the focus group are showing in Table 7.1.

Table 7.1 Questions used to lead the focus group discussions

1. How are university organizations tackling the significant challenge of artificial intelligence?
2. What practices and policies have been implemented at your university to integrate AI?
3. What benefits do you see from using AI in the teaching-learning process and research?
4. What potential risks emerge from artificial intelligence in higher education?
5. What ethical issues should teachers and students consider when using AI in education?

Data Collection and Analysis Methods

This qualitative study utilized a thematic analysis approach. In particular, Barun and Clarke (2008) implemented thematic analysis within this framework. The data analysis involved five steps: familiarization with the data, initial coding, searching for themes, reviewing, and defining and naming themes. The data analysis included integrating interview content and closely analyzing the texts for trends. This process recognized the qualitative nature of interviews and their contributions. The next phase focused on coding, beginning with identifying key primary codes in the data. These codes were enumerated to provide a quantitative overview of their frequency. The primary codes aligned with the research questions, ensuring the analysis addressed the study's objectives. Similar codes were consolidated to streamline data and reduce redundancy. A crucial step was verifying that the number of codes was sufficient to capture the depth of the interview data. Finally, the created classes were revised by identifying similarities and differences among the codes. This process resulted in the arrangement of recognized themes, providing a structured and coherent framework for interpreting the findings.

Findings and Discussion

The analysis identified seven themes. These themes were: 1) AI Policies and Response Challenges in Higher Education; 2) AI Integration in Teaching and Learning Practices; 3) AI in Student Assessment: Balancing Transparency and Innovation; 4) Next-Gen Skills for Teaching, Learning, and Innovation; 5) Perceived Benefits of AI in Education: Enhancing Learning and Innovation; 6) Concerns and Perceived Risks: Dependency, Bias, and Decline of Critical Thinking; 7) Ethical Issues and Future Paths for AI Research in Education.

Theme 1: AI Policies and Response Challenges in Higher Education

In recent months, universities have begun adopting essential policies and strategies related to the use of artificial intelligence (AI) by students and researchers. Several faculties and departments have introduced workshops for educators, researchers, and students to highlight the opportunities presented by AI and promote ethical practices in its application to scientific research. As one focus group participant shared: "Recently, they started offering workshops for my department's students. They aim to help students benefit from AI and introduce ethical ways to use it in research."

Despite these efforts, the prevailing perception suggests that such initiatives are insufficient to address both current and anticipated challenges. Another participant noted:

> We need to have a serious and robust discussion about AI, strengthen its use, and, why not, establish standards for how we can use it in our research [...] We were introduced to some AI tools and how we can use them, how we can benefit from them in our study. But I don't believe there is a strong and serious discussion about those issues.

This theme reveals that institutional engagement with AI often remains task-oriented—focused on using tools to complete assignments or assist with research—while lacking a broader critical or meta-reflective perspective at the faculty and institutional levels. The discussion underscores the need for more transparent, analytical dialogue around the role of AI in education, particularly concerning how and why it should be used (Zanotti et al., 2024). AI should not be viewed merely as a technological tool, but as a catalyst for an epistemological paradigm shift. Emerging research is beginning to explore the deeper foundations of educational technology, including how knowledge is produced, how assumptions shape edtech development and innovation, and how controversies arise when AI is integrated into academic environments (Perrotta & Selwyn, 2020).

In this context, the Diffusion of Innovation Theory (DIT) offers a valuable framework for understanding how GAI is adopted and disseminated in higher education, highlighting the connections between innovation, communication channels, social systems, and time within different cultural contexts (Rogers et al., 2014). According to Jin et al. (2025),

DIT can illustrate the ways GAI can be incorporated into educational systems and assist in developing policy guidelines designed to optimize the advantages of this new technology while reducing its possible risks.

Theme 2: AI Integration in Teaching and Learning Practices

During the focus group discussion, it became apparent that expertise must be cultivated to effectively integrate artificial intelligence into instructional and research methodology modules, which remain in their developmental phases. As a researcher affirmed:

> We need to use artificial intelligence with students in the classroom; otherwise, they will use it without guidance, and it's important to utilize these tools effectively.

Integrating AI necessitates foundational knowledge and skills and an understanding of information and communication technology as applied to teaching. Teachers cannot guide students with AI unless they are first familiarized with it.

The prevailing view suggests that achieving a comprehensive understanding of how to effectively integrate AI and its implications for learning and social-emotional aspects is necessary. A participant added:

> We are exploring AI's technical potential in our learning system. Additionally, we want to understand and explain the emotional and social aspects of using AI to build confidence in producing effective learning outcomes. Therefore, we aim to develop a framework for the deeper integration of AI, but first, we need to grasp everything involved.

While ethical standards are essential for fostering trust in artificial intelligence systems, their existence alone does not ensure responsible use. Responsible implementation requires that individuals and institutions actively engage with, understand, and adopt these principles. Integrating AI into education calls for a structured approach that includes comprehensive teacher training, the cultivation of students' critical thinking skills, and targeted investments to bridge both technological and cultural divides. A proactive strategy in higher education can help mitigate the negative impacts and biases associated with AI in research, while also providing a roadmap for stakeholders—from educators to administrators—that highlights the importance of strategic planning in navigating the AI-driven transformation of academia (George & Wooden, 2023).

Theme 3: AI in Student Assessment: Balancing Transparency and Innovation

One of the most frequently discussed topics at the classroom level is the role of artificial intelligence in student assessment. Participants described various ways educators are using AI for grading, feedback, and assessment design—such as automated scoring systems and real-time performance analysis—to support evaluation practices. As one participant noted, "Our recent programs feature many tools primarily for evaluating student progress."

Participants emphasized the importance of transparency, particularly in essay-based assessments. One remarked, "We need to be more transparent about our expectations from students in our institute. Since our evaluations are predominantly essay-based, this transparency becomes crucial. We should communicate what resources students can or cannot use, as leaving this vague creates unnecessary difficulties. Students are also uncertain about what is permissible in their work."

Acknowledging the need for clear and structured rules to ensure assessment practices accurately reflect students' learning, some participants proposed a more integrated approach. This would involve enabling students to reflect on content and its relevance through collaborative tasks, presentations, and peer feedback. A researcher explained:

> We let the students use AI in whatever way they choose. So, we just give them a program and a weekly class. We set up the program and provided them with the outlines. When they all come next week, they will present their ideas, and we won't check what they write in the book or anything like that. Instead, we scored them based on their participation and how they presented their ideas...60% of the class was based on the scoreboard derived from class participation.

In contrast, others referenced more restrictive policies for students who use AI to produce written work. One participant explained: "We have a basic AI policy for students, and our regulations include a provision on this topic. In the curriculum, we need to define how to evaluate students who use AI. What are the limitations? Is it permissible or not? We must clarify the score if they utilize AI."

The focus groups shows the coexistence of two distinct approaches to AI in assessment: a mitigation approach and an integrative approach. The mitigation approach seeks to limit or eliminate AI use in evaluations by establishing strict standards and guidelines. These assessments often avoid AI involvement and aim to preserve authenticity by replicating real-world, professional skills. Tools like the AI Assessment Scale (AIAS) offer frameworks for ethically and transparently incorporating GenAI into assessment processes ("The Artificial Intelligence Assessment Scale (AIAS)," 2024; Perkins et al., 2024). The integrative approach, on the other hand, supports the development of innovative assessment strategies aligned with intended learning outcomes. By embedding AI thoughtfully into curriculum and instruction, this model promotes curriculum coherence, fosters critical thinking, self-regulated learning, and problem-solving, while also maintaining academic integrity through the responsible use of GenAI tools (Schultz et al., 2022; Bakare et al., 2023).

Theme 4: Next-Generation Skills for Teaching, Learning, and Innovation

Regarding the skills issue, participants emphasized the importance of continuous professional development to manage innovation effectively. In particular, there is a growing need to understand how AI works—examining its foundational principles to better grasp its limitations and risks (Gillani et al., 2023). As one participant noted: "We need to understand how you produce information, because otherwise, this kind of information feels like a black box to us. It doesn't represent fair play regarding the type of information we have access to." Thus, being competent in AI for researchers goes beyond simply using AI tools in their studies, teaching, or research activities. It also requires an effort to "open the black box" and understand how AI systems function. One participant explained:

> Understanding how AI works means examining who designs it, the values they hold, and how those values shape the content. There's confusion about whether designers are truly neutral and objective, especially since all AI-generated content ultimately reflects the input from its creators.

Another participant added:

> We need to be more aware of our actions and methods, because automation is a specific form of human–technology interaction. We have to think about what we are programming machines to do—and what behaviors machines, in turn, encourage us to produce.

Generational factors further complicate the skill landscape. Focus group participants confirmed findings from Chan and Lee (2023), which highlight differing perceptions of AI across Generation Z, Generation X, and Generation Y, as well as variations in their skillsets. Generation Z, for instance, is often praised for entrepreneurial problem-solving, fast information access, and adaptability. However, they tend to lack strong critical thinking and information literacy skills.

Findings from the focus groups also align with Gerlich's research (2025), which found a negative correlation between frequent AI tool use and critical thinking among younger users. This trend is attributed in part to increased cognitive offloading (Risko & Gilbert, 2016). Older students, by contrast, may start with lower digital proficiency but bring valuable life experience that helps them reflect more critically on AI use. As one participant shared:

> We have many older students, so those who come in later may face a generational issue. They might be less digitally proficient, but they have developed basic skills to think through certain issues. Younger generations are still in the learning process.

In sum, this discussion underscores the importance of helping students acquire foundational skills, tailoring the learning experience to different groups, and striking a balance between automation and critical thinking (Nguyen et al., 2024). One participant offered this insight: "Teachers should also indicate when AI should not be used for certain exercises or courses—and explain why. I'm trying to teach you the fundamental skills essential for your future use of AI."

Ultimately, the recommended strategy centers on raising student awareness and engagement in the learning process, while clarifying when and how to use AI appropriately for academic work.

Theme 5: Perceived Benefits of AI in Education: Enhancing Learning and Innovation

All the researchers interviewed agreed on the numerous benefits of AI in teaching and research. Chatbots, for instance, can significantly streamline responses to common student inquiries, granting students immediate access to a wide range of resources. This reduces the workload for both students and instructors, allowing them to focus more critical aspects of teaching and learning. As one participant noted, "It can generate insights and new ideas, helping students improve their critical thinking."

Educators can also use digital avatars to create interactive and immersive learning environments. These avatars—often representing historical figures, scientists, or subject-matter experts—offer students a more dynamic and engaging educational experience (Steele, 2023). One participant explained:

> We produce digital avatars … in our learning system, and AI generates an interface for a learning course based on the content. We also collect student feedback—for example, we take small steps by using a chatbot to answer common questions. Our next goal is to train AI to work solely with lecture materials. We aim to use generative AI to identify which teaching content can be incorporated into chatbot responses.

Another key benefit is the automation of repetitive and time-consuming tasks, which enables students to focus on more complex projects and develop higher-order thinking skills. AI supports student learning by handling routine tasks, thereby freeing up time for deeper exploration.

Additionally, AI can present diverse perspectives, fostering critical reflection and debate. This encourages students to engage with alternative viewpoints, expanding their intellectual horizons and enhancing their analytical abilities. One participant emphasized that AI tools open new opportunities for students to grasp more complex concepts. AI also simplifies academic tasks such as literature reviews and research storytelling. As one interviewee shared: "AI tools are assisting us in writing literature reviews, helping us understand the material and construct a coherent narrative—which used to be very difficult. Since we aim to publish internationally, we must write in English."

AI technologies also benefit non-native English speakers by improving their reading, writing, and comprehension skills, ultimately boosting engagement with academic content. As one participant remarked, "AI fascinates non-native speakers, especially when it helps with reading and writing English papers and understanding the study context.

The findings affirm what existing literature has highlighted: AI offers the potential to create more personalized and efficient learning experiences by supporting customization, reducing repetitive tasks, aiding translation, improving resource access, and fostering creative thinking (Algabri et al., 2021; Chaka, 2023; Boguslawski et al., 2025; Malik et al., 2023; Manditereza & Chamboko-Mpotaringa, 2024).

Interestingly, support for AI in evaluation processes did not emerge as a clear benefit. Instead, focus group participants raised concerns about its application in assessment, citing ongoing controversies regarding the consistency and validity of AI-generated feedback and its effectiveness in supporting genuine learning. These concerns echo recent studies (Gamage et al., 2023; Aad & Hardey, 2025).

Theme 6: Concerns and Perceived Risks: Dependency, Bias, and Decline of Critical Thinking

The benefits highlighted, however, also leave room for concerns and perceived risks: "Of course, it could be a powerful tool for developing critical thinking, but only if it's used as a complement to human judgment rather than, let's say, a replacement."

Recent studies indicate that participants emphasize how AI can reinforce existing biases and produce false or manipulated content (King, 2023; Leong & Zhang, 2025). One major concern is that students are becoming overly reliant on AI, which leads them to lose critical thinking skills and the ability to work independently (Zhang & Xu, 2025).

Additionally, there are concerns about the gradual decline in relationships and social engagement among students and researchers due to excessive use of AI, highlighting the need to balance its usage and return to a more embedded experience. A participant shared:

> It's reducing the depth of the relationship and social engagement. The keyword is balanced. We should find the balance between AI and real life. How to commit and to be connected, not very connected, and not to be disconnected. The main goal is to design a solution that fosters inclusivity. Still, we should maintain the authenticity of social relationships, and I don't know if this is possible.

Additionally, using AI in our teaching environment and methodologies influences students' learning processes along their unique learning paths:

> This point is significant because artificial intelligence can diminish students' efforts in shaping their learning experiences, reducing their opportunities to practice essential skills, attitudes, talents, and resources.

Another critical element that has emerged and has already been highlighted in the literature is the friction in the learning process (Malaguti et al., 2025; Chen & Schmidt, 2024; Kirschner & Hendrick, 2020). While AI can simplify learning (*frictionless*), an overly fluid experience may diminish the necessity for active engagement, ultimately compromising the depth of understanding: Even in research, too much of a frictionless experience can lead to a lack of depth and originality in academic work, compromising the validity and credibility of findings. A participant pointed out that:

> These tools have a customer service ideology. They tend to present solutions that guide us in certain ways and not others, making some knowledge more visible while rendering others more invisible. They promote some critical aspects of our thinking but not others. This creates a different type of learning that undoubtedly has positive and negative aspects.

Theme 7: Ethical Issues and Future Paths for AI Research in Education

From the discussions on the opportunities and risks associated with AI in education, a range of ethical challenges emerged—raising concerns and points of attention that should guide future behaviors and research agendas.

Participants were particularly concerned about privacy violations and the potential exposure of sensitive information when AI is used in professional and educational contexts. One participant noted that many students feel uncomfortable with how AI systems collect and utilize their personal data.

In addition, participants highlighted the difficulty of distinguishing between content generated by AI and the inherent biases or inaccuracies that such content may contain. Concerns were also raised about growing social disparities, the risk of disconnection from reality, and the urgent need for transparency in how AI systems function, particularly given their perceived lack of clarity and integrity. On participant pointed out:

> One major issue is academic integrity. There are concerns that students use AI to bypass personal effort, which could compromise authentic learning. Another challenge is equitable access to technology, as students from less privileged backgrounds may be disadvantaged.

Conclusion

The impact of AI on the education system is both profound and far-reaching. Human agents, machines, institutions, and environmental factors actively generate new knowledge through a sophisticated, contextualized, embodied, distributed, and relational process. While this study primarily explored themes inductively and narratively, Table 7.2 reorganizes the sub-themes into a deductive framework to provide an actionable, easy-to-interpret overview of the opportunities, risks, and ethical challenges associated with AI that are facing practitioners in Europe and beyond.

Tapping into these AI opportunities, mitigating risks, and navigating ethical pitfalls will require a collective effort within the scientific community to critically examine the nature of this paradigm and establish a methodological framework that includes ontological and epistemic dimensions. This framework would respond more effectively to ongoing ethical and socio-political challenges. Therefore, universities and the broader educational system must reassess and create platforms for social critique, facilitating open inquiry into the purposes and roles of digital technology in scientific research processes.

Our exploratory study aims to thoroughly investigate the main emerging themes related to AI in higher education and the changes in research and teaching methods resulting from AI. It also identifies the key implications for academic research and acknowledges the researcher's subjectivity in navigating the ongoing disruptive transition.

Our findings suggest that a more comprehensive, epistemological, and relational approach to educational development is essential for addressing emerging challenges. The complexities of living and working as scholars in a digital world have significant implications for how knowledge is created and shared. Data literacy skills become meaningful and applicable when researchers deepen their thinking discipline. This discipline involves

Table 7.2 Opportunities, risks, and ethical challenges

Primary subtheme	*Secondary subtheme*	*Concepts*
Opportunities	Teaching/ Learning Practices	Support educators in creating more engaging and personalized learning experiences, benefiting both teachers and students (e.g., digital avatars) (P10, P1, P5, P6); use of chatbot to answer students' usual questions (P10); Providing instant access to vast amount of information of resources (P7); Generation of some insight and new idea (P7); Streamline repetitive and time-consuming tasks, freeing up time for deeper learning and exploration (P1, P5, P2); Encourage reflection and the ability to argue by presenting multiple perspectives, inviting users to consider alternative viewpoints (P7)
	Research work	Simplify complex academic processes, such as literature reviews and research storytelling, allowing students to focus on higher-level thinking (P1, P5); opportunity for non-native English speakers to improve their reading, writing, and comprehension skills, enhancing their ability to engage with academic materials (P5, P1); empowering researchers to explore new ideas (P5, P2); AI should enhance human judgment instead of replacing it (P7).
Risks	Teaching/ Learning Practices	Uncorrected information and bias in contents (P1); Poor reliability of sources and undermine critical thinking, creativity and student ability to work independently and with integrity (P1, P10, P8); Reduction of relationship and social engagement of students (P3); Reduction of opportunities for students to build their learning process ad to practice and refine essential skills (P10); AI and the frictionless experience in the learning process (P4); Importance of prior knowledge and the theoretical foundation for critically using AI (P7, P4, P10); Conformism (P7).
	Research work	Negative impact of AI on research work quality if not used appropriately (P1, P3, P10, P5); AI and the frictionless experience in the research process (P4, P10)

(*continued*)

Table 7.2 (continued)

Primary subtheme	*Secondary subtheme*	*Concepts*
Ethical challenges	Concerns	Fear of privacy violations and the leakage of sensitive information due to AI usage in professional environments (P1); Challenges in discerning AI-generated content and its potential biases or inaccuracies (P3, P1, P10); Rising inequalities, risk of losing touch with reality (P3); AI as black box, we need to know how AI works (P7, P4).
	Emerging Issues	The context in which AI is used raises ethical questions and highlights the values associated with that technology. The framework surrounding AI also reflects its value implications (P4, P10); AI and the reshaping of social relations and time dimension (P10); Impact of cultural dimension in the AI usage (P4, P5).

Note: The label *Pn* following each concept denotes the participant's code number from the interview
Source: Author's analysis

reflecting in and on action, enabling the exploration of reality by questioning preconceived knowledge while being aware of participation in a scientific community and a specific cultural context. It also requires a readiness to reflect on experience and thought.

We need to move beyond the dichotomy of viewing technological advancements as symbols of progress and expanded possibilities for humanity, versus perceiving these innovations as potential threats to human autonomy and freedom. A third perspective should highlight the importance of promoting ethical decision-making and critical thinking within governance processes. As noted in the focus groups, this objective may be achieved by critically examining various factors, such as technological advancements, political and economic dynamics, and historical contexts, that influence the reconfiguration of learning and literacy and fundamentally shape the evolution and adaptation of education systems.

Competing Interests The study was part of the Jean Monnet Erasmus+ Project *BuTH-AI—Building Trust in Human-Centric Artificial Intelligence* (Project number: 101127627). The agreement was duly signed on September 13, 2023

Ethics Approval All research activities of the BuTH-AI project respected all individuals involved, as well as their rights, interests, dignity, freedom, and privacy, in accordance with the principles of the European Commission (EC, 2024).

Try It Out: Learn about European and non-European participation in Erasmus

Did you know Non-European countries can participate in the the European Union's flagship interntional exchange program, Erasmus?

De Angelis's chapter was developed within the context of an Erasmus+ project. While many non-European readers may be familiar with Erasmus as a flagship EU exchange program, fewer may realize that numerous non-EU countries—referred to as *Partner Countries* within the Erasmus+ framework—are fully eligible to participate in a wide range of program activities. These include higher education, youth engagement, and capacity-building initiatives. Although Erasmus+ was originally designed to support mobility and cooperation within the European Union, it has since expanded globally. Institutions and organizations from outside the EU can apply for funding by partnering with *Program Countries* (EU Member States and select associated nations).

Non-EU participants can engage in international credit mobility, joint degree programs, and cross-border digital collaboration projects. The program emphasizes four key horizontal priorities: inclusion and diversity, environmental sustainability, democratic participation, and—critically—digital transformation. Erasmus+ supports projects that advance digital literacy, online and blended learning, and educational technology innovation.

One of the U.S.-based editors of this volume first connected with Maria Chiara De Angelis through their mutual participation in an Erasmus+-affiliated research symposium, illustrating the program's powerful role in fostering meaningful international academic collaboration. In a further example of the program's reach, the editors' students collaborated with Finnish students through an Erasmus+-supported partnership with Laurea

University in Finland. Together, they participated in a research and project presentation symposium focused on how businesses in both the United States and Finland are using artificial intelligence. Their collaborative findings were published in *Laurea Publications 223*, which is available online: https://www.theseus.fi/bitstream/handle/10024/859016/Laurea%20Publications%20223.pdf?sequence=2&isAllowed=y. This initiative reflects Erasmus+'s commitment to advancing digital transformation through global educational exchange.

Non-EU institutions interested in participating are encouraged to consult the annually updated Erasmus+ Programme Guide and learn more at the official website: https://erasmus-plus.ec.europa.eu.

Questions for Reflection and Discussion

1. What parallels do you see between the researchers' experiences in this chapter and your own institution's efforts to engage with AI in higher education?
2. In your local context, what opportunities or barriers exist for faculty and researchers to shape how AI is integrated into teaching, learning, or research?
3. How does your institution support (or limit) cross-border or interdisciplinary collaboration on emerging technologies like AI? Are you aware of programs like Erasmus+ that can help facilitate these partnerships?
4. How do ethical concerns raised in the chapter—such as inclusion, transparency, or academic freedom—resonate with challenges you're seeing in your own work or learning environment?

References

Aad, S., & Hardey, M. (2025). Generative AI: hopes, controversies and the future of faculty roles in education. *Quality Assurance in Education, 33*(2), 267–282. https://doi.org/10.1108/QAE-02-2024-0043

Abbasi, B. N., Wu, Y., & Luo, Z. (2025). Exploring the impact of artificial intelligence on curriculum development in global higher education institutions. *Education and Information Technologies, 30*(1), 547–581. https://doi.org/10.1007/s10639-024-13113-z

Abbass, H. A. (2019). Social integration of artificial intelligence: Functions, automation allocation logic and human-autonomy trust. *Cognitive Computation, 11*(2), 159–171. https://doi.org/10.1007/s12559-018-9619-0

Alam, A. (2023). Harnessing the power of AI to create intelligent tutoring systems for enhanced classroom experience and improved learning outcomes. In *Intelligent communication technologies and virtual mobile networks* (pp. 571–591). Springer. https://doi.org/10.1007/978-981-99-1767-9_42

Algabri, H. K., Kharade, K. G., & Kamat, R. K. (2021). Promise, threats, and personalization in higher education with artificial intelligence. *Webology, 18*(6), 2129–2139. https://www.webology.org/abstract.php?id=1965

Al-Zahrani, A. M. (2024). Unveiling the shadows: Beyond the hype of AI in education. *Heliyon, 10*(9). https://doi.org/10.1016/j.heliyon.2024.e30696

The Artificial Intelligence Assessment Scale (AIAS): A Framework for Ethical Integration of Generative AI in Educational Assessment. (2024). *Journal of University Teaching and Learning Practice, 21*(06). https://doi.org/10.53761/q3azde36

Baidoo-Anu, D., & Ansah, L. O. (2023). Education in the era of generative artificial intelligence (AI): Understanding the potential benefits of ChatGPT in promoting teaching and learning. *Journal of AI, 7*(1), 52–62. https://doi.org/10.2139/ssrn.4337484

Bakare, O. D., Oladokun, T., Quadri, G. O., & Idowu-Davies, T. O. (2023). ChatGPT and other generative Artificial Intelligence (AI) tools in teaching and learning as integrative pathways to contemporary university education. In J. Keengwe (Ed.), *Creative AI tools and ethical implications in teaching and learning* (pp. 168–180). IGI Global Scientific Publishing. https://doi.org/10.4018/979-8-3693-0205-7.ch009

Barros, A., Prasad, A., & Śliwa, M. (2023). Generative artificial intelligence and academia: Implication for research, teaching and service. *Management Learning, 54*(5), 597–604. https://doi.org/10.1177/13505076231201445

Berente, N., Gu, B., Recker, J., & Santhanam, R. (2021). Managing artificial intelligence. *MIS Quarterly, 45*(3), 1433–1450. https://hdl.handle.net/2144/44096

Boguslawski, S., Deer, R., & Dawson, M. G. (2025). Programming education and learner motivation in the age of generative AI: student and educator perspectives. *Information and Learning Sciences, 126*(1/2), 91–109. https://doi.org/10.1108/ILS-10-2023-0163

Braun, V., & Clarke, V. (2008). Using thematic analysis in psychology. *Qualitative Research in Psychology, 3*(2), 77–101. https://doi.org/10.1191/1478088706qp063oa

Chaka, C. (2023). Fourth industrial revolution—A review of applications, prospects, and challenges for artificial intelligence, robotics and blockchain in higher education. *Research and Practice in Technology Enhanced Learning, 18*(2), 1–39. https://doi.org/10.58459/rptel.2023.18002

Chan, C. K. Y. (2023). A comprehensive AI policy education framework for university teaching and learning. *International Journal of Educational Technology in Higher Education, 20*(1), 38. https://doi.org/10.1186/s41239-023-00408-3

Chan, C. K. Y., & Lee, K. K. W. (2023). The AI generation gap: Are Gen Z students more interested in adopting generative AI such as ChatGPT in teaching and learning than their Gen X and millennial generation teachers? *Smart Learning Environments, 10*, 60. https://doi.org/10.1186/s40561-023-00269-3

Chan, C. K. Y., & Tsi, L. H. Y. (2023). The AI revolution in education: Will AI replace or assist teachers in higher education? arXiv.Org, abs/2305.01185. https://doi.org/10.48550/arXiv.2305.01185

Chen, Z., & Schmidt, R. (2024). Exploring a behavioral model of "Positive Friction" in Human-AI interaction. In A. Marcus, E. Rosenzweig, & M. M. Soares (Eds.), *Design, user experience, and usability. HCII 2024* (Lecture Notes in Computer Science) (Vol. 14713). Springer. https://doi.org/10.1007/978-3-031-61353-1_1

Corrao, S. (2000). *Il focus group*. FrancoAngeli.

Cotton, D. R., Cotton, P. A., & Shipway, J. R. (2024). Chatting and cheating: Ensuring academic integrity in the era of ChatGPT. *Innovations in Education and Teaching International, 61*(2), 228–239. https://doi.org/10.1080/14703297.2023.2190148

De Angelis, M. C. (2024). The impact of digitalisation in scientific research: Risks, opportunities and ethical challenges. *Quaderni Di comunità. Persone, Educazione E Welfare Nella Società, 5.0*(3), 195–226. https://doi.org/10.61007/QdC.2023.3.159

De Angelis, M. C., & Velardi, A. (2024). E-Research: Emerging challenges and ethical issues in the algorithms age. *SOCIOLOGIA, 3*, 28–33. ISSN: 0038-0156

ERC. (2023). *Current position of the ERC Scientific Council on AI*. https://erc.europa.eu/sites/default/files/2024-03/report-AI.pdf

Fukushima, K. (1980). Neocognitron: A self-organizing neural network model for a mechanism of pattern recognition unaffected by shift in position. *Biological Cybernetics, 36*, 193–202. https://link.springer.com/article/10.1007/BF00344251

Galih, A. P., & Barát, Á. H. (2024). Data literacy and artificial intelligence in higher education. In O. Eybers & A. Muller (Eds.), *AI approaches to literacy in higher education* (pp. 150–168). IGI Global Scientific Publishing. https://doi.org/10.4018/979-8-3693-1054-0.ch007

Gamage, K. A. A., Dehideniya, S. C. P., Xu, Z., & Tang, X. (2023). ChatGPT and higher education assessments: More opportunities than concerns? *Journal of Applied Learning and Teaching, 6*(2), 358–369. https://doi.org/10.37074/jalt.2023.6.2.32

Gao, C. A., Howard, F. M., Markov, N. S., et al. (2023). Comparing scientific abstracts generated by ChatGPT to real abstracts with detectors and blinded human reviewers. *npj Digital Medicine, 6*, 75. https://doi.org/10.1038/s41746-023-00819-6

George, B., & Wooden, O. (2023). Managing the strategic transformation of higher education through artificial intelligence. *Administrative Sciences, 13*(9), 196. https://doi.org/10.3390/admsci13090196

Gerlich, M. (2025). AI tools in society: Impacts on cognitive offloading and the future of critical thinking. *Societies, 15*(1), 6. https://doi.org/10.3390/soc15010006

Ghnemat, R., Shaout, A., & Abrar, M. (2022). Higher education transformation for artificial intelligence revolution: Transformation framework. *International Journal of Emerging Technologies in Learning, 17*(19), 224–241. https://doi.org/10.3991/ijet.v17i19.33309

Gillani, N., Eynon, R., Chiabaut, C., & Finkel, K. (2023). Unpacking the "Black Box" of AI in education. *Educational Technology & Society, 26*(1), 99–111. https://doi.org/10.48550/arXiv.2301.01602

Grassini, S. (2023). Shaping the future of education: Exploring the potential and consequences of AI and ChatGPT in educational settings. *Education Sciences (Basel), 13*(7), 692. https://doi.org/10.3390/educsci13070692

Javaid, M., Haleem, A., Singh, R. P., Khan, S., & Khan, I. H. (2023). Unlocking the opportunities through ChatGPT Tool towards ameliorating the education system. *BenchCouncil Transactions on Benchmarks, Standards and Evaluations, 3*(2), 100115. https://doi.org/10.1016/j.tbench.2023.100115

Jin, Y., Yan, L., Echeverria, V., Gašević, D., & Martinez-Maldonado, R. (2025). Generative AI in higher education: A global perspective of institutional adoption policies and guidelines. *Computers and Education: Artificial Intelligence, 8*, 100348. 10.48550/arXiv.2405.11800.

King, M. R. (2023). A conversation on artificial intelligence, chatbots, and plagiarism in higher education. *Cellular and Molecular Bioengineering, 16*, 1–2. https://doi.org/10.1007/s12195-022-00754-8

Kirschner, P. A., & Hendrick, C. (2020). *How learning happens: Seminal works in educational psychology and what they mean in practice*. Routledge. https://doi.org/10.4324/9780429061523

Kok, C. L., Ho, C. K., Koh, Y. Y., Thanh, N. T. C., & Teo, T. H. (2024). Collaborative learning environments facilitated by AI technologies. In TENCON 2024–2024 IEEE Region 10 Conference (TENCON) (pp. 1841–1844). IEEE. https://doi.org/10.1109/TENCON61640.2024.10902974

Krause, S., Panchal, B. H., & Ubhe, N. (2025). Evolution of learning: Assessing the transformative impact of generative AI on higher education. *Frontiers of Digital Education, 2*, 21. https://doi.org/10.1007/s44366-025-0058-7

Leong, W. Y., & Zhang, J. B. (2025). AI on academic integrity and plagiarism detection. *ASM Science Journal, 20*(1), 10.32802/asmscj.2025.1918.

Lin, H., & Chen, Q. (2024). Artificial intelligence (AI)—Integrated educational applications and college students' creativity and academic emotions: students and teachers' perceptions and attitudes. *BMC Psychol, 12*, 487. https://doi.org/10.1186/s40359-024-01979-0

Lund, B. D., Lee, T. H., Mannuru, N. R., & et al. (2025). AI and academic integrity: Exploring student perceptions and implications for higher education. *Journal of Academic Ethics.* Advance online publication. https://doi.org/10.1007/s10805-025-09613-3

Malaguti, P., Karran, A. J., Le, D., Mortin, H., Coursaris, C. K., Sénécal, S., & Léger, P. M. (2025). Investigating interaction friction in generative AI: Improving user experience and decision-making. *SIGHCI 2024 Proceedings, 26.* https://aisel.aisnet.org/sighci2024/26

Malik, A. R., Pratiwi, Y., Andajani, K., Numertayasa, I. W., Suharti, S., & Darwis, A. (2023). Exploring artificial intelligence in academic essay: Higher education student's perspective. *International Journal of Educational Research Open, 5*, 100296. https://doi.org/10.1016/j.ijedro.2023.100296

Manditereza, B., & Chamboko-Mpotaringa, M. (2024). Generative AI and its implications for higher education students' creativity. In *Impacts of generative AI on creativity in higher education* (pp. 177–192). IGI Global. https://doi.org/10.4018/979-8-3693-2418-9.ch007

McCarthy, J., Minsky, M. L., Rochester, N., & Shannon, C. E. (2006). A proposal for the Dartmouth summer research project on artificial intelligence, August 31, 1955. *AI Magazine, 27*(4), 12. https://doi.org/10.1609/aimag.v27i4.1904

McGuire, A. (2023). Leveraging ChatGPT for rethinking plagiarism, digital literacy, and the ethics of Co-authorship in higher education: A position paper and comparative critical reflection of composing processes. *Irish Journal of Technology Enhanced Learning, 7*(2), 21–31. https://doi.org/10.22554/ijtel.v7i2.131

Michel-Villarreal, R., Vilalta-Perdomo, E., Salinas-Navarro, D. E., Thierry-Aguilera, R., & Gerardou, F. S. (2023). Challenges and opportunities of generative AI for higher education, as explained by ChatGPT. *Educ. Sci. (Basel), 13*(9), 856. https://doi.org/10.3390/educsci13090856

Nguyen, A., Kremantzis, M., Essien, A., Petrounias, I., & Hosseini, S. (2024). Enhancing student engagement through Artificial Intelligence (AI): Understanding the basics, opportunities, and challenges. *Journal of University*

Teaching and Learning Practice, 21(6), 1–13. https://search.informit.org/doi/10.3316/informit.T2024092900003101199694011

Perkins, M. (2023). Academic integrity considerations of AI large language models in the post-pandemic era: ChatGPT and beyond. *Journal of University Teaching and Learning Practice, 20*(2), 1–24. https://search.informit.org/doi/10.3316/informit.T2024111300009591751711095

Perkins, M., Furze, L., Roe, J., & MacVaugh, J. (2024). The Artificial Intelligence Assessment Scale (AIAS): A framework for ethical integration of generative AI in educational assessment. Journal of University Teaching and Learning. *Practice, 21*(6), 49–66. https://doi.org/10.53761/q3azde36

Perrotta, C., & Selwyn, N. (2020). Deep learning goes to school: Toward a relational understanding of AI in education. *Learning, Media and Technology, 45*(3), 251–269. https://doi.org/10.1080/17439884.2020.1686017

Risko, E. F., & Gilbert, S. J. (2016). Cognitive Offloading. *Trends in Cognitive Sciences, 20*, 676–688. https://doi.org/10.1016/j.tics.2016.07.002

Rogers, E. M., Singhal, A., & Quinlan, M. M. (2014). Diffusion of innovations. In *An integrated approach to communication theory and research* (pp. 432–448). Routledge.

Schultz, M., Young, K., Gunning, T., & Harvey, M. L. (2022). Defining and measuring authentic assessment: A case study in the context of tertiary science. *Assessment & Evaluation in Higher Education, 47*(1), 77–94. https://doi.org/10.1080/02602938.2021.1887811

Silverman, D. (2013). *Doing Qualitative Research: A Practical Handbook* (4th ed.). Sage Publications.

Sozon, M., Sia, B. C., Pok, W. F., & Alkharabsheh, O. H. M. (2024). Academic integrity violations in higher education: A systematic literature review from 2013–2023. *Journal of Applied Research in Higher Education*, Vol. ahead-of-print No. ahead-of-print. https://doi.org/10.1108/JARHE-12-2023-0559

Steele, J. L. (2023). To GPT or not GPT? Empowering our students to learn with AI. *Computers and Education: Artificial Intelligence, 5*, 100160. https://doi.org/10.1016/j.caeai.2023.100160

Strauss, A., & Corbin, J. (2008). *Basics of qualitative research: Techniques and procedures for developing grounded theory* (3rd ed.). SAGE Publications.

Su, J., & Yang, W. (2023). Unlocking the power of ChatGPT: A framework for applying generative AI in education. ECNU Review of Education, 6(3), 355-366. https://doi.org/10.1177/20965311231168423 (Original work published 2023)

Šumak, B., et al. (2024). AI-based education tools for enabling inclusive education: Challenges and benefits. In *2024, 47th MIPRO ICT and Electronics Convention (MIPRO)* (pp. 472–477). IEEE. https://doi.org/10.1109/MIPRO60963.2024.10569714

Tripathi, A., & Thakar, S. V. (2024). Ethical use of AI For academic integrity: Preventing plagiarism and cheating. *Ethical Frameworks in Special Education: A Guide for Researchers, 91.*

Turing, A. M. (1950). Computing machinery and intelligence. *Mind, 59*(236), 433–460. https://doi.org/10.1093/mind/LIX.236.433

Udeh, C. G. (2025). The role of generative AI in personalized learning for higher education. *World Journal of Advanced Engineering Technology and Sciences, 14*(2), 205–207. https://doi.org/10.30574/wjaets.2025.14.2.0077

Välimaa, J. (1998). Culture and identity in higher education research. *Higher Education, 36*(2), 119–138.

Välimaa, J. (2008). Cultural studies in higher education research. In J. Välimaa & O. H. Ylijoki (Eds.), *Cultural perspectives on higher education*. Springer. https://doi.org/10.1007/978-1-4020-6604-7_2

Van Audenhove, L., Vermeire, L., Van den Broeck, W., & Demeulenaere, A. (2024). Data literacy in the new EU DigComp 2.2 framework how DigComp defines competences on artificial intelligence, internet of things and data. *Information and Learning Sciences, 125*(5/6), 406–436. https://doi.org/10.1108/ILS-06-2023-0072

Wayahdi, M. R., & Zaki, M. (2025). The role of AI in diagnosing student learning needs: Solutions for more inclusive education. *International Journal of Educational Insights and Innovations, 2*(1), 1–7. https://ijedins.technolabs.co.id/index.php/ijedins/article/view/6

Yu, H. (2023). Reflection on whether Chat GPT should be banned by academia from the perspective of education and teaching. *Frontiers in Psychology, 14*, 1181712. https://doi.org/10.3389/fpsyg.2023.1181712

Zaman, B. U. (2023). Transforming education through AI, benefits, risks, and ethical considerations. *TechRxiv*. https://doi.org/10.36227/techrxiv.24231583.v1

Zanotti, G., Chiffi, D., & Schiaffonati, V. (2024). AI-related risk: An epistemological approach. *Philosophy & Technology, 37*, 66. https://doi.org/10.1007/s13347-024-00755-7

Zhai, C., Wibowo, S., & Li, L. D. (2024). The effects of over-reliance on AI dialogue systems on students' cognitive abilities: A systematic review. *Smart Learning Environments, 11*(1), 28. https://doi.org/10.1186/s40561-024-00316-7

Zhang, L., & Xu, J. (2025). The paradox of self-efficacy and technological dependence: Unraveling generative AI's impact on university students' task completion. *The Internet and Higher Education, 65*, 100978. https://doi.org/10.1016/j.iheduc.2024.100978

Zhang, S., Zhao, X., Zhou, T., et al. (2024). Do you have AI dependency? The roles of academic self-efficacy, academic stress, and performance expectations on problematic AI usage behavior. *International Journal of Educational Technology in Higher Education, 21*, 34. https://doi.org/10.1186/s41239-024-00467-0

CHAPTER 8

Cicada Safari: Mapping Insects with Citizen Science and AI

Gene Kritsky, Oliver Oniate, and Rebecca J. Allen

Introduction

Citizen science is when people help collect or sort data for scientific projects, such as snapping photos of plants, tracking wildlife sightings, or identifying stars in telescope images (Fraisl et al., 2025). One of the oldest examples of citizen science was to determine when and where periodical cicadas emerged (Kritsky, 2020). Periodical cicadas are insects with piercing-sucking mouthparts and belong to the insect order *Hemiptera* (the group that also includes true bugs, lanternflies, and stink bugs). Although there are 3400 species of cicadas worldwide, the seven periodical cicada species with their red eyes and orange-colored wing veins only occur in the eastern United States. Periodical cicadas are further separated into year classes called broods, with life cycles of seventeen or thirteen years (Kritsky, 2021).

G. Kritsky (✉) • O. Oniate • R. J. Allen
Center for IT Engagement (cITe), Mount St. Joseph University,
Cincinnati, OH, USA
e-mail: gene.krtisky@msj.edu; oliver.oniate@msj.edu; rebecca.allen@msj.edu

R. J. Allen, A. Nakonechnyi (eds.), *Using and Understanding AI in Higher Education*,
https://doi.org/10.1007/978-3-031-99754-9_8

When periodical cicadas emerge, they do so in very large numbers (Fig. 8.1), which attracts considerable public attention.

When the periodical cicadas emerged in 1634 at Plymouth Colony, the Pilgrims took notice and recorded their appearance. The cicadas also sang so loudly that people could not ignore them, and then, as quickly as they appeared, they disappear for 17 or 13 years. There was considerable confusion about cicadas in the two centuries that followed the 1634 emergence. These insects were thought to be locusts, and there was doubt about the length of their life cycle. When scientists started to take notice, the patterns of their life cycles and distributions were discerned. Today, the emergence of periodical cicadas is a predictable event, like waiting for a total eclipse of the sun or the return of Halley's Comet. However, it was not clear how many broods there were or what the distribution of the broods was. That changed when the entomologist Gideon B. Smith started in the 1840s to use citizen science to learn where periodical cicadas were emerging (Kritsky, 2021).

Fig. 8.1 A group of periodical cicadas. (Photograph by Gene Kritsky)

Smith was a resident of Baltimore, Maryland, and he was working as the assistant to the editor of the newspaper *The American Farmer*. It was through this connection that Smith learned about periodical cicadas from the writings of the physician Dr. Nathaniel Potter. Potter first noticed the periodical cicadas during their 1783 emergence, and he decided to "jump" into cicada research "with all enthusiasm." However, his patient load was too large for him to do any real research during the next two emergences in 1800 and again in 1817. Potter was disappointed that scientific knowledge of periodical cicadas had not advanced since 1783 (Potter, 1839). He lamented the lack of information in a short article he wrote in 1829 and published in *The American Farmer*. Gideon Smith, in his role as assistant to the editor at that time, read Potter's paper. The now 64-year-old Potter needed help when the cicadas next emerged in 1834, so he enlisted Smith to help with his research. In 1839, Potter wrote:

> As [my] professional avocations would not permit [me] to devote [my] whole time to the [study of cicadas], it became necessary to call in the aid of a colleague whose knowledge of entomology, and industry could be relied on. These qualifications were found and well exemplified in Mr. Gideon B. Smith. Should our labours reflect any light on so obscure a subject, the credit is equally due to him. (Potter, 1893 as cited by Kritsky, 2020, p. 50)

With Smith's help, Potter published the first stand-alone publication on periodical cicadas, *Notes on the Locusta*, in 1839. This publication included the first color illustrations of the cicadas (Potter, 1839). Although Potter died in 1843, Smith continued the work of mapping the distribution of periodical cicada emergences. Smith accomplished this on a much larger scale than Potter by writing letters to national newspapers asking their readers to write him if they saw periodical cicadas emerging in their areas. Smaller local papers would reprint Smith's letters, thus increasing their coverage. By the time of Smith's death in 1867, he had documented the existence of all the broods through this early use of citizen science. Smith's work earned him a national reputation, and his efforts extended the continuity of cicada records through the mid-nineteenth century (Kritsky, 2020).

It was the Bureau of Entomology at the United States Department of Agriculture in 1902 that created the first national campaign to encourage citizens to submit cicada records for what is now called Brood X (Ten).

The USDA, under the leadership of L. O. Howard and Charles Marlatt, sent out 15,000 letters to superintendents of schools, postmasters, and railway station conductors asking if cicadas had emerged in their locations. They also led a media campaign, issuing USDA press releases that asked the public to send in observations of cicada sightings (Kritsky, 2020).

The USDA's 1902 campaign for cicada records received 992 replies, the largest dataset up to that time. These records, combined with Smith's lists, provided the foundation for where cicada emergences would occur (see Fig. 8.2).

The USDA continued the solicitation of periodical cicada records with variable success until 1940. World War II interrupted the citizen science collection of cicada records, and it fell to university entomologists to continue the mapping efforts within their states. Fortunately, all the USDA records for two of the largest broods were compiled and published in

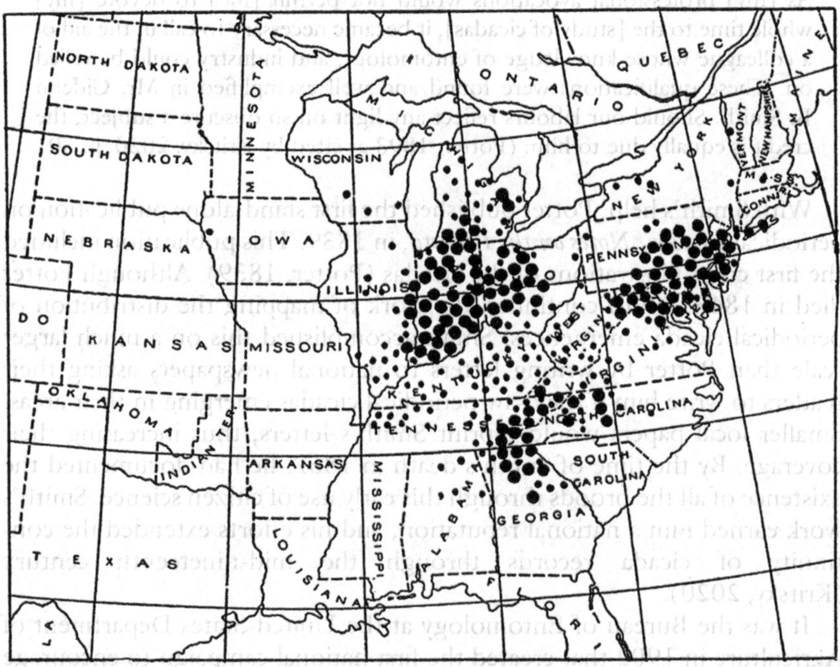

Fig. 8.2 The 1902 periodical cicada emergence mapped with the USDA 1902 data

1935 for Brood X and in 1940 for Brood XIV. These, combined with the efforts of several individual entomologists, created distribution maps that are still used today. There are several problems with these maps: they are not very granular (often being county-level records), and the surveys were incomplete in their coverage, not documenting several smaller broods (Kritsky, 2021a).

A fundamental problem with all the records from Smith's 1843–1867 work, the USDA records, and several isolated state surveys was the lack of specimens or voucher photographs. Were people really reporting periodical cicadas, or were they reporting annual cicadas? How did the USDA verify the accuracy of the historic records? They didn't. They accepted the assertion that the reports were accurate. For future research, entomologists needed more than a dot on a map. They needed a way to check the data for accuracy.

What has changed since Smith's pioneering work, of course, is the advent of modern communication technologies—and more recently, the rise of artificial intelligence (AI) as a tool for scientific analysis. Whereas nineteenth-century researchers relied on handwritten letters and newspaper reprints to track cicada sightings, today's scientists have access to geotagged images and real-time public input through mobile apps. But while this technological shift makes it easier than ever to gather data, it also introduces new challenges: the sheer volume of submissions can quickly overwhelm researchers, and verifying the accuracy of each observation remains essential. This is where AI offers transformative potential. With tools like computer vision and machine learning, scientists can now train algorithms to recognize species in photos, detect patterns in emergence data, and flag possible errors for human review. As Fraisl et al. (2025) note, AI can enhance citizen science by improving data quality and making large-scale participation more manageable. In the case of periodical cicadas, a unique collaboration between entomologists, students, and the public is beginning to demonstrate how these technologies can work together. In the following sections, we explore how the Cicada Safari project used artificial intelligence to scale up citizen science, improve data verification, and engage students in shaping the tools that help us understand one of nature's most remarkable phenomena.

Development of the Cicada Safari App

In Chap. 3, this book pointed out that the advent of AI systems as we know them today would not be possible without the internet and modern hardware. The iPhone was released in 2007, and with subsequent improvements—including cameras, built-in GPS capabilities, and apps designed specifically to facilitate citizen-science projects—there was now a widely available device in the hands of tens of thousands of people, enabling them to help map scientific phenomena. GPS-powered location accuracy, combined with photos to back up observations, represented a major leap forward.

Drawing on these technological advances, the Cicada Safari app (Fig. 8.3) was created by the Center for IT Engagement (cITe) at Mount St. Joseph University. cITe began designing Cicada Safari during the spring of 2018. Key to its success would be its ease of use.

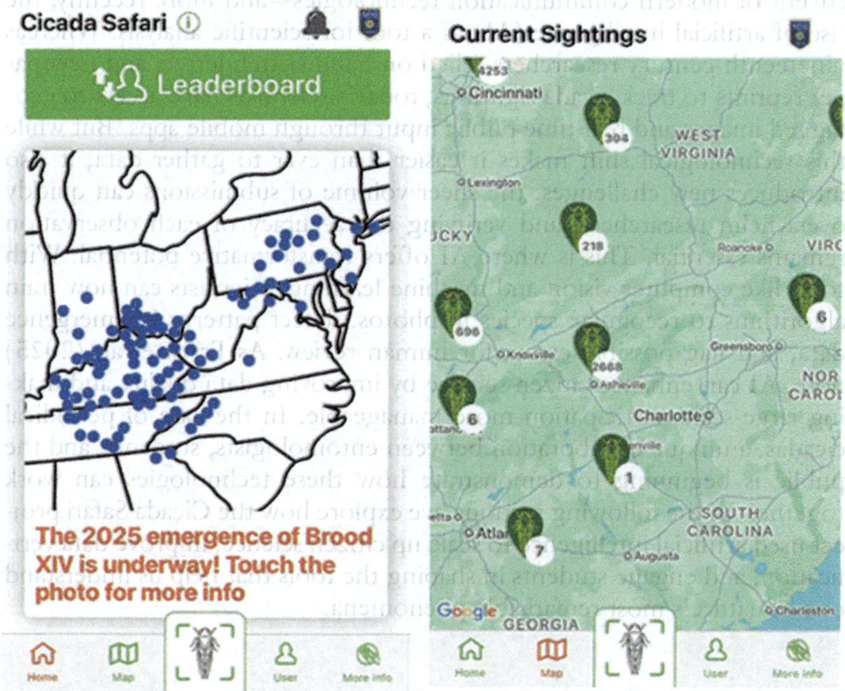

Fig. 8.3 The example screen shots of the Cicada Safari app

To launch the development process, the team first created a storyboard covering login, information on periodical cicadas, how to take a good photograph, opening the camera, taking the photograph with metadata, and photograph submission. We also outlined what we wanted to receive, including the photograph, date, longitude, latitude, username, the photograph's URL, and whether the photo was of a periodical or annual cicada.

There were other apps used to identify and map wildlife, but these apps often relied on users inputting details such as location information. In contrast, users of Cicada Safari would only need to take pictures. The app relies on the smartphone's metadata—attached to the photos and/or extracted from location sharing—to capture the date, time, longitude, and latitude of the photographed cicadas. This ease of use would prove key to obtaining as many submitted photos as possible.

We invited app developers to submit prototypes for evaluation. The major requirement was that the prototype be completed by April 1, 2019, as periodical cicada Brood VIII was emerging in May 2019, and we wanted to test the app with that emergence. The original idea of the app was that, as photographs were submitted, trained individuals would verify each photograph as a periodical cicada, and its location would be added to a map, enabling users to see where cicadas were emerging in real time.

The app also needed to educate users about what cicadas are and how to take proper photos. The app uses photographs with embedded articles to help users learn about cicadas and how best to use the app. Articles are shown in order of importance as the user scrolls down. Touching the article's photograph reveals the article's text. Topics include an invitation to help map the emergence, what periodical cicadas are, how to take a good photograph to permit accurate identification, a map of where the emergence will take place, which periodical species are emerging, the differences between annual and periodical cicadas, cicada morphology, and a list of supporting partners.

Raising Public Awareness about the App

The Cicada Safari team launched a media campaign to raise awareness about the app, drawing inspiration from earlier public-relations efforts such as those led by Smith between 1843 and 1867 and by the USDA in 1902 (Kritsky, 2021a). To expand outreach, the team actively recruited partners with an interest in insect mapping. Early collaborators included Mount St. Joseph University, the Indiana Academy of Science, the Ohio

Biological Survey, the University of Connecticut, and the popular website Cicadamania. Since 2018, the number of supporting organizations has grown to 15.

To complement the app, the team created a dedicated website (cicadasafari.org) designed for both desktop and mobile users. The site offers detailed information about cicada emergence, frequently asked questions, educational resources for schools, and recommended books and websites. The app links directly to this site. A proprietary press kit, featuring high-quality images, maps, and key information for both print and digital media, was also made available. Access to the press page was restricted to media requests, allowing the team to manage the use of copyrighted materials more effectively (Kritsky, n.d.).

Testing and Refining the App

Testing was critical for quality control. Cicada Safari was ready for testing in 2019 with a small brood (Brood VIII) that occurred in northeastern Ohio, western Pennsylvania, and extreme northern West Virginia. As photos were submitted, entomologists randomly selected approved reports and traveled to those locations to verify that cicadas were present. In this first test, 5721 reports were verified (Kritsky, 2021).

Based on the results of that first survey, the app was updated to streamline the verification process and to accept eleven-second videos with sound, permitting species identification from recorded cicada chorusing. This update was launched prior to the emergence of Brood IX in May 2020 for further testing (Kritsky, 2021). The 2020 test of Cicada Safari was even more successful than in 2019, with 7721 approved reports, including 804 videos. Not only was the app effective in mapping Brood IX—which was expected to emerge in southern West Virginia, western Virginia, and northwestern North Carolina—it also verified the off-cycle emergences of cicadas belonging to four different broods (Fig. 8.4). Finding and verifying these short-lived off-cycle emergences had been very difficult before the app. The extent of these off-cycle emergences had never been documented before (Kritsky, 2021).

The app continued to uncover new findings that would have been difficult to document otherwise. The first 2020 reports of periodical cicadas came from Georgia and were quickly followed by reports from South Carolina and eastern North Carolina. These locations were part of Brood XIX, a 13-year brood, and the cicadas were emerging after only nine years.

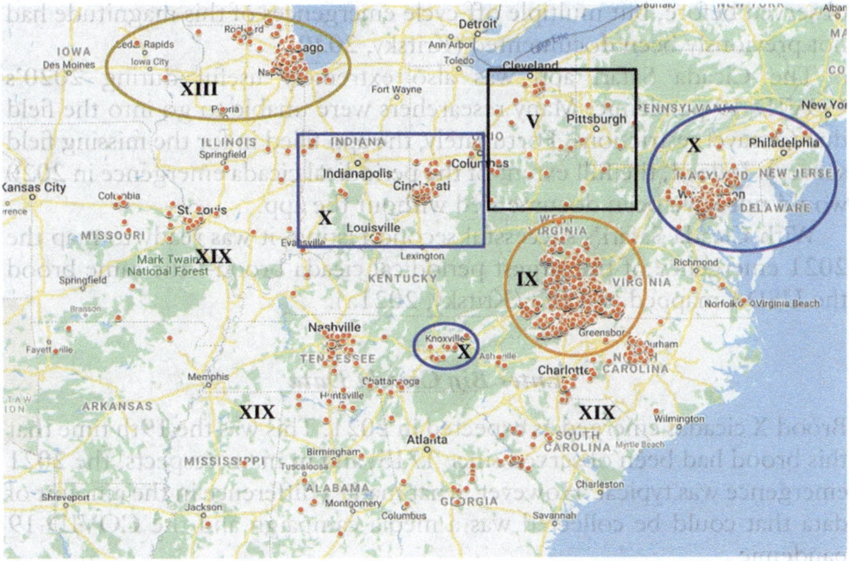

Fig. 8.4 The 2020 emergence of periodical cicadas using the Cicada Safari data (Kritsky 2021)

These reports were soon joined by sightings from Missouri, Mississippi, Alabama, Kentucky, and Illinois. Videos from west of St. Louis documented an emergence with light, sustained chorusing. Physical surveys from Brood XIX areas in North Carolina found that the emergences there were light and heavily decimated by predators (Kritsky, 2021).

Other off-cycle cicadas were reported in 2020 from Cincinnati, Washington, DC, Louisville, and near Bloomington, Indiana. These reports were of Brood X cicadas emerging one year early. They were mostly isolated stragglers, and only intermittent, isolated calls were heard. No mating was noted. That was not the case in greater Chicago, where large emergences of four-year-early Brood XIII cicadas were reported. Submitted videos and photographs showed widespread chorusing, mating, and egg laying (Kritsky, 2021).

A few scattered observations of four-year-late Brood V cicadas were also reported from eastern Ohio and western Pennsylvania, though no chorusing or oviposition was noted among these isolated sightings. These four-year-early 17-year and 13-year off-cycle emergences had been observed before, but multiple off-cycle emergences of this magnitude had not previously been documented (Kritsky, 2020).

The Cicada Safari app was also extremely useful during 2020's COVID-19 pandemic. Many researchers were unable to go into the field due to travel restrictions. Fortunately, the app filled in for the missing field surveys. Indeed, the full extent of the periodical cicada emergence in 2020 would not have been documented without the app.

With Cicada Safari's successful second testing, it was ready to map the 2021 emergence of the largest periodical cicada brood—the same brood the USDA mapped in 1902 (Kritsky, 2021a).

Enter Big Cicada Data

Brood X cicadas emerged as expected in 2021. This was the 19th time that this brood had been observed since 1715, and in many respects, the 2021 emergence was typical. However, what made a difference in the amount of data that could be collected was a media campaign and the COVID-19 pandemic.

Before the emergence, a media campaign whetted the public's appetite, encouraging people to download the app and contribute to the mapping effort. The COVID pandemic was still a concern, but one of the few activities people could enjoy during that time was hiking in nature. Tens of thousands of people, spurred on by media coverage, hiked in search of periodical cicadas with the goal of supporting the mapping project. Documenting what was happening at the time, Kritsky writes:

> The first adults were reported emerging on 18 April at the southern edge of Brood X's range in northern Georgia. By the end of April, light emergences of cicadas had been reported in Georgia, Alabama, Tennessee, South Carolina, North Carolina, Maryland, and Washington, DC. The emergence increased during the first two weeks of May, with large numbers emerging in Georgia, Tennessee, Maryland, and Washington, DC. A cold spell delayed the emergence in Brood X's western range, but that changed on 13 May, when warmer temperatures moved into Ohio, Indiana, and eastern Illinois. Chorusing was reported throughout Brood X's range by 18 May, reaching its loudest peaks during the last week of May and into the first week of June. The chorusing sound levels were noticeably quieter by mid-June, and the last isolated calls were heard in Cincinnati on 2 July. (Kritsky, 2021a, p. 95)

As the number of adult cicadas declined, the impact of egg-laying became more obvious, with widespread flagging—broken branches caused by cicadas laying eggs at the ends of tree branches. The 2021 emergence ended in Ohio on July 2 (Kritsky, 2021a).

What was unexpected about the 2021 emergence was the amount of data captured by the app. The University's Information Services and Support (ISS) office monitored the servers supporting the app. Once the 2021 emergence began, server usage increased by 50%. As more people downloaded the app, the strain on the servers grew—but careful monitoring of the quantity of photographs being submitted allowed ISS to take the necessary actions to keep everything running, even when usage nearly exceeded capacity (Graber-Stiehl, 2021). Specifically:

The public interest in the emergence was staggering, with thousands of photos being submitted to Cicada Safari every day at the height of the emergence (see Fig. 8.5).

Sunday, May 30, over 8000 people were online using the Cicada Safari app at the same time. By the end of the 2021 emergence, over 197,000 users had downloaded Cicada Safari, and the number of verified *Magicicada* photographs exceeded 551,000.

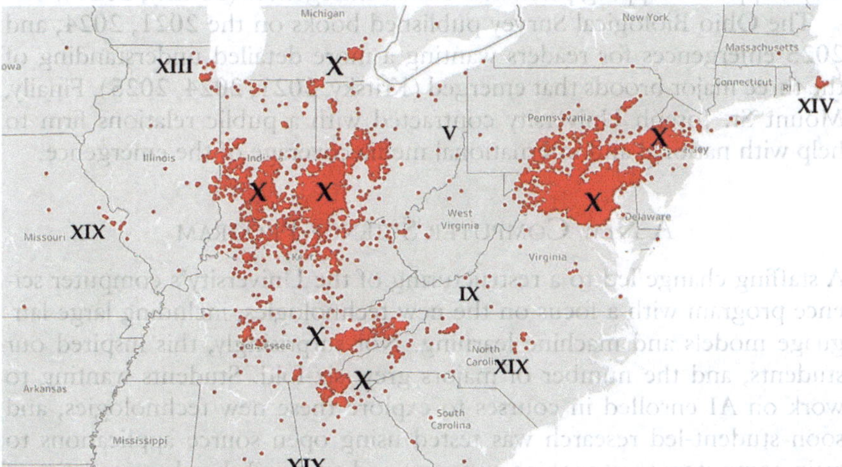

Fig. 8.5 The 2021 emergence of periodical cicadas using the Cicada Safari data (Kritsky, 2021)

The volume of images to be examined required the efforts of 23 trained people. Whereas technology enabled us to get better location data with voucher photographs, the sheer number of images being submitted often outstripped our ability to keep up with verifications. The obvious answer was integrating machine learning into the verification process to handle the easily identified photographs of cicadas, thus permitting trained personnel to focus on evaluating the more difficult images (Kritsky, 2021).

Uncovering New Patterns in Cicada Emergences

Similar to what happened in 2020, several periodical cicada sightings were reported outside of the historical range of past Brood X emergences. These emergences occurred in western West Virginia, Virginia, Illinois, Iowa, Missouri, central Georgia, parts of eastern North and South Carolina, and Massachusetts. These were not Brood X cicadas, but cicadas belonging to other broods that emerged off-cycle in 2021.Using historical periodical cicada brood distributions, it was possible to assign many of these 2021 stragglers to other broods. Cicadas belonging to Broods V, IX, XIII, XIV, and XIX also emerged during 2021. As occurred during the previous year, Cicada Safari exceeded expectations and has become the major app for mapping periodical cicada emergences (Kritsky, 2021)!

The Ohio Biological Survey published books on the 2021, 2024, and 2025 emergences for readers wanting a more detailed understanding of the three major broods that emerged (Kritsky, 2021, 2024, 2025). Finally, Mount St. Joseph University contracted with a public relations firm to help with national and international media coverage of the emergence.

A New Computer Science Program

A staffing change led to a restructuring of the University's computer science program with a focus on the new technologies, including large language models and machine learning. Not surprisingly, this inspired our students, and the number of majors grew six-fold. Students wanting to work on AI enrolled in courses to explore these new technologies, and soon student-led research was tested using open source applications to train computers to recognize an insect and to "see" the characteristics of periodical cicadas.

Using Machine Learning to Identify Cicada Safari Data

Most approaches to artificial intelligence require very large datasets. A major issue with citizen science is the verification that the submitted data is accurate, because bad data can be worse than no data. Moreover, the verification process, depending on how large the dataset is, can involve considerable time and expense. Implementing AI as a verification process can be a non-biased tool to improve the quality of the dataset.

Thus, automating verification of the large amounts of data that Cicada Safari collected was much needed. The students used supervised machine learning with Python's Ultralytics library, better known as YOLO (You Only Look Once). They chose YOLO as it was the leading standard in the computer vision space, primarily for its object detection features and ease of access. Starting a project focused on machine learning, we were originally overwhelmed by the complexities of TensorFlow, PySpark, and several other deep-learning systems. YOLO, on the other hand, largely simplified the process of creating a computer vision model while still providing the desired results.

The students were divided into different roles and responsibilities within the project. At first, they focused on annotating images, while others focused on data analytics surrounding the cleanliness and usability of our images. After a sufficient number of images were annotated, emphasis shifted to training different models based on these images, adjusting hyperparameters or datasets to improve the models' accuracy. Finally, a Python script was written that uses these models to approve or reject images within a database.

The process started by manually annotating a training dataset of 557 images of cicadas. This involved drawing boxes around different features, such as the entire insect, their characteristic red eyes, and their wings, and labeling them accordingly (Fig. 8.6). Afterward, the students used image augmentation, including mirroring and rotation, to create a final dataset of 1451 images that were used to train a prototype of the cicada detection model. Testing YOLO's feedback features allowed the students to tweak hyperparameters and learn what kinds of images and labeling processes worked best, which gradually improved the model (Torres, 2024; Ultralytics, 2023).

A script was written to auto-annotate images, and a recursive process was born. This script was used to annotate images using our existing model, which could then be used for further training. This continued to

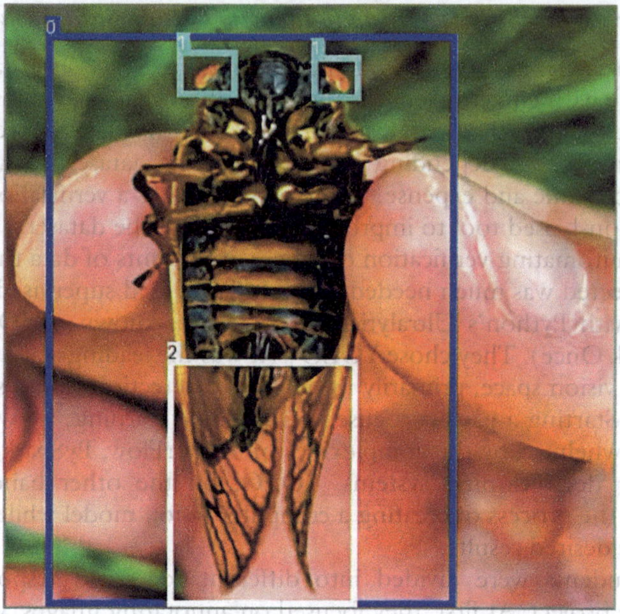

Fig. 8.6 The bounding boxes that were selected to teach the app how to identify periodical cicadas included the body, the red eyes, and the wings

expand the cicada dataset to 1318 original images and 3426 images after using image augmentation. After training several variations of the cicada detection models, a Python script was introduced that regularly pulled images from a database and checked for periodical cicadas.

An issue that came up in the early stages of the project was the model detecting recurring background features as periodical cicadas. Occasionally, the model labeled sticks as cicadas. However, using a more robust dataset of common cicada features gradually corrected that problem. The AI was learning. The software learned to recognize an adult cicada as an insect approximately 86% of the time. When the cicada's characteristic red eyes were added to the learning, the accuracy increased to approximately 94%. This holds the promise of greatly speeding up the verification process of the photographs. If applied to the 2021 dataset, it would have reduced the number of photographs that needed human eyes for verification from 551,000 to 33,000.

Plans for Future Research

This year, the 17-year Brood XIV is set to emerge, and we plan to test the AI component to review the thousands of photographs expected. To improve the accuracy, we incorporated a box on the camera's screen to guide the user to get closer to the insect. The next two periodical cicada emergences will occur in 2027 and 2028—Broods XXII and XXIII, respectively. The 2027 emergence is expected to occur in two areas: the southern Mississippi River area in Louisiana and over 12 counties in southern Ohio and northern Kentucky. The Ohio/Kentucky emergence was only verified in 2014, having been missed over two centuries of fieldwork. It is possible that periodical cicadas may occur in other areas along the Ohio and Mississippi River valleys. If so, the Cicada Safari app may be the only way these possible isolated cicada emergences might be found. Brood XXIII is a much larger brood, ranging from Illinois south to Louisiana in the Mississippi River valley. Cicada Safari will also be there to produce the most detailed distribution map of the brood.

The integration of AI in Cicada Safari will continue to prove beneficial by making large-scale data verification faster and more accurate. As future emergences are expected to generate hundreds of thousands of images, AI models can efficiently filter clearly identifiable cicadas, allowing human reviewers to focus on ambiguous cases. With each new dataset, it is anticipated that the model will improve, creating a feedback loop where public participation enhances both research and AI accuracy. This scalable approach ensures that citizen science can keep pace with growing participation—advancing ecological research through the combined power of community engagement and machine learning.

Incorporating a human-in-the-loop (HITL) process within Cicada Safari would enable a more interactive, adaptive, and participatory model of citizen science. In this framework, users could be invited to assist in expanding and refining training datasets by labeling new images or verifying AI-generated classifications—particularly when the algorithm is uncertain or assigns low confidence to a prediction. This human feedback would not serve as a final or sole decision point but would function as one feature among many in the model, helping improve the robustness and generalizability of the AI system over time. Although individual lay users may introduce some degree oflabeling error, HITL designs benefit from aggregation, redundancy, and probabilistic weighting, allowing the model to learn patterns from imperfect data and balance human input with other algorithmic signals (Fortson et al., 2024; Mahajan & Helbing, 2025). In this way, layperson contributions can strengthen the AI model without requiring expert-level precision at the individual level. Furthermore, the participatory nature of this process empowers community members to play a direct role in shaping the accuracy and ethical dimensions of the system, enhancing trust and inclusivity in citizen science platforms (Fraisl et al., 2025).

We plan to continue to refine Cicada Safari by increasing user participation in both design feedback and usability testing. Gathering input through surveys or in-app prompts will help ensure the app is intuitive, accessible, and engaging for diverse users. This participatory approach can guide feature improvements and make the app more effective during high-activity periods like cicada emergences (Mahajan & Helbing, 2025).

We are exploring the development of a white-label version of Cicada Safari that would allow communities, educators, and researchers to repurpose the citizen science data collection functionalities in the app to collect data for other projects. The white-label version could be used to collect and classify observations on a range of topics—such as invasive species, pollinators, or seasonal plant changes—based on issues that matter most to specific regions or groups. By giving users control over the app's focus and appearance, this approach empowers communities to engage in meaningful, place-based science and fosters broader participation in environmental data collection (Fraisl et al., 2025).

Conclusion

The Cicada Safari project illustrates the remarkable evolution of citizen science, from nineteenth-century newspaper letters to twenty-first-century mobile apps powered by supervised machine learning. By combining public participation, educational outreach, and AI tools, the platform has dramatically scaled data collection and verification efforts during cicada emergences.

Looking ahead, our goals include expanding user involvement in app design, refining AI models through human-in-the-loop processes, and developing a white-label version to support community-driven science on a wide range of ecological topics. As technology and public engagement continue to intersect, Cicada Safari stands as a model for participatory science in the digital age.

Acknowledgments A major component of any successful citizen science initiative is publicity. Some of Gene's images and maps have been made publically available as part of press kits and used across mass media outlets and the blogsphere. Gene Kritsky is the owner of all images aside from Fig 8.2.

The map used in Fig. 8.2 was published in 1907 by the USDA and is in the pubic domain.

Try It Out: Download Cicada Safari Yourself

You can visit Cicada Safari's website at cicadasafari.org to learn more about the project and download the free mobile app, which has already been downloaded over 245,000 times. While the Cicada Safari team would certainly appreciate your help in photographing any periodeical cicadas (if they are in your area), exploring the app is also a valuable way to explore how design choices impact the success of a citizen science project powered by AI.

As you explore the app, pay close attention to how it educates users about what to look for and how to take usable photos. In machine learning, having a large dataset is helpful—but the quality of that data is equally important. A blurry, misframed, or mislabeled image can introduce noise into the training process. To address this, the Cicada Safari team recently introduced a helpful design feature: a framing box that appears on the camera screen, guiding users to center and properly scale cicadas in their photos. This simple UI addition helps ensure the submitted images are not only plentiful, but also consistently structured for machine learning analysis.

In this way, Cicada Safari becomes more than just an app—it's a window into how thoughtful interface design, community participation, and AI come together to support large-scale biodiversity monitoring. Engaging with the app firsthand will bring the technical themes of this chapter to life in a very practical, visual way.

Questions for Reflection

1. What design features make citizen science apps like Cicada Safari easy or hard to use?
2. What are the potential consequences of using machine learning to verify citizen science data without sufficient human oversight, especially when models are trained on imperfect or limited datasets?
3. If you could create your own citizen science app, what would it track and how would AI help?

References

Fortson, L., Crowston, K., Kloetzer, L., & Ponti, M. (2024). Artificial intelligence and the future of citizen science. *Citizen Science: Theory and Practice, 9*(1), 32. https://doi.org/10.5334/cstp.812

Fraisl, D., et al. (2025). Leveraging the collaborative power of AI and citizen science for sustainable development. *Nature Sustainability, 8*(2), 125–132.

Graber-Stiehl, I. (2021). To study swarming cicadas, it takes a crowd. *Science, 372*(6546), 1022–1023. https://doi.org/10.1126/science.372.6546.1022

Kritsky, G. (2020). Gideon B. Smith: America's forgotten entomologist. *American Entomologist, 66*(4), 48–53.

Kritsky, G. (2021). *Periodical Cicadas: The Brood X edition*. Ohio Biological Survey.

Kritsky, G. (2021a). One for the books: The 2021 emergence of the periodical cicada Brood X. *American Entomologist, 67*(4), 40–46.

Kritsky, G. (2024). *A Tale of Two Broods: The 2024 Emergence of Broods XIII and XIX*. Ohio Biological Survey.

Kritsky, G. (2025). *The Pilgrims' Promise: The 2025 Emergence of Brood XIV*. Ohio Biological Survey.

Kritsky, G. (n.d.). *Cicada Safari: Mapping the emergence of Brood XIV in 2025*. https://cicadasafari.org

Mahajan, S., & Helbing, D. (2025). *Co-designing AI systems with value-sensitive citizen science. ACM*. 10.1145/XXXXXXX (Note: Replace with actual DOI when available).

Potter, N. (1829). Locusts. *American Farmer, 11*(1): 125–126. Accessed through Google Books. https://tinyurl.com/unwymmc

Potter, N. (1839). *Notes on the Locusta septendecim americanæ decim septima*. R. Robinson. https://www.biodiversitylibrary.org/item/56537#page/11/mode/1up

Torres, J. (2024, September 9). *What is box loss in Yolov8?*. YOLOv8. https://yolov8.org/what-is-box-loss-in-yolov8/

Ultralytics. (2023, November 12). *Performance metrics deep dive*. Ultralytics YOLO Docs. https://docs.ultralytics.com/guides/yolo-performance-metrics/

CHAPTER 9

Patterns That Matter: AI-Driven Insights into College Attendance and Student Achievement

Alex Nakonechnyi, *Olena Holub*, *and Rebecca J. Allen*

Introduction

College dropout rates in the United States remain a significant concern for higher education stakeholders, with a recent report from the Educational Data Initiative indicating that 39% of first-time, full-time bachelor's degree-seeking students fail to complete their programs within an eight-year period (Hanson, 2024). The report highlights the cumulative impact of college dropout—the phenomenon of "some college, no credential" (SCNC) now encompasses over 41.9 million adults nationally, disproportionately affecting younger populations, with 67% of SCNC individuals having been under the age of 35 at the time of their last enrollment (Hanson, 2024). In terms of causes of dropout, financial hardship emerges as the most frequently cited cause of attrition, reported by 42% of former

A. Nakonechnyi (✉) • O. Holub • R. J. Allen
Center for IT Engagement (cITe), Mount St. Joseph University, Cincinnati, OH, USA
e-mail: alex.nakonechnyi@msj.edu; olena.holub@msj.edu; rebecca.allen@msj.edu

R. J. Allen, A. Nakonechnyi (eds.), *Using and Understanding AI in Higher Education*,
https://doi.org/10.1007/978-3-031-99754-9_9

students, followed by familial obligations and academic challenges (Hanson, 2024). These findings underscore the pressing need for targeted interventions that address financial, academic, and social support structures within postsecondary institutions (Hanson, 2024).

Reducing attendance barriers and encouraging students to attend class are not the only ways to improve graduation outcomes, but they represent a tangible and effective action step. Research over the past three decades has consistently demonstrated that student attendance is closely tied to persistence and retention in higher education. For instance, Tinto (1993) theorized that students are more likely to persist when they are meaningfully integrated into the academic and social fabric of the institution, with class attendance and active participation serving as key pathways for achieving that integration. Moreover, subsequent empirical studies have reinforced this theory. Specifically, Credé, Roch, and Kieszczynka's (2010) meta-analysis found that class attendance is a stronger predictor of college grades than either standardized test scores or high school GPA, both of which are traditional indicators of retention potential. Similarly, Kassarnig et al. (2017) measured class attendance among nearly 1,000 undergraduate students and found a strong positive correlation between early, consistent attendance and higher academic performance. Their study also revealed that students tended to mirror the attendance behaviors of their social peers, suggesting that peer influence plays a meaningful role in shaping attendance habits. More recently, post-COVID studies have continued to affirm the relationship between attendance and academic success across a variety of student populations, including medical students (Kassab et al., 2022), sports management students (Gough et al., 2021), and students with autism (Flegenheimer & Scherf, 2022).

Capturing attendance data, therefore, appears critical for institutions aiming to support student success. However, collecting accurate attendance data is neither straightforward nor universally practiced. Scholars have noted that attendance data collection is often contingent on faculty workload, willingness, and reliance on manual methods that are time-consuming and error-prone (Budi et al., 2018; Khan et al., 2020). In large classes, traditional paper-based systems may be particularly impractical (Buechele, 2020). To address these challenges, a variety of technological interventions have been proposed. One approach is tracking students' smartphone and mobile device locations to automate attendance recording (Panca et al., 2020). Another method involves using facial recognition technology to verify student presence (Essien & Ansa, 2023). A further alternative is fingerprint scanning, offering biometric confirmation of attendance (Khan et al., 2020). Additionally, some researchers have explored the gamification of attendance, using game-based incentives to encourage student engagement (Pinter et al., 2020). Each of these strategies offers potential advantages but also raises significant concerns, particularly regarding privacy, the ethical use of biometric data, and the burden of implementation. Thus, any adoption of new attendance systems must carefully balance efficiency gains against the need to safeguard student rights and institutional trust.

Even when attendance data is successfully captured, it must be used thoughtfully and purposefully. Simply promoting attendance without context is unlikely to be effective. While attending class is undeniably important—absenteeism often initiates a downward spiral of confusion and disengagement (Kassarnig et al., 2017)—addressing absenteeism requires acknowledging the broader socioeconomic factors that influence student behavior. Financial insecurity, transportation difficulties, and limited support networks are all significant contributors to college absenteeism (Buechele, 2020). Thus, supporting attendance means supporting students as whole people, with socioemotional, physical, and economic needs. Moreover, collecting data solely for its own sake is not only ineffective but potentially harmful; data must be harnessed to create actionable, evidence-based supports that meaningfully improve student outcomes.

Given the well-established relationship between attendance and academic success, the central research question guiding this chapter is: How can attendance data be captured, analyzed, and translated into actionable, student-centered interventions within a university context? To address this question, the chapter proceeds in several stages. First, we describe the methods used to collect, structure, and analyze student attendance and academic performance data at our university. In this section, we provide both a layperson-friendly overview as well as a traditional methods description to serve diverse readers. Second, we present findings from a linear regression analysis examining the relationship between attendance and final course grades. Third, we apply machine learning techniques—specifically, K-means clustering—to identify and characterize patterns of attendance behavior. Fourth, we explore ethical considerations related to the collection, analysis, and use of attendance data. Finally, we propose a set of practical, equity-focused interventions and outline next steps for future research and institutional implementation. Our chapter aims to offer both empirical insights and practical guidance for leveraging attendance data in ways that genuinely support student success. While reading a single chapter about machine learning will not transform a non-technical reader into an AI expert, we have intentionally included reader supports throughout the chapter to make the material accessible to academic audiences from diverse disciplinary backgrounds. In doing so, we aim to help non-computer science experts begin to build foundational knowledge about how machine learning methods might be used to improve student outcomes within higher education settings.

Methods

One of the primary goals of this book is to make AI and machine learning accessible to readers who are not computer scientists. To support this goal, we have included two methods sections: *(1) a shorter, layperson-friendly overview, and (2) a more traditional, detailed methods section.*

Layperson, Plain-Language Methods

It could be that vast bodies of research using machine learning on topics of interest to you exists, but much may remain inaccessible to you because of dense jargon. Using our own research as a case study, let us break down a typical machine learning project, and make clear what is happening—if you follow along with us, the next time you encounter a machine learning article, reading it will be much easier.

For readers who may be less familiar with AI and computer science, Table 9.1 provides a clear breakdown of the steps we undertook: data aggregation (collecting the data), cleaning and normalization (organizing the data for use), analysis (using Python primarily) and visualization (making figures). The second column lists the tools, programming languages, and libraries we used—most of which are common in the field. What we are trying to make evident is that when authors, like us, say that "we analyzed the data with AI," it does not mean that a single, magical "AI tool" completed the work. Rigorous AI-driven research closely mirrors traditional quantitative research, relying on a sequence of clearly defined steps and multiple distinct tools to complete the analysis. The quality and trustworthiness of AI-based research ultimately depend not on the mystique of artificial intelligence itself, but on the accuracy, relevance, and soundness of the methods and tools applied throughout the process.

Table 9.1 Steps undertaken in the AI attendance data analysis

Step number and what we did	*Technical tools/Approaches (see definitions in Table 9.1)*
Data Aggregation	
1. Recorded student attendance for each class session.	Google Sheets
2. Centralized attendance and final grades into a database.	SQLite Database (sqlite3 module)
Data Cleaning and Normalization	
3. Filtered out students who dropped or withdrew.	SQL Queries, pandas
4. Excluded sessions with missing attendance data.	pandas (data filtering)
5. Normalized attendance entries into binary values (1 = attended, 0 = absent).	pandas (data normalization)
6. Calculated attendance metrics: attendance proportion, longest absence streak, number of absence gaps, and attendance split by semester half.	Custom Python scripts, pandas
Analysis	
7. Conducted linear regression to examine the relationship between attendance and final grades.	scikit-learn LinearRegression, scipy.stats linregress
8. Calculated Pearson correlation coefficients and p-values.	scipy.stats pearsonr
9. Standardized attendance metrics for clustering analysis.	scikit-learn StandardScaler
10. Applied K-Means clustering to group students based on attendance patterns.	scikit-learn KMeans
11. Used the Elbow Method to determine the optimal number of student clusters.	Elbow Method using matplotlib, scikit-learn
Visualization	
12. Created visualizations (boxplots) to interpret attendance and clustering results.	matplotlib.pyplot

As you read, you likely noticed the second column of Table 9.1. Many of those tools may be unfamiliar to you—many of the listed tools are Python (a programming language) libraries (ready to use code) that are very common in machine learning. You do not have to necessarily learn how to use every one if you yourself will not be doing machine learning, but becoming conversant with the terminology will go a long way in being able to make sense of machine learning research; thus we have provided a further explanation of the tools we used in Table 9.2.

Table 9.2 Explanation and definition of tools used

Tool/Approach	*Layperson-friendly explanation*
Google Sheets	An online spreadsheet program (similar to Excel) that teachers used to keep track of attendance.
SQLite Database (using Python's sqlite3)	A simple digital filing cabinet that stored all the attendance and grade records together in one place. Accessed with a small set of Python tools called sqlite3.
SQL Queries	Special commands that help search, organize, and pull specific information from a database.
pandas (Python library)	A collection of ready-to-use tools in Python that makes it easy to clean up, organize, and analyze data arranged in tables (like spreadsheets).
Custom Python Scripts	Small programs written by the researchers in Python to perform specific tasks, like calculating percentages or finding patterns.
scikit-learn LinearRegression (Python library)	A tool in Python used to draw a straight line that best fits the data, helping show how two things (like attendance and grades) are related.
scipy.stats linregress (Python library)	Another Python tool that calculates the straight-line relationship between two sets of numbers, giving a sense of how strong the connection is.
scipy.stats pearsonr (Python library)	A Python tool that measures how closely two variables move together (e.g., attendance and final grades).
scikit-learn StandardScaler (Python library)	A tool in Python that adjusts different types of data so they are all measured in a similar way, making comparisons fair and meaningful.
scikit-learn KMeans (Python library)	A machine learning tool that sorts students into groups based on similar attendance habits.
Elbow Method (with matplotlib and scikit-learn)	A simple graphing method that helps decide how many groups best fit the data by looking for a "bend" or 'elbow' shape in a chart.
matplotlib.pyplot (Python library)	A tool used in Python to create graphs and charts that make the data easier to see and understand.

Traditional Methods Section

Data Collection and Integration

This study is a secondary analysis of departmental student attendance data. The original student attendance data were collected using Google Sheets, where faculty recorded attendance for each class session throughout the semester. Each spreadsheet represented a single course and was periodically exported and integrated into a centralized SQLite database, accessed and managed using Python's built-in sqlite3 module. Final grades, awarded to students at the end of each course based on metrics outlined in the respective syllabi, were also recorded and stored within the same SQLite database, allowing for efficient cross-referencing with attendance records.

Data Preprocessing

The attendance dataset that we used had names and course names anonymized. Once the data were loaded into the database, SQL queries were used to retrieve table names dynamically, supporting automated data processing across multiple courses. Records for students whose final grades were labeled as "DROPPED" or "W" were filtered out using pandas, a Python library for data organization and analysis, to maintain consistency and ensure meaningful correlations between attendance and academic performance. Additionally, if data for a specific class session were missing, that session was disregarded and excluded from all downstream calculations to minimize bias or distortion in the computed metrics.

Attendance Normalization and Metric Calculation

Attendance entries were normalized by converting them into binary values using pandas. An attended session was marked as 1, and an absence was marked as 0. Based on this binary format, several attendance metrics were calculated using custom Python scripts. Attendance proportion was computed by summing a student's attended sessions and dividing by the total number of valid (non-missing) sessions. Longest absence streak was determined by identifying the maximum sequence of consecutive zeros (absences) using a sliding window approach. The number of absence gaps was calculated, defining gaps as discrete blocks of absences separated by attended sessions. First-half and second-half attendance proportions were calculated separately to assess behavioral changes over the course of the semester.

Regression Analysis of Attendance and Performance

Final numeric grades were used as the outcome variable in a regression analysis. A linear regression model was applied using the LinearRegression module from the scikit-learn library, with attendance proportion as the independent variable. To further assess the strength and significance of the relationship between attendance and academic performance, Pearson correlation coefficients and p-values were calculated using the pearsonr function from the scipy.stats library.

Clustering Analysis of Attendance Patterns
For clustering analysis, all attendance-related metrics were standardized using the StandardScaler function from scikit-learn to ensure comparability across different measures. K-Means clustering, implemented with sklearn.cluster.KMeans, was then performed to group students based on their attendance behavior patterns. Selection of the optimal number of clusters (k) was performed using the elbow method by plotting distortion scores across k-values ranging from 2 to 9, with visualizations generated using the matplotlib.pyplot library. Finally, boxplots and other graphical summaries were produced to support the interpretation of cluster characteristics and highlight meaningful differences across student groups.

Findings

We used both traditional statistics and machine learning to understand the data. First, we examined linear regression in each course and across all courses combined. Secondly, we then grouped students by their attendance patterns, using K-means.

Course-Level Regression Results

A linear regression analysis was conducted for each course to examine the relationship between student attendance and final course grades. Attendance proportion—the percentage of attended sessions out of the total number of valid class sessions—served as the independent variable, while final numeric grades were used as the dependent outcome variable.

The strength of the relationship between attendance and academic performance varied across courses. Several courses demonstrated strong positive correlations, with Pearson r values greater than 0.75 and r^2 values exceeding 0.50. Other courses exhibited moderate or weak relationships.

Table 9.3 summarizes the correlation and regression statistics by course. To preserve confidentiality, course identifiers have been anonymized. The table is ordered from strongest to weakest observed associations, allowing for both detailed course-specific insights and an overview of broader trends.

Table 9.3 Correlation and regression statistics by course (anonymized and ordered by strength of association)

Course	R^2	*Pearson r*	*p-value*	*Interpretation*
Course 401	0.73	0.85	0.007	Strong
Course 215	0.70	0.83	< 0.001	Strong
Course 097	0.65	0.81	< 0.001	Strong
Course 170	0.60	0.77	0.072	Moderate
Course 193	0.58	0.76	0.002	Strong
Course 120	0.56	0.75	< 0.001	Strong
Course 220	0.55	0.74	0.014	Strong
Course 106B	0.55	0.74	< 0.001	Strong
Course 105A	0.53	0.73	< 0.001	Strong
Course 230	0.46	0.68	0.001	Moderate
Course 187	0.43	0.66	0.002	Moderate
Course 350	0.38	0.61	0.272	Moderate
Course 106A	0.36	0.60	0.002	Moderate
Course 180A	0.34	0.58	0.005	Moderate
Course 174C	0.30	0.55	0.007	Moderate
Course 120B	0.28	0.52	0.007	Moderate
Course 174B	0.13	0.36	0.074	Weak
Course 172	0.02	0.14	0.582	Weak
Course 098	0.01	0.11	0.615	Weak
Course 180B	0.01	0.09	0.653	Weak
Overall	0.29	0.54	< 0.001	Moderate

Note: Course identifiers have been anonymized

Combined Courses Regression Results

Across all courses combined, a moderate positive correlation was observed between attendance and academic performance ($r = 0.536$, $p < 0.001$). The regression model produced an R^2 value of 0.288, indicating that approximately 28.8% of the variance in final grades could be explained by attendance alone. As shown in Fig. 9.1, the model's slope was 4.91, with an intercept of −1.46, suggesting that for every one-unit increase in attendance proportion, final grades increased by nearly five points.

K-Means Clustering

Following the correlation analysis between attendance and academic performance, K-Means clustering was applied to further examine patterns among students. K-Means is an unsupervised machine learning method

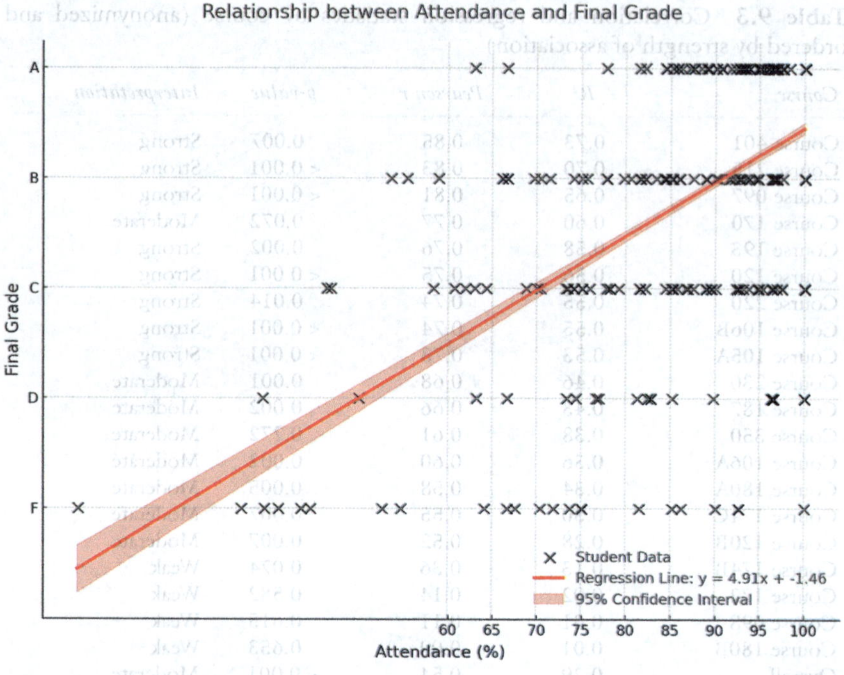

Fig. 9.1 Relationship between attendance proportion and final course grade (with 95% confidence interval)

that partitions a dataset into a specified number of clusters by grouping observations that share similar characteristics. Each observation is assigned to the cluster with the nearest mean (or "centroid"), minimizing the distance between the data point and the center of its assigned group. In this way, K-Means identifies natural groupings within the data without relying on pre-existing categories or labels. The resulting clusters summarize underlying patterns and simplify complex datasets by grouping similar cases together.

The number of clusters for the K-means was selected based on the Elbow Method, which evaluates the within-cluster sum of squares (WCSS) across different numbers of clusters. In this analysis, a clear inflection point was observed at four clusters (see Fig. 9.2), suggesting that additional clusters beyond four would yield minimal further reduction in variance.

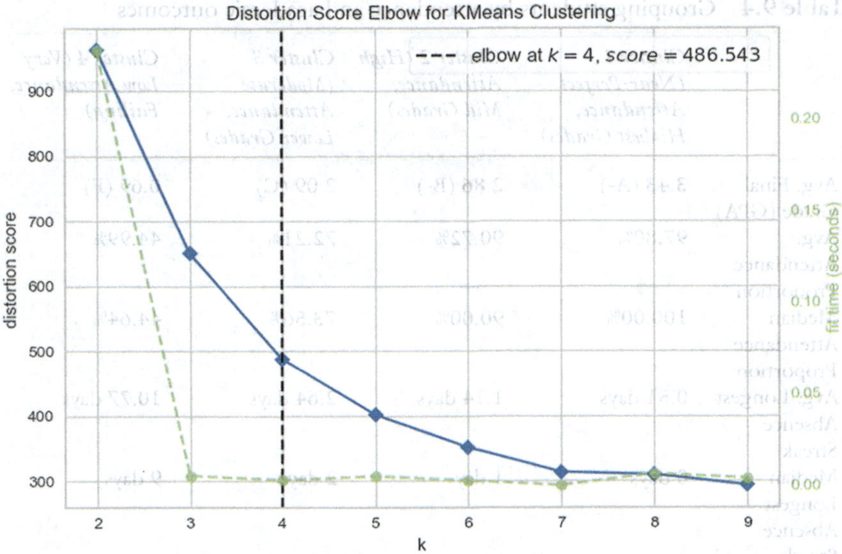

Fig. 9.2 Distortion score elbow for K-means clustering

Students were clustered based on two primary variables: overall attendance proportion and final course grade (numeric GPA). These variables captured both students' academic engagement and their academic achievement. In addition, two further descriptors—longest absence streak and number of distinct absence gaps—were calculated to enrich the characterization of attendance patterns. Longest absence streak measured the maximum number of consecutive days missed, reflecting sustained disengagement, while absence gaps measured how often periods of attendance were interrupted by one or more missed sessions.

Based on the K-Means clustering analysis, four distinct student profiles emerged. The results are summarized in Table 9.4 and described below.

Cluster 1, labeled "Near-Perfect Attendance, Highest Grades," comprised students who maintained nearly complete attendance and achieved the highest academic outcomes. The average final grade in this group was an A- (GPA 3.43), with an average attendance proportion of 97.80%. Median attendance was a perfect 100%, indicating that more than half of these students attended every scheduled class session. These students had minimal disruptions in attendance, with an average longest absence streak

Table 9.4 Grouping students by attendance and academic outcomes

	Cluster 1 (Near-Perfect Attendance, Highest Grades)	*Cluster 2 (High Attendance, Mid Grades)*	*Cluster 3 (Moderate Attendance, Lower Grades)*	*Cluster 4 (Very Low Attendance, Failing)*
Avg. Final Grade (GPA)	3.43 (A-)	2.86 (B-)	2.09 (C)	0.69 (F)
Avg. Attendance Proportion	97.80%	90.72%	72.21%	44.99%
Median Attendance Proportion	100.00%	90.00%	73.56%	44.64%
Avg. Longest Absence Streak	0.51 days	1.14 days	2.64 days	10.77 days
Median Longest Absence Streak	0 days	1 day	2 days	9 days
Avg. Absence Gaps	1.69 gaps	4.84 gaps	7.36 gaps	6.54 gaps
Median Absence Gaps	2 gaps	5 gaps	7 gaps	6 gaps
Avg. First-Half Attendance	97.76%	86.85%	73.02%	57.45%
Median First-Half Attendance	100.00%	87.50%	75.00%	59.38%
Avg. Second-Half Attendance	96.60%	88.32%	64.87%	20.18%
Median Second-Half Attendance	100.00%	88.24%	63.07%	20.83%
Number of Students	185	129	58	13

of just 0.51 days and very few absence gaps (average of 1.69 gaps). Their attendance remained consistently high throughout the semester, with little variation between the first and second halves.

Cluster 2, labeled "High Attendance, Mid Grades," included students with strong attendance patterns but more moderate academic performance. Their average final grade was a B- (GPA 2.86), with an average attendance proportion of 90.72%. The median longest absence streak for this group was one day, and students typically had around five distinct absence gaps across the semester. Attendance remained stable between the first and second halves of the term, though slightly lower than Cluster 1.

Cluster 3, labeled "Moderate Attendance, Lower Grades," captured students with lower attendance and correspondingly lower academic achievement. Students in this group had an average final grade of approximately a C (GPA 2.09) and an average attendance proportion of 72.21%. Their attendance behavior was characterized by longer absence streaks (averaging 2.64 days) and more frequent interruptions, with an average of 7.36 absence gaps. Attendance showed a slight decline across the semester, reflecting reduced engagement over time.

Cluster 4, labeled "Very Low Attendance, Failing Grades," represented the most academically at-risk group. Students in this cluster earned an average final grade of 0.69 (failing) and had an average attendance proportion of just 44.99%. Their attendance patterns were marked by extremely long absence streaks (average of 10.77 days) and relatively few recoveries (6.54 absence gaps). Notably, their second-half attendance dropped sharply to an average of 20.18%, suggesting that disengagement deepened as the semester progressed.

Together, these clusters reveal significant links between attendance behaviors and academic performance. While higher attendance was generally associated with better grades, the clustering also highlights that frequent, sustained absences—not just lower overall attendance rates—were strongly associated with poor academic outcomes (Fig. 9.3).

Discussion

This study explored the relationship between class attendance and academic performance within a small, private university setting. Consistent with prior research, our findings revealed a positive and statistically significant correlation between higher attendance rates and higher final course grades across a variety of math and computer science courses. Through

Fig. 9.3 Students can be divided into attendance patterns and resultant academic outcomes. This image was generated with DALLE and was used with faculty locally to encourage them to submit attendance for future data analysis and point out that patterns of late drop off in attendance are troubling and should be followed up on

linear regression analysis, we found that attendance alone accounted for nearly 29% of the variance in final grades, representing a substantial effect size in the context of educational research. Further, K-Means clustering analysis identified distinct patterns of attendance behavior—it is especially important to note that not just absences, but absence streaks matter, and that drop-offs in attendance mostly happen in the second half of the semester. Let us now discuss some ways these findings can be interpreted and translated into action.

First, let us understand the findings a bit more deeply. Although aggregate data clearly showed that class attendance was correlated with academic performance, the question remains: does attendance itself cause academic success, or is it simply an outward marker of other factors such as motivation, financial stability, or access to resources (e.g., transportation, childcare, employment flexibility)? Correlation alone cannot rule out alternative explanations. However, multiple studies suggest that there is a genuine causal link between attendance and performance. For example, Dobkin et al. (2010) implemented a mandatory attendance policy in large economics classes and found that a 10-percentage point increase in attendance led to a 0.17 standard deviation rise in final exam scores. Similarly, Chen and Lin (2008) conducted a randomized experiment and found that attending lectures improved exam scores by 9.4% to 18%, substantially larger than effects estimated by prior correlational studies. These findings strengthen the argument that attendance itself exerts a meaningful, independent influence on academic outcomes.

Second, we must also understand that student absences are not randomly distributed; beyond overall attendance rates, deeper patterns emerged. Students at risk of failing did not abruptly stop attending classes; rather, their attendance often declined gradually over time. Many continued to attend sporadically late into the semester, suggesting that initial motivation was present and that opportunities for re-engagement remained. These findings urge institutions to look beyond simple present/absent counts and recognize that students with irregular attendance may still be seeking ways to reconnect. Early identification of declining attendance could allow institutions to intervene before deeper disengagement occurs, offering students realistic pathways back to success. Used thoughtfully, attendance data can support proactive, equity-centered efforts to promote persistence and academic achievement.

However, using attendance data to guide interventions also raises important ethical considerations. If attendance patterns are interpreted without proper context, there is a risk of unfairly labeling students as disengaged or at-risk. Without careful attention to equity, interventions could inadvertently penalize first-generation, low-income, or marginalized students. Attendance tracking should therefore be transparent, proportional, and used for supportive—not punitive—purposes. Presenteeism (students coming to class without being engaged), infantilization of adults, and punitive policies are a possible risk to overselling attendance (Macfarland, 2013). Institutions must balance the opportunity to help students with a commitment to safeguarding privacy, autonomy, and trust (Florea and Florea, 2020). There often is no one-size-fits-all solution to promoting attendance, but below we describe some departmental interventions that we are developing and researching.

Interventions and Future Directions

Building on these findings, we have begun implementing several practical interventions designed to support students in non-punitive, inclusive ways. One initiative involves distributing baskets filled with snacks and flyers promoting campus support resources, such as food pantries and financial aid, to classes. Importantly, no individuals are singled out; the entire class benefits, reducing stigma while increasing awareness of available supports.

We have also found that personalized text messaging is an especially effective way to re-engage students. Text outreach tends to elicit quicker and more receptive responses than emails or phone calls, helping students reconnect with academic supports. This observation aligns with research showing that mobile instant messaging (MIM) fosters higher levels of behavioral engagement compared to traditional forums (Tang & Hew, 2022). In response to these insights, we successfully advocated for a new feature within the university's student information system that allows instructors and academic support staff to send text messages directly to students, provided they have opted in.

Previously, our institution, like many others, lacked standardize methods for attendance taking. Some instructors take attendance on the learning management systems (LMS) in which data is not available for central aggregation, other instructors used paper which is cumbersome to digitalize, still other instructors use spreadsheets in which the formatting varied, and finally some instructors did not take attendance at all. Recognizing the importance of reliable attendance data collection and aggregation for early intervention, we also collaborated with IT staff to integrate two flexible, technology-supported attendance options into the university's student information system and mobile app. In one option, students can enter a PIN into MountRoar (the campus smartphone app) to generate a unique QR code, which instructors scan using their smartphones to record attendance. The instructor interface is shown in Fig. 9.4).

In the other option, instructors can quickly take attendance through a point-and-click page displaying student names and photos, synchronized

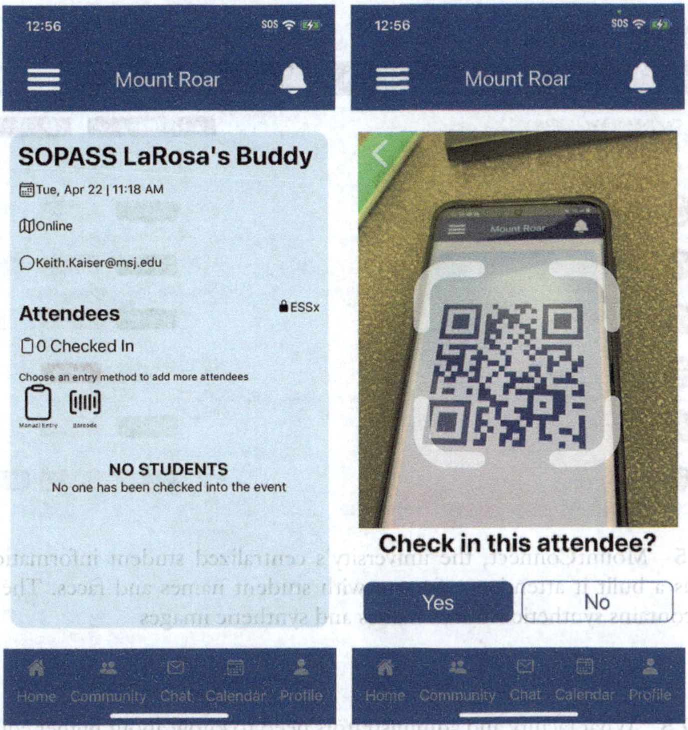

Fig. 9.4 To facilitate more accurate data collection our campus app has introduced an attendance QR feature that can be used for classes or events. The class/event owner can either take attendance manually or scan attendees' generated QR codes

with the centralized database. These tools were designed to minimize faculty burden, promote consistent data collection, and support sustainable, real-time tracking of student engagement (Fig. 9.5).

Finally, looking forward to what can be done next, emerging research also points to gamification as a promising strategy for boosting attendance and participation. Limonova et al. (2023) demonstrated how integrating AI and gamification strategies—such as rewards, feedback loops, and dynamic personalization—can improve engagement in higher education settings. Similarly, Pinter et al. (2020) reported substantial gains in attendance after implementing a gamified system using points, badges, and leaderboards. While gamification must be thoughtfully designed to avoid unintended consequences, it offers a motivational complement to traditional academic supports (Table 9.5).

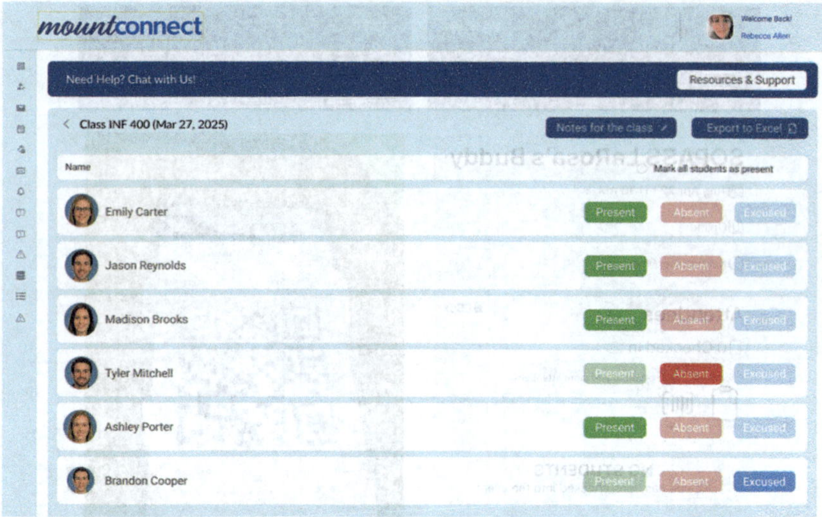

Fig. 9.5 MountConnect, the university's centralized student information system, has a built it attendance feature with student names and faces. The image below contains synthetic student names and synthetic images

Table 9.5 What faculty and administrators need to know about higher education student attendance

This study showed…
1. Attendance is independently correlated with academic outcomes.
2. Absence streaks as opposed to just absences were associated with poor academic outcomes.
3. In students with poor academic outcomes, attendance trails off the second half the semester. Students do still reappear from time to time though.
The broader literature supports…
1. Acquiring reliable attendance data is difficult. Simplification of the process for instructors is needed.
2. Reasons for absences vary. Non-punitive social supports are needed.
3. Text messaging as opposed to emails may result in better engagement.
4. Gamification of attendance may be beneficial.

Limitations

Several limitations should be acknowledged when interpreting the findings or contemplating replication of our local responses to our data. First, the research was conducted at a small, private Catholic university, which may limit the generalizability of results to larger or more diverse institutions. Second, the data were collected exclusively from math and computer science courses, disciplines that may have distinct attendance norms compared to fields such as the humanities or social sciences. Third, although faculty made consistent efforts to record attendance accurately, manual entry into Google Sheets introduces the possibility of human error or missing data. Finally, the observational nature of the study, while strong in establishing correlations, restricts our ability to make definitive causal claims despite supportive external evidence.

Conclusion

This study reinforces the critical role of class attendance as a meaningful, actionable indicator of student success. While technological and ethical challenges must be navigated carefully, our findings demonstrate that capturing and thoughtfully using attendance data can offer valuable insights for supporting students. By combining machine learning analysis with human-centered interventions, we are beginning to translate attendance patterns into opportunities for proactive outreach. Moving forward, it will be essential to continue developing non-punitive, equity-focused strategies that respect student autonomy while maximizing the potential of attendance data to promote persistence, engagement, and academic achievement.

Try It Out: Learn No-Code Machine Learning Analysis

This chapter explores how attendance data, when thoughtfully analyzed, can uncover important trends and inform student success strategies. Working with your own data to carry out similar analyses may be more feasible than you think via no-code and low code appoaches.

Untangling the Approaches

As discussed in Chap. 2 ("Machine Learning vs. Traditional Statistics"), the same mathematical techniques can serve different purposes depending on the intended outcome.To ground your exploration, it is helpful to understand how different analytical approaches—statistical and machine learning—frame problems and produce insights. Before beginning the exercises, consider the methods used in this chapter and how they influence both the questions we ask and the conclusions we are able to draw.

Regression appears in both statistics and machine learning, but the goals and assumptions often differ: Think of it this way: Statistical regression asks, "What is the relationship, and how sure are we?"Machine learning regression asks, "How well can we predict what comes next?"In statistics, regression is used for explanation—to understand how variables relate, to test hypotheses, and to estimate confidence in results. These models typically rely on assumptions such as linearity, normality, and independence, and they are designed to be interpretable.

In machine learning, regression is used for prediction. The focus is on producing accurate outputs for new, unseen data. Machine learning regression is often embedded within larger models, such as neural networks, and may rely on algorithmic optimization rather than strict statistical assumptions.

Because of this, machine learning regression is frequently not explainable in a traditional sense. A model may generate highly accurate predictions, but it may not be possible to trace precisely why a particular prediction was made or which variables had the greatest influence.

This chapter used a traditional statistical approach (linear regression) to examine the relationship between attendance and course grades. This method was chosen for its ability to maximize transparency and interpretability.

The chapter also employed an unsupervised machine learning technique called clustering to identify common attendance patterns. Although clustering can be less explainable, it is useful for discovering group-level trends when no outcome variable is specified in advance.

No-code and Low-code Approaches to Machine Learning

The data analyst, Holub, conducted her analysis using Python, a programming language she was already familiar with. What many people do not realize is that in both statistics and machine learning, more than one tool can often be used to accomplish the same task. Whether to use Python, R, SPSS, or even Excel may reflect personal preference, institutional context, or comfort level rather than a fundamental difference in analytic power. The important thing is to understand the reasoning behind the analysis, regardless of which platform is used. In fact, if more people recognized that tools they already know—such as spreadsheets—can be used to explore data patterns and apply basic analytic methods, they might find data science and machine learning less intimidating and more accessible.

From our own teaching experience, anecdotally, we have had notable success introducing machine learning concepts through spreadsheets before transitioning to code. This approach seems to lessen the cognitive load for new learners, especially those who are still developing fluency with programming syntax. By starting with a familiar interface and focusing on the logic of the methods first, students often gain confidence and conceptual clarity that prepares them for later work in Python or R.

Example of a No-Code Approach to Machine Learning

If you have a little Excel proficiency, using an Excel add-on can enable you to perform analyses similar to the ones described in this chapter. A handy tool that Rebecca and Olena have often used to introduce machine learning concepts is XLSTAT, available from Lumivero (the makers of NVivo). XLSTAT integrates with Excel to provide user-friendly options for regression, clustering, and other analytical techniques without requiring programming experience. It was selected in part because it offers highly accessible video tutorials that walk users through how to perform common statistical and clustering tasks step-by-step. We have no relationship with XLSTAT or Lumivero, but we have found it to be a useful, no-code tool for teaching applied data analysis.

You are encouraged to replicate the regression and clustering analyses from this chapter using your own data. The tips and steps below can help you do this:

Obtain your data ethically. Use only de-identified or aggregate data, or ensure that you have proper consent if individual-level data is involved. Protect student privacy at every step.

Clean your dataset before analysis. This includes checking for missing values, ensuring consistent formatting, and confirming that all records align with your variables of interest.

Handle missing data thoughtfully. In this chapter, Holub excluded class sessions with missing attendance data from all downstream calculations. This approach helps maintain the integrity of metrics like attendance proportion and longest absence streak. If missingness is minimal and appears random, this method is both sound and transparent.

Format attendance using a binary structure. Assign a value of 1 for each session attended and 0 for each absence. This simple format makes the data easy to work with and interpret for both regression and clustering.

Run your regression and clustering analyses. Again, the video tutorials **offered by XLSTAT make this much easier. They offer step by step guidance on where to click.**

Compare your results to those in this chapter. Do you observe similar patterns—such as declining attendance in the second half of the semester or a strong relationship between attendance and final grades?

We would love to hear what you discover. If you try one of these analyses and find something interesting—or unexpected—please email us and let us know what you found.

Questions for Reflection and Discussion

What are the primary takeaways from the regression and clustering analyses presented in this chapter? How do these statistical and machine learning approaches complement one another in revealing attendance trends?

How did the use of a dual-methods section (plain-language and traditional) support the authors' goals of accessibility and rigor? Would this structure benefit other types of research dissemination?

Cluster 4 students had very low attendance and failing grades, but also showed evidence of sporadic re-engagement. What interventions might be both realistic and respectful to support students in this group?

What is the significance of "absence streaks" and "second-half drop-off" patterns in student attendance? How might these insights inform the design of midsemester supports or early alert systems?

The chapter cautions against punitive uses of attendance data. What ethical considerations should institutions keep in mind when using behavioral data to drive interventions?

The authors argue that collecting attendance data must be coupled with context-sensitive interpretation. How can institutions avoid reinforcing bias when identifying students as "at risk" based on attendance?

Several attendance-tracking technologies are described (e.g., QR codes, facial recognition, Wi-Fi-based detection). What are the pros and cons of these tools in terms of accuracy, scalability, and student privacy?

If your institution were to implement a centralized attendance tracking system, what key design features would you prioritize? Consider student burden, faculty workload, and data usefulness.

References

Budi, S., Karnalim, O., Handoyo, E. D., Santoso, S., Toba, H., Nguyen, H., & Malhotra, V. (2018). IBAtS—Image based attendance system: A low cost solution to record student attendance in a classroom. In *Proceedings of the 2018 IEEE International Symposium on Multimedia (ISM 2018)* (pp. 259–266). IEEE. https://doi.org/10.1109/ISM.2018.00037

Buechele, S. (2020). *Evaluating the link between attendance and performance in higher education: The role of classroom engagement dimensions.* Joint Discussion Paper Series in Economics by the Universities of Stefan Büchele.

Chen, J., & Lin, T. F. (2008). Class attendance and exam performance: A randomized experiment. *Journal of Economic Education, 39*(3), 213–227.

Credé, M., Roch, S. G., & Kieszczynka, U. M. (2010). Class attendance in college: A meta-analytic review of the relationship of class attendance with grades and student characteristics. *Review of Educational Research, 80*(2), 272–295. https://doi.org/10.3102/0034654310362998

Dobkin, C., Gil, R., & Marion, J. (2010). Skipping class in college and exam performance: Evidence from a regression discontinuity classroom experiment. *Economics of Education Review, 29*(4), 566–575. https://econpapers.repec.org/RePEc:eee:ecoedu:v:29:y:2010:i:4:p:566-575

Essien, U. D., & Ansa, G. O. (2023). A deep learning-based face recognition attendance system. *Global Journal of Engineering and Technology Advances, 17*(1), 9–22. https://doi.org/10.30574/gjeta.2023.17.1.0165

Flegenheimer, C., & Scherf, K. S. (2022). College as a developmental context for emerging adulthood in autism: A systematic review of what we know and where we go from here. *Journal of Autism and Developmental Disorders, 52*(5), 2075–2097. https://doi.org/10.1007/s10803-021-05088-4

Florea, D., & Florea, S. (2020). Big data and the ethical implications of data privacy in higher education research. *Sustainability, 12*(20), 1–11. https://doi.org/10.3390/su12208744

Gough, L. A., Duffell, T., & Eustace, S. J. (2021). The impact of student attendance on assessment-specific performance in sport degree programs. *Journal of Hospitality, Leisure, Sport and Tourism Education, 29*, 100323. https://doi.org/10.1016/j.jhlste.2021.100323

Hanson, M. (2024). College dropout rates. *Education Data Initiative*.. https://educationdata.org/college-dropout-rates

Kassab, S. E., El-Sayed, W., & Hamdy, H. (2022). Student engagement in undergraduate medical education: A scoping review. *Medical Education, 56*(7), 703–715. https://doi.org/10.1111/medu.14799

Kassarnig, V., Bjerre-Nielsen, A., Mones, E., Lehmann, S., & Lassen, D. D. (2017). Class attendance, peer similarity, and academic performance in a large field study. *PLoS ONE, 12*(11), e0187078. https://doi.org/10.1371/journal.pone.0187078

Khan, N. I., Mustafina, S. N., Jhumu, F. F., Zobyer, A. H. M., Mahin, M. H., Tarek, M. A. I., Rahman, R., & Islam, M. N. (2020). Towards developing an automated attendance management system using fingerprint sensor. In *Proceedings of the 2020 International Conference on Emerging Technology in Computing, Communication and Electronics (ETCCE)*. IEEE. https://doi.org/10.1109/ETCCE51779.2020.9350882

Limonova, E., Terzieva, V., & Kaloyanova, K. (2023). Maximising attendance in higher education: How AI and gamification strategies can boost student engagement and participation. In I. Maglogiannis, L. Iliadis, & E. Pimenidis (Eds.), *Artificial Intelligence Applications and Innovations* (pp. 502–512). Springer. https://doi.org/10.1007/978-3-031-60225-2_39

Macfarlane, B. (2013). The surveillance of learning: A critical analysis of university attendance policies. *Higher Education Quarterly, 67*(4), 358–373. https://doi.org/10.1111/hequ.12017

Panca, B. S., Paulus, Y., & Karnalim, O. (2020). An automated attendance system in academia with implicit authentication via mobile devices and Wi-Fi connection. *International Journal of Online and Biomedical Engineering, 16*(7), 86–94. https://doi.org/10.3991/ijoe.v16i07.13869

Pinter, R., Maravić-Čisar, S. M., Balogh, Z., & Manojlović, N. (2020). Enhancing higher education student class attendance through gamification. *International Journal of Emerging Technologies in Learning (iJET), 15*(20), 166–181. https://doi.org/10.3991/ijet.v15i20.15059

Tang, Y., & Hew, K. F. (2022). Effects of using mobile instant messaging on student behavioral, emotional, and cognitive engagement: A quasi-experimental study. *International Journal of Educational Technology in Higher Education, 19*(1). https://doi.org/10.1186/s41239-021-00306-6

Tinto, V. (1993). *Leaving college: Rethinking the causes and cures of student attrition*. University of Chicago Press.

CHAPTER 10

Conclusion: Shaping AI with Purpose—Reflections and Next Steps for Collaborative Practice

Rebecca J. Allen and Allison J. Lester

Introduction

But lo! Men have become the tools of their tools. The man who independently plucked the fruits when he was hungry is become a farmer; and he who stood under a tree for shelter, a housekeeper. We now no longer camp as for a night, but have settled down on earth and forgotten heaven. (Thoreau, 1854, *Economy*)

R. J. Allen (✉)
Center for IT Engagement (cITe), Mount St. Joseph University, Cincinnati, OH, USA
e-mail: rebecca.allen@msj.edu

A. J. Lester
Leadership, Empowerment, and Academic Development (LEAD)/Success by Design, Arizona State University, Tempe, AZ, USA
e-mail: allison.lester@asu.edu

R. J. Allen, A. Nakonechnyi (eds.), *Using and Understanding AI in Higher Education*,
https://doi.org/10.1007/978-3-031-99754-9_10

Whether welcomed or resisted, AI, like many tools before it, is revolutionizing how humans work. The AI genie is already out of the bottle. Higher education policy-makers and educators must now confront a critical question: how will we harness AI's potential and adapt to the changes it brings?

The changes AI is bringing about are, of course, mixed. In Chap. 3, the authors discussed some real and pressing issues surrounding AI ethics. In Chap. 5, the authors overviewed how some of these ethical issues are playing out in staff, faculty, and students' concerns—and hopes—for AI adoption. Yet, on that note of caution, we have quite a bit of hope. Looking forward to our higher education classrooms, there is quite a lot of good that is coming even now—and can come—from AI. AI promises to automate our drudgery, bridge literacy gaps, personalize learning, and inspire new ways of teaching—these are all good things (Rasul et al., 2023).

The trick, though, is how we will harness that good. In Chap. 4, when we discussed technology adoption and the ways it has been theorized, we noted that much of the work has been quantitative and framed from the top down. While participatory frameworks are beginning to emerge in AI education, traditional approaches to technology adoption have remained largely hierarchical and researcher-driven as we overview in Chap. 4. The idea of student-centered teaching—a focus on student communication and collaboration, an environment in which a professor facilitates rather than dictates—is not a new idea. But increasingly, generative AI has brought about a paradigm shift. Before generative AI, faculty largely had a choice as to whether content was delivered in a professor-centered or student-centered method, and that choice of delivery method largely remains—for now. The shift though, is with the availability of content itself. The fact is, that many models of generative AI are trained on corpora (i.e. knowledge-bases) multiple times more expansive than any human expert-faculty. Generative AI can give answers and explanations to domain-specific questions in mere seconds. So while faculty remain in charge of delivery of content—content is available to anyone with an internet connection and some basic prompting skills.

Having said all of this, we have to acknowledge the inherent tension that we foreshadowed with the historical quote at the start of the chapter—technological change has long been sometimes scary, and, sometimes, for better or worse, irreversible. In the university context, the displacement of faculty as experts is a threat to the identities of many. As generative AI increasingly performs tasks traditionally associated with faculty—such as writing and analyzing content—research has shown that generative AI raises concerns about professional relevance and identity in higher education. These concerns have led to resistance behaviors, including skepticism, avoidance, or rejection of AI tools, often rooted in fears of being replaced or devalued (Zhou et al., 2025).

These faculty identity-related fears and feelings, while valid, are often not validated. AI education is an emergent and rapidly evolving field, but much of the hyperkinetic focus thus far has centered on what we want students to do or not do with AI, or on pedagogical techniques designed to help students use AI more effectively. All of this emphasis on what to teach and how to teach is necessary, and we too are energized by the possibilities that generative AI brings. However, as we emphasized earlier, the reality is that faculty ultimately choose how they teach. Without holding space for faculty concerns and supporting their sense of agency, a significant portion of educators in our institutions will continue to resist integrating generative AI into their classrooms (Zhou et al., 2025). Faculty need more than scattered how-to resources; they need why-to—and, just as importantly, they need the foundational training that enables them to act on that why.

One of the core goals of this book is to provide that prerequisite foundation. Chapters 2 and 3 explore how AI works, along with its historical roots and ethical implications. There are already many excellent books offering practical, how-to guidance on prompt writing and classroom use (a list of recommended resources is included at the end of this chapter). But as we conclude this volume, our aim is to move toward a more human-centered why-to by sharing first-person teaching narratives. Through these stories, we hope to demonstrate how we—university educators ourselves—are engaging with AI within our institutions and classrooms.

In that spirit, I, invited Allison—a graduate school classmate and fellow higher education faculty member—to share her own story and work with me on this chapter. As case studies, Allison shares what she is doing as a higher education teacher, and I share my perspective as a higher education chair. We then zoom out and look at what we have shared, what has happened in this book, and what next steps for AI in higher education may be.

Narrative Case Study: Allison Lester

In reflecting upon how she and her institution have handled the rather sudden emergence of (particularly generative) artificial intelligence, Allison, shares:

As artificial intelligence became more visible in education, many institutions, including my own, grappled with how to respond (McDonald et al., 2024). The shift was not gradual. Almost overnight, students had new tools at their fingertips—tools that could draft essays, generate ideas, or simulate conversations—often before faculty had a chance to fully understand what was happening. Policies often emerged *after* students had already begun using AI tools in learning, filling the gap in ways that were creative, cautious, or sometimes conflicted (Ghimire & Edwards, 2024). In those early moments, it became clear that a top-down approach alone would not be enough. Students needed a seat at the table from the start.

Rather than handing students a pre-written AI policy, I invited learners to co-create it alongside me. In our digital literacy course, the process began with critical conversations: *What do we fear about AI? What excites us? Where do we see potential for harm? What counts as learning, creativity, and originality when AI is in the room?* These were not easy questions. They surfaced different positionalities, different literacies, and at times, different comfort levels with uncertainty. Yet it was precisely this discomfort that mattered. By collaboratively developing the norms and boundaries for AI use in our class, students did more than agree to a set of rules: they practiced ethical decision-making, critical reflection, and collective ownership of the learning environment itself.

The co-designed policy covered principles and practices. Students agreed that transparency mattered most. If AI tools were used in any assignment or project, students would disclose how they were used, what prompts were given, and what parts of the work reflected AI input versus their own. Several students voiced the need for AI to support thinking, not replace it. As one student put it, "It should help me do the work, not do the work for me." Another emphasized, "I still want my voice to come through."

To deepen our shared understanding, I asked follow-up questions like: *How will we know if AI is helping you think more deeply versus taking over your thinking? What signs would tell you if you crossed that line?* Through those discussions, students proposed practices like maintaining original drafts, documenting decision points, and using AI for brainstorming, organization, and expansion—not for generating full, final submissions.

The policy became more than a list of rules. It became a living document that shaped how we approached our work together. In ASU 121: *Creative Solutions in Action*, a course where students use action research to design solutions to community needs important to their lives, the policy became the foundation for building a custom GPT tailored specifically to our work. We trained and shaped it based on our shared priorities. We programmed the GPT to prioritize student agency, to always ask clarifying questions before offering solutions, to model stakeholder empathy, and to avoid producing polished final drafts. We gave it context about our action research cycle, details about our projects, including problem statements, timelines, and task lists. In short, we built the GPT to act less like an answer machine and more like a thoughtful collaborator, tuned to the complex, iterative work of real-world problem solving.

Students used the GPT to role-play stakeholder meetings, seek advice on grant funding proposals, generate early prototype ideas, analyze survey responses, and translate complex research into accessible language for community partners. Because the policy emphasized transparency, critical use, and student agency, the GPT became an extension of their thinking. It amplified their voice and helped move ideas forward in ways that stayed grounded in student-driven inquiry.

This participatory approach has useful implications for the broader conversation about AI literacy in higher education (Ryall & Abblitt, 2024). Teaching students about AI is important, yet it is equally essential to teach with learners—modeling critical, adaptive, and ethical practices that can travel beyond any single course or technology. Co-designing policy becomes a method of building thoughtful users, active decision-makers, and reflective practitioners who are prepared to navigate an AI-shaped world.

Narrative Case Study: Rebecca Allen

One of the reasons I invited Allison to share her story is that I had been both a graduate school classmate of hers and, more recently, an observer of her public scholarship on AI and higher education via social media. Her ideas caught the attention of colleagues at my institution as we began grappling with how to approach AI in our own teaching and departmental planning. She offered models I wanted to learn from, adapt, and promote as we built our local approach; I was interested in participatory and grassroots approaches to AI education.

Even so, my role has been somewhat different from Allison's. While she teaches primarily as a faculty member, I serve as chair of my department—a position that has given me a unique vantage point to observe how AI has affected both faculty and students in our programs. Undergraduate education is an important spoke of what I do, but also, there is a need to create a broader culture that supports innovation among students and faculty alike.

The Computer Science Department's overarching aim, thus, was to create a space for dialogue, experimentation, and awareness-raising about AI. As was shared in Chap. 5, we called this initiative the AI Café. This semester, in AI Café, as part of a credit-bearing research capstone, a small group of six students interviewed faculty, staff, and peers to assess AI needs across campus. They then analyzed the data, scripted and produced a series of how-to AI videos, and published them on a website they built themselves.

Of course, there is no shortage of AI training content online. Thus, our goal was not just to make more videos. Rather, given that literature suggests case studies help with adoption (Kurtz et al., 2024), we hoped to create materials localized to our institution—featuring familiar faces, voices, and campus contexts—and to use this project as a starting point for dialogue. Ultimately, our aim is to build bridges between the computer science department and other disciplines, foster curiosity, and promote a culture of thoughtful AI exploration.

The AI Café is a promising example within a broader array of training opportunities. Through project-based learning, undergraduate research, and treating students as Partners, the AI Café helps students develop research, facilitation, and leadership skills, plants seeds for long-term culture change, and importantly, invites them in as co-partners in navigating the advent of GenAI. As we noted in Chap. 4, technological adoption is rarely a "one-and-done" event. Moving forward, the AI Café aims to offer a number of ways for faculty and students to continue to engage with AI training. At press, currently, we have run a pilot for our online social media driven focus groups about AI teaching and syllabus policy formation—we want to obtain student input when forming syllabus policies. We, like Allison's institution, are also launching project-based undergraduate courses that feature generative AI in the fall. Students from the AI Café will act as near-peers (e.g. teaching assistants who do not assess work)—providing support and mentorship for first year peers.

Implications and Future Directions

As generative AI tools have become increasingly accessible, universities are facing new opportunities to rethink how they teach, assess, and support students. In this section, we briefly contemplate alternative theoretical conceptualization of AI and move ahead to what institutions and faculty can tangibly do with AI. The real objective is to ensure that everyone becomes conversant with the emergent and here-to-stay technology, even if some choose not to use it actively (Kurtz et al., 2024).

How We Think About AI

One of the core goals of this book has been to promote AI literacy. Not all faculty will—or should—use AI for every task. In conducting trainings around the world, I have observed that many educators conflate knowledge of AI with an unabashed endorsement of its use. However, understanding a tool does not mean one must embrace it uncritically or apply it universally. While I believe AI holds tremendous promise, I also acknowledge its significant limitations and potential harms. My aim in writing this book has been to foster AI literacy—because, as Paulo Freire (2000) reminded us, meaningful change begins with understanding and literacy. Educators, already literate across many domains, now need to become literate in AI—not only to integrate it thoughtfully, but also to critique it sensibly and challenge it when necessary.

This book discusses AI ethical issues in Chap. 3—those possible ethical pitfalls mean we need to be careful in how we promote AI. In Chap. 5, we noted that students are often far ahead of professors when it comes to adopting these tools. The need for faculty training comes up again and again in the literature (Kurtz et al., 2024; Nikolopoulou, 2024; Hutson et al., 2022; Naik et al., 2024).

The tone of AI training that we are advocating for, and indeed, the tone of AI books like this one needs to be non-prescriptive. As with so many organizational challenges in higher education, top-down mandates rarely work. Long before AI entered the classroom, Mager and Pipe (1997, p. 151) warned against the simplicity of "telling":

> All you have to do is tell. But it isn't as simple as that, is it? Even if telling worked—which it seldom does—someone has to decide how the telling will happen. Will someone prepare a memo for all the instructors? Will someone sit down in a group with them and tell? Or meet with them individually and tell?... [Telling] may be quick and easy to do; but even for a solution of dubious effectiveness, there is likely to be "cost" in terms of someone's time, at the very least.

It is also worth considering that fear is often a root cause of resistance among faculty (Saccenti et al., 2024). If we want to build an environment where educators can engage meaningfully with AI, we must offer supportive, trust-building strategies—not just instructions.

Generative AI threatens faculty identities by disrupting traditional ideas of expertise, authority, and instructional value in higher education. Faculty have long served as content experts and knowledge gatekeepers—conveying information, interpreting ideas, and modeling critical thinking. Generative AI systems have, for several years now, demonstrated the ability to surpass experts across a wide variety of domains (Guo et al., 2023). This tension is compounded by the fact that, as we saw in Chap. 5, students are often quicker to adopt and adapt to these tools, placing some instructors in the unfamiliar position of learning from their students about emerging technologies. As faculty strive to maintain relevance, the traditional identity of the professor as "the one who knows" is destabilized.

The good news is that faculty have empathy, expertise, and context that LLMs do not have. While generative AI can mimic or summarize content, it lacks the ability to truly understand student struggles, build trust, or tailor instruction based on the complex dynamics of a classroom. Faculty bring not only subject matter expertise but also pedagogical insight and institutional knowledge that AI systems cannot replicate. There are practical, tangible, and needed ways to teach in the area of generative AI—such as helping students critically evaluate AI-generated content, guiding them in ethical use, and framing assignments that emphasize human judgment, creativity, and reflection. Educators can scaffold student learning in ways that acknowledge the presence of AI while reinforcing foundational academic skills that machines cannot replace.

From Literacy to Practice: Strategies for Faculty Engagement

There are many practical steps one could take toward AI integration in university teaching. Here, we offer some starting points for your consideration.

Prompt Engineering. In developing AI literacy, one of the first places that faculty should start with students is prompt engineering (Nikolopoulou, 2024). If you are not familiar with the concept of prompt engineering, this book provides a brief overview and some jumping-off points at the end of Chap. 2. Prompt engineering involves using natural language to prompt LLMs to achieve the most useful and accurate output possible.

Without it, it is hard to generalize experiences with LLMs beyond "ChatGPT doesn't do that well." Prompt engineering gives us a solid framework to describe how we interact with LLMs; we suggest that it is a vital skill that should be taught alongside first-year writing and research skills.

For example, a faculty member in a composition course might ask students to use ChatGPT to generate a first draft of an argumentative essay. Then, the students revise the draft using peer feedback and instructor input, reflecting on how the AI-generated draft shaped their thinking. This practical application enables students to critically assess AI outputs and refine their writing in iterative cycles.

Coming Out of Our Silos. Silos have long been derided in higher education, but still, cross-disciplinary collaboration is sporadic. Nevertheless, generative AI increasingly demands that we work and think across disciplines. While not all disciplines or faculty members may adopt generative AI tools in the short term, the reality is that students already have access to these technologies—regardless of instructor or disciplinary preference. This ubiquity means that AI literacy must be addressed across the curriculum. Hence, we need AI expert faculty and staff to support non-AI expert faculty and staff.

Hutson et al. (2022) emphasize integrating AI even into liberal arts and humanities instruction. For example, students might use AI to perform text analysis on literature or explore stylistic differences in writing. In a history class, students could prompt ChatGPT to summarize a primary source document, then critique and correct the output—developing both content knowledge and critical thinking skills.

For AI to be addressed cross-curricularly, universities will need to support co-teaching models. We will need AI experts to support other content areas. Yet, as one colleague told me when I suggested co-teaching, "they won't pay you for that." We need more flexible—not necessarily more expensive—structures that allow for collaboration.

Designing for Diversity. Integrating AI across disciplines helps dismantle structural barriers in education by supporting personalized learning. Nikolopoulou (2024) identifies tools such as intelligent tutoring systems that deliver targeted feedback and recommend supplementary resources. A writing center might implement an AI assistant that provides real-time grammar suggestions or citation help. Hutson et al. (2022) suggest such adaptability can serve as a model for broader academic applications.

In addition, AI tools offering real-time translation or text-to-speech functionality can support multilingual learners and students with disabilities. Universities and instructors will need to consider carefully their policies which may discourage the recording of class content, particularly when recordings can be adapted and translated in ways that can be transformative for diverse learners.

Valuing Participation and Co-Creation. Moving beyond instructional support, a particularly innovative approach described by Kurtz et al. (2024) involves treating students as co-creators in the classroom's use of AI. Faculty are encouraged to involve students in decisions about how AI is used, as well as the ethical implications of its use. For instance, students might co-author classroom policies on acceptable AI applications or lead discussions on academic integrity in the GenAI era. Some classes may feature student-led workshops where peers demonstrate how they use ChatGPT for brainstorming or revision. This participatory approach not only empowers students but also deepens their understanding of AI, aligning with inclusive teaching philosophies.

Rethinking Assessment. Artificial intelligence also provides a practical toolkit for rethinking assignments and assessments. Kurtz et al. (2024) recommend redesigning traditional assignments to integrate AI tools like ChatGPT or Midjourney. For example, students might generate an initial draft using AI and then submit a reflective critique comparing the AI's work to their own revised version. This approach promotes critical analysis, supports academic integrity, and fosters metacognitive awareness.

Faculty can also leverage AI to generate quiz questions, scaffold learning with tiered exercises, or provide immediate formative feedback. Nikolopoulou (2024) reinforces this, noting AI's potential to automate grading and create adaptive assessments that adjust to student performance, enhancing both efficiency and engagement. Of course, care needs to be taken to use FERPA-compliant tools and approaches, but in Chap. 6 the authors talked about ways that ChatGPT can complement traditional assessment pratices.

Creating AI Policies for Success. AI policy development in higher education is both essential and complex, requiring institutions to address ethical, legal, pedagogical, and operational concerns associated with generative technologies such as ChatGPT. These policies are increasingly necessary to safeguard academic integrity, student privacy, and responsible AI integration while offering guidance to faculty and students (McDonald et al., 2024).

However, enforcing such policies proves difficult due to the rapid pace of AI development, disciplinary variability, and lack of consensus on acceptable use. Many institutions lack clear guidelines on large language models (LLMs), and even when policies exist, they are often vague on important issues such as transparency, bias, and student data protection (McDonald et al., 2024; Ghimire & Edwards, 2024). Furthermore, faculty face burdens in interpreting and applying AI-related policies without sufficient institutional support (McDonald et al., 2024).

On a practical level, detecting AI-generated text is ill-advised and often inaccurate, putting policymakers in the unenviable position of developing policies that can are difficulty be enforced. Nevertheless, students do want clear guidance on what they can and cannot do with AI, and they are afraid of being accused of AI-driven dishonesty. Given these complexities, institutions must design flexible, iterative policy frameworks that support ethical and enforceable AI adoption practices in higher education (Ghimire & Edwards, 2024). Even still, higher education has not figured out policy formation. This gap in AI policy formation certainly needs to be addressed in higher education.

Reducing Administrative Burden. One incentive for faculty to consider learning about generative AI is that it can streamline administrative and student support functions within higher education. Nikolopoulou (2024) highlights the use of virtual assistants and chatbots to address frequently asked questions regarding coursework, deadlines, or logistics—tools that remain accessible around the clock. Instructors might also use AI to automate routine tasks such as attendance tracking or composing email reminders. Naik et al. (2024) describe the implementation of custom GPTs tailored to institutional contexts, capable of advising students on course selection or policy navigation. These applications enhance operational efficiency while improving responsiveness and equity in academic services.

Conclusion

In this chapter, we shared narratives of our own experiences with AI and given a quick overview some possible strategies for faculty and institutions to engage with AI. Table 10.1 overviews these strategies.

In this book as a whole the authors have explored technologies will change faster than we can predict. It is likely that the systems explored in this book—large language models, custom GPTs, emerging AI

Table 10.1 Summary of AI assumptions or concerns

AI Assumptions or Concerns	*Practical Strategies for Faculty and Institutions*
AI literacy requires endorsement or constant use.	Reframe literacy as informed critique (Freire, 2000); understanding a tool doesn't mean embracing it universally.
Faculty are being replaced as experts.	Acknowledge identity concerns (Zhou et al., 2025); emphasize what AI lacks: Empathy, context, and pedagogical judgment.
Faculty fears are not relevant to implementation.	Validate identity disruption and offer trust-building supports, not just instructional mandates (Saccenti et al., 2024).
Students know how to use AI; they don't need help.	Support structured AI literacy across disciplines (Hutson et al., 2022); students may adopt quickly, but not always critically.
Top-down policies and trainings are sufficient.	Shift to participatory, co-created approaches (Mager & Pipe, 1997; McDonald et al., 2024); avoid the 'just tell them' model.
AI use is inherently unethical or encourages cheating.	Design reflective assessments and transparent use policies (Kurtz et al., 2024); distinguish between support and substitution.
We can ignore AI in non-technical disciplines.	Showcase liberal arts use cases (e.g., text analysis, critique); support cross-disciplinary co-teaching even if not compensated (Hutson et al., 2022).
Student voice doesn't belong in AI policy design.	Use co-created policies to teach ethics and ownership (Allison's narrative; Ghimire & Edwards, 2024).
GPTs are just content generators.	Build collaborative GPTs that prompt inquiry, clarify context, and uphold student agency (ASU 121 case study).
We already have enough AI resources online.	Create institution-specific content (e.g., AI Café's videos) to foster relevance, dialogue, and local engagement.

platforms—may feel outdated for future readers. What remains timeless is the practice of participatory learning, helping students navigate, critique, and shape technology with agency and purpose, no matter what comes next.

Try It Out: Take the Next Steps

This book has laid the groundwork for AI literacy and provided several examples of interdisciplinary applications of AI. Yet for many readers, the question remains: *What's next?* As discussed in Chap. 1, the AI educational landscape can be confusing and difficult to navigate.

To support your continued learning, we recommend consulting the Appendix, "Resources to Learn More About AI," which offers an ordered and annotated list designed to help you become progressively more familiar with key AI skills and tools.

Questions for Reflection and Discussion

1. The chapter emphasizes that AI threatens traditional notions of faculty expertise. In what ways do you see generative AI challenging—or potentially enriching—your own identity or role as an educator?
2. Allison's case study describes a co-created classroom policy on AI. What are the benefits and challenges of involving students in this kind of participatory decision-making? Would you try it in your own classroom? Why or why not?
3. Rebecca describes the AI Café as a local, student-led initiative grounded in research and collaboration. How might initiatives like this shift broader campus culture around AI? What would it take to start something similar at your institution?
4. The chapter argues that understanding AI does not require constant use or endorsement. How might this view help reduce resistance among faculty and promote more inclusive conversations about AI?
5. The authors propose moving from "how-to" to "why-to" in AI education. What kinds of faculty development activities or supports would you need to explore your own "why" with AI?
6. Participatory teaching, interdisciplinary collaboration, and flexible policy design are presented as essential strategies. Which of these feels most urgent—or most difficult—in your current institutional context?

References

Freire, P. (2000). *Pedagogy of the oppressed* (30th anniversary ed., M. B. Ramos, Trans.). Continuum.

Ghimire, A., & Edwards, J. (2024). From guidelines to governance: A study of AI policies in education. *arXiv*. https://doi.org/10.48550/arXiv.2403.15601

Guo, B., Zhang, X., Wang, Z., Jiang, M., Nie, J., Ding, Y., Yue, J., & Wu, Y. (2023). How close is ChatGPT to human experts? Comparison corpus, evaluation, and detection. *arXiv*. https://doi.org/10.48550/arXiv.2301.07597

Hutson, J., Jeevanjee, T., Vander Graaf, V., Lively, J., Weber, J., Weir, G., Arnone, K., Carnes, G., Vosevich, K., Plate, D., Leary, M., & Edele, S. (2022). Artificial intelligence and the disruption of higher education: Strategies for integrations across disciplines. *Creative Education, 13*(12), 3953–3980. https://doi.org/10.4236/ce.2022.1312253

Kurtz, G., Amzalag, M., Shaked, N., Zaguri, Y., Kohen-Vacs, D., Gal, E., Zailer, G., & Barak-Medina, E. (2024). Strategies for integrating generative AI into higher education: Navigating challenges and leveraging opportunities. *Education Sciences, 14*(503). https://doi.org/10.3390/educsci14050503

Mager, R. F., & Pipe, P. (1997). *Analyzing performance problems: Or, you really oughta wanna: How to figure out why people aren't doing what they should be, and what to do about it* (3rd ed.). Center for Effective Performance.

McDonald, N., Johri, A., Ali, A., & Hingle, A. (2024). Generative artificial intelligence in higher education: Evidence from an analysis of institutional policies and guidelines. *arXiv*. https://doi.org/10.48550/arXiv.2402.01659

Naik, N., Raj, J., Johnson, T., & Shah, P. (2024). AI-empowered teaching assistants: Enhancing learning experiences with generative language models. In *Proceedings of the 2024 IEEE International conference on Technology for Education (T4E)* (pp. 153–160). https://doi.org/10.1109/T4E59213.2024.1243437

Nikolopoulou, K. (2024). Generative artificial intelligence in higher education: Exploring ways of harnessing pedagogical practices with the assistance of ChatGPT. *International Journal of Changes in Education, 1*(2), 103–111. https://doi.org/10.47852/bonviewIJCE42022489

Rasul, T., Nair, S., Kalendra, D., Robin, M., de Oliveira Santini, F., Ladeira, W. J., et al. (2023). The role of ChatGPT in higher education: Benefits, challenges, and future research directions. *Journal of Applied Learning and Teaching, 6*(1), 41–56.

Ryall, A., & Abblitt, S. (2024). Co-designing an artificial intelligence (AI) literacies framework for learning designers: Knowledge, skills, and mindsets for a post-AI profession. *ASCILITE Publications*. https://doi.org/10.14742/apubs.2024.1136

Saccenti, D., Buattini, M., Grazioli, S., & Torres, D. (2024). Navigating the AI frontier: Should we fear ChatGPT use in higher education and scientific research? Finding a middle ground through guiding principles and practical applications. *Possibility Studies & Society, 2*(4), 415–437. https://doi.org/10.1177/275386992412318

Thoreau, H. D. (1854). *Walden; or, life in the woods*. Project Gutenberg. https://www.gutenberg.org/ebooks/205

Zhou, J., Lu, Y., & Chen, Q. (2025). GAI identity threat: When and why do individuals feel threatened? *Information & Management, 62*, 104093. https://doi.org/10.1016/j.im.2024.104093

Appendix

Resources to Learn More About AI

The goal of this book is to build AI literacy in a way that empowers readers to develop functional AI skills, engage meaningfully in classroom discussions about AI, and identify credible applications within their own research. While this book may have provided the foundational knowledge and vocabulary to get started, navigating the next steps in AI education can still feel overwhelming—as we noted in Chap. 1.

So, what comes next? Below, we offer an overview of specific books and tools that we've used and can confidently recommend for teaching and learning. We've arranged these resources in a sequence that reflects a typical learner's journey—from refining prompt engineering skills to gradually building basic coding abilities and, eventually, developing a deeper understanding of how AI works behind the scenes.

One point of pride in our computer science program is our commitment to Open Educational Resources (OERs) and free library-supported materials. In compiling this list, we intentionally prioritized tools and texts that are freely available or commonly accessible through university libraries, making them realistic options for many institutions and learners.

Han, J., Qiu, W., & Lichtfouse, E. (2024). *ChatGPT in Scientific Research and Writing: A Beginner's Guide.* Springer Nature Switzerland.

R. J. Allen, A. Nakonechnyi (eds.), *Using and Understanding AI in Higher Education*,
https://doi.org/10.1007/978-3-031-99754-9

This book is a strong resource for new and experienced researchers alike. It shows how ChatGPT can support tasks like literature review, writing, editing, peer review, and instrument design. It also thoughtfully addresses common concerns such as intellectual property, privacy, and ethical issues in academic contexts. We like the abundance of prompts that could be copy-pasted and adapted.

Eduonix Learning Solutions. (2024). *Driving business success with ChatGPT—A comprehensive guide* [Video course]. Packt Publishing.

This highly practical course focuses on applied prompt engineering for business use cases. It is ideal for students and professionals in business, marketing, and communication fields. While it does not cover advanced technical concepts or model deployment, it excels at demonstrating how AI can solve everyday business problems.

DataCamp. (n.d.). *DataCamp for universities.* Retrieved May 17, 2025, from https://www.datacamp.com/universities

DataCamp offers a structured platform for learning data science, analytics, and Python programming. We've used it successfully in both undergraduate and applied graduate education. The browser-based interface is especially beginner-friendly, although students sometimes find the shift to real coding environments overwhelming. Customer support has been helpful even on the free academic plan, and the free certifications provide great value.

Tableau. (n.d.). *Academic programs.* Retrieved May 17, 2025, from https://www.tableau.com/community/academic

Tableau is a leading data visualization platform that supports the communication of insights from AI and analytics workflows. Though not an AI tool in itself, it plays a key role in exploring and interpreting data. We use Tableau in our undergraduate courses to build foundational data literacy, and its free academic program offers generous access and training resources.

Hall, V. A. (2024). *Coding with ChatGPT and other LLMs: Navigate LLMs for effective coding, debugging, and AI-driven development.* Packt Publishing.

This book is a highly practical resource for students and educators in computer science. It offers clear, grounded examples of how to use ChatGPT for debugging and improving code, while also engaging thoughtfully with the ethical concerns surrounding large language models. Although the section explaining how LLMs work is technically dense, the book stands out for integrating real-world coding practices with a critical awareness of AI's limitations. Unlike many coding texts, it neither ignores the existence of LLMs nor glosses over the risks of using them uncritically—something we found refreshingly rare.

Addinsoft. (n.d.). *Educational pricing*. XLSTAT. Retrieved May 17, 2025, from https://www.xlstat.com/pricing/education

Referenced in Chap. 9, XLSTAT is a no-code Excel add-in for running machine learning algorithms. Though not free for universities—only available at a discounted rate—its beginner-friendly interface and clear instructional videos make it one of the most accessible tools for non-technical users seeking to explore data and machine learning.

Google. (n.d.). *Google Colaboratory*. Retrieved May 17, 2025, from https://colab.research.google.com/

Google Colab is a free, web-based Python coding environment that removes the barrier of local setup and installation. It's an ideal place for beginners to explore AI programming using tools like TensorFlow and scikit-learn. Colab supports both scripting and notebook-style documentation, making it perfect for early experimentation.

Botsonic. (n.d.). *AI agents: Build your own custom GPT-powered AI agents*. Retrieved May 17, 2025, from https://botsonic.com/ai-agents

Botsonic is an affordable and easy-to-use tool for deploying AI chatbots on websites. We recommend it for students transitioning from using LLMs through browser interfaces to building real implementations with minimal coding. It's particularly useful for early developers looking to take their first steps toward AI deployment.

Glass, L., Dickinson, M., Brew, C., & Meurers, D. (2023). *Language and computers*. Language Science Press. https://langsci-press.org/catalog/book/454

We've used the first edition of this open-access book in our introductory computer science course to help students understand how computers process language. It's a conceptually rich and accessible resource covering formal language theory, NLP, and ethics. It includes abundant examples from second language acquisition—highly relevant to the NLP field and something we personally enjoyed—though not all students found those examples relatable. The availability of a free PDF adds to its accessibility.

Index

R. J. Allen, A. Nakonechnyi (eds.), *Using and Understanding AI in Higher Education*,
https://doi.org/10.1007/978-3-031-99754-9

9783031997532